Mary Aspinwall 1697-1736
heiress of Sir Gilbert
Ireland of Hale and Hutt

Bamber Gascoyne I
1725-91 of
Bifrons, Barking
eldest son of Sir
Crisp Gascoyne,
Lord Mayor of
L
a
B heiress of
D John Bamber
of Bifrons,
Barking 1667-1753

=

Mary Greene
1729-99 lady of
the manors of
Childwall, West
Derby, Wavertree,
Everton and Much
and Little
Woolton

General Isaac Gascoyne
1770-1841 of Raby Hall,
Liverpool and 71 South
Audley Street, M.P. for
Liverpool 1802-30

=

Mary Williamson of
Liverpool

and had issue 3 sons 3 daughters

4
Blanche Mary
Harriet 1825-72
m. James Balfour
of Whittinghame
and had issue 5
sons 3 daughters
of whom the
eldest son Arthur
Balfour was
Prime Minister
1902-05

5
Evelyn Georgiana
Geraldine 1827-8
no issue

6
Robert Arthur
Talbot 1830-1903
Viscount Cran-
borne 1865 3rd
Marquess of
Salisbury 1868
K.G., P.C. Prime
Minister 1885-92
and 1895-1902 m.
Georgina
daughter of Sir
Edward Alderson
and had issue 5
sons 3 daughters

7
Eustace Brownlow
Henry 1834-
1921 m. Lady
Louisa Scott
and had issue

THE GASCOYNE HEIRESS

THE GASCOYNE HEIRESS

The Life and Diaries of Frances Mary Gascoyne-Cecil
1802–39

by

CAROLA OMAN

HODDER AND STOUGHTON

Printed in Great Britain for Hodder and Stoughton Limited,
St. Paul's House, Warwick Lane, London, E.C.4,
by Butler & Tanner Ltd, Frome and London.

Foreword

The Duke of Wellington was her father-figure. He gave away the heiress at her wedding. But Fanny Gascoyne (1802–39) brought far more than a Liverpool fortune to the house of Cecil. Her husband, her father and both her grandfathers were Members of Parliament. She was passionately interested in politics at a crucial date. She was an enthusiastic but humble patron of the Arts and a compulsive reader and traveller. She observed and criticized the social scene from Regency days to the first years of the reign of Queen Victoria. The memory of his witty, beautiful, high-spirited mother was tenderly cherished by her sixth child, Robert, afterwards third Marquess of Salisbury and Prime Minister, who lost her when he was a shy sensitive boy of nine.

Her Diaries have never left Hatfield House, where, together with the letters of her parents and grand-parents which tell her story up to her marriage, they form part of the Cecil Papers.

Mr. Richard Gunton, private secretary to the Prime Minister, and after his retirement Librarian, copied the Diaries and the Letters of the Duke of Wellington to the second Marquess and Marchioness of Salisbury in a wonderfully clear small round long-hand. They were made available to Sir Herbert Maxwell who quoted some passages in his life of the Duke of Wellington in 1899.

The Diaries, written in a slanting somewhat spidery hand, in faded gritty black ink, fill nine note-books and are here published for the first time by permission of the great-grandson of the writer, the fifth Marquess of Salisbury, to whom also the editor must record gratitude for the illustrations, all of which except two come from the collection at Hatfield House.

The Diaries are at first sight uniform, but actually, although all measure about 8 inches by 9 inches, they differ in almost every respect. All have stiff covers and most contain pages of good quality paper, well bound. The covers of several are of marbled paper with leather spines and corners — red, blue, olive. The first is the smallest and thinnest, written on paper water-marked "J. Whatman 1811".

The two written in 1828, one opening "Vienna" were perhaps bought there. They are bound in soft emerald green leather, but their paper is ribbed and yellowing. Only one has "Commonplace Book" on the spine. The 1824 volume was bought at Gray, Sons and Fell, 60 Piccadilly. That for 1833 is majestic in full red leather.

The diarist's three foreign tours have been omitted. They cover upwards of two hundred pages and would make a whole book, and of another sort. Otherwise, where passages have been omitted it is generally because they were repetitive or contained only lists of guests or figures of polls and votes. An omission is indicated by three dots . . . Square brackets enclose the editor's explanations. All references to the Cecil Papers refer to the Cecil Family papers at Hatfield House. Where proper names are spelt variously, the majority style has been chosen. The spelling has usually been left untouched but the punctuation has been augmented.

The editor wishes to thank, firstly the Marquess of Salisbury for his kind permission to edit the diaries and for much information about the family papers. Miss Clare Talbot, Archivist and Librarian at Hatfield House, has given the editor sympathetic and outstanding help at every juncture. The Gorhambury Papers were kindly made available by the Earl of Verulam. The editor also wishes to express her indebtedness to Mr. Ian Fraser, Archivist at the library, University of Keele, for assistance over the Sneyd Papers (and also for long and vain search amongst the sketches of Charlotte Sneyd for one of Robert Cecil in youth — the one infant apparently not sketched). Mr. Peter Walne, Archivist at Hertford County Record Office, and his staff, have given valuable assistance, and Professor Ernest Jacob, Librarian of the Codrington Library, All Souls College, Oxford, has supplied every detail for footnotes on the Diarist's fascinating description of her visit to the University attending the Duke of Wellington on his first appearance as Chancellor.

The author wishes to thank Mr. Basil King who took the photographs at Hatfield House for her book.

C.O.

Contents

Contents

Illustrations

9

By Sir George Hayter; reproduced by permission of the National Portrait Gallery

"Went with the Duke to the private exhibition of the Royal Academy, the first time of it being placed in the National Gallery. Hayter's portrait of the Queen abominable— like, but disagreeably so."

(From the Diary of the 2nd Marchioness, May 4th, 1838

All the illustrations, with the exception of the two separately acknowledged, come from the collection at Hatfield House and are reproduced by permission of the Marquess of Salisbury.

PART I
1729–1822

I

Mary Greene (1729–99)

Grandmother

When his motherless daughters were twenty and nineteen it was represented to Isaac Greene of Childwall Hall, Lancashire, that it was his duty to take them to London.

He came of yeoman stock: his ancestors had owned property in the parish of Prescot as early as 1490. But he had been apprenticed to the law as an attorney at an early age. His father, who had been a considerable merchant in Liverpool, had failed in business, gone overseas and died. This was a piece of ill-luck, for Liverpool had obvious possibilities. The old borough, lying between the pool and the Mersey, was a sad muddle of narrow alleys, and during the sixteenth and seventeenth centuries was visited by plague – but there was a continued slope down to the estuary, and as the site had a dry subsoil and fine natural drainage it was naturally healthy. With the Restoration commerce began to expand; Liverpool exported wool and got wine and iron. By 1709 the manufacturers of South Lancashire and the opening of the American and West India trade had made the harbour inadequate, and a wet dock had been constructed. Isaac Greene had lived at Childwall for a quarter of a century before Liverpool got a Town Hall, built in the Corinthian manner, but although he had prospered fishing in troubled waters, his fortune was assured before the West Indies were the source of most Lancashire riches. The times had been very disturbed, giving much scope for a hardworking and long-headed lawyer. Charles I, when Parliament had refused him funds, had sold a thousand manors in Lancashire. Many estates which had been sequestrated by the Commonwealth, and mortgaged, were being gradually recovered. Childwall stood in a park once Stanley property, amongst splendid beechwoods, on the hills east of the estuary. Isaac Greene had rebuilt it and re-named the old manor house before 1728. It was about five miles outside Liverpool, and the view from its terrace was breathtaking.

It looked towards Liverpool, not London, and Isaac, who had begun to buy land before he was thirty-four, was reported to have said that "if he had his days over again he would have all Lancashire in his hands". The daughters of such a man should be taken to London.

The elder Miss Greene kept a diary.

"*Friday, February ye 12th* (1747–8) We set out from Childwall in our own coach, went thro' Prescott to Warrington where Mrs. Grimes came to see us. We stayed all night.

"*Saturday (13th)* Din'd at Holmschappel, in the road from there to Lawton lost one of our small wheels, so walk'd to Lawton and stay'd there. Then the coach was mended. And look'd at the Church, nothing remarkable in it. Lodg'd at Talk [o' th'Hill].

"*Sunday (14th)* Stay'd at Newcastle all day, went to church in the afternoon ldg'd there that night.

"*Monday (15th)* Breakfasted at Stone, din'd at Whooseley Bridges, lay at Litchfield.

"*Tuesday (16th)* Din'd at Coleshill and lay at the King's Head in Coventry. These two last days excessive cold, hard frost with a little snow."

Their journey took them nine days. On the very afternoon of their arrival "safe in London", Mr. Nicholas Fazakerley, Member of Parliament for Preston, his sister and her sister-in-law, Mrs. Lutwyche of Holm Rook, were announced. Next day came Lady Strange, wife of the eldest son of the Earl of Derby, with the Ladies Stanley. Lady Sidney Beauclerk, wife of the fifth son of the Duke of St. Albans, followed. (She had been Miss Mary Norris of Speke.) Their circle contained a good many clients of Isaac, Jacobites and Roman Catholics. The girls bought materials at The Wheatsheaf in Covent Garden, took them to the mantua makers, and entered on a life of gaiety. They went to "An Oratorio call'd *Judas Maccabeus* by Mr. Handel", Queen Street Chapel, the Ridotto at Vauxhall, Drury Lane, Ranelagh and a large number of routs, card parties and tea-drinkings. The sad entry "Stayed at home all day" appeared only four times in their three London months.

Next year they repeated the happy experience, at almost exactly the same dates, but rode on horseback for the first two days, as far as Holme Chapel. Their London lodgings were this time mentioned — "a house in Southampton Street, Bloomsbury". They saw five of the children of the Prince of Wales at a performance of *Henry IV*, Mrs. Woffington as Calista, in *The Fair Penitent*, Mr. Garrick in one of his star parts — Abel Drugger — and the fireworks to celebrate the Peace, with Mr. Handel's music in the Green Park. Playing at Lottery Tickets at Mrs. Starkie's (*née* Miss Farington of Preston), they met "Mr. Will. Pitt", then aged forty and Paymaster-General.

They got home in May again, in "excessive hot weather" and started six weeks later for another haunt of fashion — Scarborough Spa. They saw the finest gardens they had ever seen at Studley, dined at Castle Howard, and took lodgings for York Races; but alas! under date July 27th, 1749, the *Gentleman's Magazine* recorded the death "of Isaac Greene of Lancashire, Esq., of an apoplexy when stepping into his coach". He had been in his seventy-second year and died intestate, but there was no question as to what should happen to his landed property and his £60,000 in hard cash. His daughters were his co-heiresses. They married happily, soon but not precipitately after losing their careful father. Ireland, who owed her unusual Christian name to the fact that their mother had been the ultimate heiress of the ancient Lancashire house of Ireland of Hale and Hutt, married Thomas Blackburne of Orford, Lancs. She was believed to have been given the first choice and was generally considered to have taken the lion's share when she asked for the manor of Hale — over thirty thousand acres of fat agricultural land. Mary got the manors of Childwall, West Derby, Wavertree, Everton and Much and Little Woolton, with less than two thousand acres. But they were going to become part of Liverpool. In the licence for her marriage to take place in King Henry VII's chapel, in Westminster Abbey, between eight and twelve a.m. on January 22nd, 1756/7, the bridegroom was described as Bamber Gascoyne, of St. Clement Danes, eldest son of Sir Crisp Gascoyne, Kt., Lord Mayor of London.[1]

[1] *Isaac Greene, a Lancashire Lawyer of the 18th Century, with the Diary of Ireland Green (Mrs. Ireland Blackburne of Hale)* 1748-9, Ronald Stewart-Brown, privately printed, Liverpool, 1921.

II

Fanny Price (1766–1820)

Mother

Eight years after Mary Greene departed to become Mrs. Bamber Gascoyne I of Bifrons, Essex, a Kentish gentleman was giving his consent to another marriage.

"Tunbridge Wells.
"September 28th, 1765.
"William Glanville Esq., M.P. to Chase Price Esq., M.P.
"Dear Sir,
"Sarah has acquainted me with the conversation that has passed between you on an affair of the highest consequence. You well know the esteem and regard I have for you, and assure you I shall be glad of a nearer and more intimate connexion with you, the terms of which we may settle at our next meeting, and must be defer'd till we meet. In general terms I agree to all your proposals and heartily wish you all health and happiness and will do all in my power to make you easy and happy, which I suppose may be obtained with £12,000 I will give her as a mark of my esteem for you and affection for her.
"I am Dr Sir, Yr affectionate Humble Servt.
"Will. Glanville."[1]

He had been born William Evelyn, but had taken the surname of his first wife, and with her fortune had bought the estate of St. Clere, near Wrotham, in Kent. She had died a month after bearing a daughter, Frances, and he had re-married. Eventually he reverted to Evelyn, but Sarah, a daughter of his second wife, married Chase Price as a Glanville. The marriage, which lasted for twelve years, was apparently happy, and from his various business and electioneering tours, a voiceful politician who was also a landowner in Shrop-

[1] Cecil Papers: Price Papers, Vol. I, 1, 221.

shire, Radnorshire and Herefordshire never failed to send his love to his "Sally" and to "Fids", "Miss Fidget", "my dear little girl". "I love you both to distraction." He had Miss Price, attended by lambs, painted by Sir Joshua. "Toby" Price had a London house in Queen Street, Mayfair, and was generally accepted as one of those who could be trusted to give dilettanti advice on interior decoration, and set the table in a roar. He died suddenly.

"14 South Audley Street.
"Monday, June 30th, 1777.
"Hon. Mrs. Edward Boscawen to Mrs. Delaney.

"I have seen Mrs. Price (my half-sister) whose shock and surprise is very great. She has gone to Brightelmstone to fetch away her girl. She received a letter from Mr. Price on Saturday evening (he had been dead then many hours) wrote on Friday in exceeding good spirits, and giving reasons why he did not himself come here as intended. He dined abroad, it seems, on Friday, and appeared to be perfectly well, for he has had a mortal disease, I am persuaded, a long time, and at length it ended him instantaneously for he appeared to be in a profound sleep when his servant found him dead on Saturday morning.

"Mr. Evelyn has got Mrs. Price, his sister, at his house (having left her girl with Lady Bathurst), where I have been all this morning, and I am now returning. He and his wife are very kind and friendly to her."[1]

Sarah Price took up life again, resolved to devote the remainder of it to "Miss Price", aged eleven. (She was destined to live for another fifty years, and die under the roof of her grand-daughter at Hatfield House, where her manuscripts came to rest amongst the archives.) She had no financial anxieties, but she prudently moved to a smaller house, in Tilney Street. On the Price side of the family, there was an antique invalid father, tyrannized over by his house-keeper, a rather colourless brother-in-law and a young nephew who showed every sign of developing into a confirmed bachelor. On the Evelyn side, relations abounded. Her principal adviser was a rock of strength, her half-sister, Fanny (widow of the elder Pitt's favourite Admiral),

[1] *Autobiography and correspondence of Mrs. Delaney*, ed. Lady Lanover, 1862, p. 229.

Mrs. Edward Boscawen, admired by Doctor Johnson, Dr. Burney, Dr. John Moore, Sir Joshua, Hannah Moore and Mrs. Montague, "Queen of the Blues". Frances Boscawen (1719–1805) had married 1742, Edward, son of 1st Viscount Falmouth. She engaged Robert Adam to decorate Hatchlands, her husband's Surrey home, and after his death divided her time between a house in London, 14 South Audley Street, and Rosedale, once the property of her favourite poet, Thomson. (It faced the Deer Park at Richmond, and has survived as the central block of the Richmond Royal Hospital.) Her family consisted of a surviving son who succeeded as Viscount Falmouth, and two daughters, Mrs. Leveson-Gower, wife of Admiral John Leveson-Gower, who lived at Bill Hill, Wokingham, and the Duchess of Beaufort, wife of Henry 5th Duke. Mrs. Boscawen, but not Mrs. Price, was a great-great-niece of John Evelyn of Wotton, the diarist.

The times were not easy for a young widow. The Duchess of Leinster, vanquished by the attempt to control her expenditure and brood of eleven young Fitzgeralds, had despairingly married her sons' Scotch tutor. Travelling, for a single woman, might entail terrifying experiences. But Mrs. Boscawen, a sailor's wife, was a stranger to self-pity. She urged on her half-sister (a hopeless sufferer from *mal de mer*) if the Continent was beyond her scope, to bigger and braver tours of beautiful Britain.

"Hon. Mrs. Edward Boscawen to Mrs. Chase Price. July 18th, 1785.

"Methinks we shall have a pleasant meeting at Badminton. I hope so. Never think of ye 70 miles. For your daughter's argument is unanswerable. Since you travel to please her, Echo answers, 'Please her'. Some friendly moon will help you on your way to Derbyshire. If not, you must borrow an hour of your pillow."[1]

Mrs. Price's tours tended westward, for she had two invariable ports of call, the homes of her step-nieces, Frances Leveson-Gower in Berkshire, and "Bess", Duchess of Beaufort, at Badminton. The Mount Edgcumbes also welcomed the Prices at Plymouth and Cotehele, and the Bathursts at Cirencester. The heavy peace of mid-Georgian afternoon settled upon the scene as Mrs. Price's

[1] Cecil Papers: Price Correspondence, I, 3.

MOTHER OF THE GASCOYNE HEIRESS

Sarah Bridget Frances, daughter of Chase Price, M.P., afterwards wife of Bamber Gascoyne II, M.P.

By Sir Joshua Reynolds. From the collection at Hatfield House.

post-chariot toiled across the landscape, from country house to country house for the improvement of Miss Price. There was a Revolution boiling up in France, but although most of their circle were interested in politics and some were in office, this undesirable foreign symptom of change was not allowed to disturb them. A letter from a Bathurst daughter to Mrs. Price's daughter, from Hastings, in July 1787 was typical.[1]

"Mrs. Price will be sure we must be completely happy when she hears we have a Bishop in the neighbourhood, the Bishop of Chichester. His place is about three miles off. We went there one evening, and by a fortunate mistake in our road drove through five or six miles of a lovely country. When our landolett was within sight of the house, one of his daughters ran out, in hopes it was a visit.

Notwithstanding the disappointment she was very civil to us, conducted us to a very fine wood, and sent a servant to show us the right road. The next day the Bishop and his daughter sent their compliments and enquiries. Whether we shall have any more inter-course with the Reverend family I know not. It is always a comfort to have a Mitre within reach.

We are going this day to visit some ladies whose father has a Place at the end of the town and is chief proprietor of the houses in it. He has civilly offered us the use of his ground to ride and walk in, and to get strawberries from his garden. This visit, you will con-ceive, is a great event and upon the strength of this acquaintance I have had my hat new trimmed."

Miss Price was shown Stourhead, Longleat, Fonthill, Stowe, Coleshill, Hunsdon, Hagley and Chatsworth. She specialized in castles — Windsor, Warwick, Wardour, Chepstow and Kenilworth. She visited the Derby ware factories, and Shakespeare's house, and Mr. Pitt's new purchase, and the Abbey at St. Albans. The chariot in which the inseparable mother and daughter travelled was hand-some. It had a trunk under the seats, two lamps, high steel springs, a box to take off, a platform budget to open in front and coats of arms on the panels. The estimate for it had been £131 5s. od. Mrs. Price kept very careful accounts. Mentions of expenditure on her own health were laconic. "Was blooded" or "Bled", occurred fairly

1 Cecil Papers: Price Correspondence, I, 3.

often. (Whether at Derby or Plymouth, the charge was the same, 10s. 6d.) Every ailment of the beloved child was meticulously entered, and even an unforgettable experience in a London fog, "That famous 18th of January, when I lost my Child in Berkeley Square".

Gradually Mrs. Price's bills ceased to be for such things as lessons in arithmetic, Atlas paper, a map of Judea, fine lake and a box of colours. From 1785, and very likely before, she made entries in small volumes called "The Ladies' Pocket Journal, or Toilet Assistant".

"Miss Price went to Court." She went to the Drawing-Room, to Almacks, to the Opera, to Lady Amherst's and Lady Bathurst's and Lady Salisbury's balls, and to concerts at Cumberland House. Lady Scarsdale wrote a very kind letter after Miss Price had visited Kedleston.

"I must not say all I think of Miss Price because she is so modest and so little aware of her own accomplishments; but without the least flattery, I never met with any young lady for whom I could so soon feel so much interested. Her turn of mind is so delightful, her judgment so far beyond her years, and her talents so many, and all this accompanied with such artless manners and so much diffidence that we are all full of admiration, but myself in particular. Miss Carson speaks of her fine singing and Julia of her sweet smile. I seldom touch upon the subject of beauty, for however pleasing to the eye, it may be only an outside cover to a very silly mind, but I can't help saying that possessing it as Miss Price does is a very great advantage, and tho she may not be a regular beauty she is something much more pleasing."[1]

The mother of a young lady who had made her entrance into the world had moved, to 33 South Street. The Prices had friends in Hertfordshire, as well as the West Country. At The Grove, Watford, they had Lord Clarendon, whose father, as a Lord of the Admiralty, had been a colleague of Admiral Boscawen. His property adjoined that of Lord Essex, at Cassiobury. In the east of the county, Sir Robert Chase of Much Hadham was fond of his niece, but terribly engrossed by his bodily ailments, and the pronouncements of his medical adviser, Pott. Pott, who sustained the fracture named after him, was physician to Johnson, whose deadly *Irene* he

[1] Cecil Papers: Price Correspondence, IV, 199–208. The pocket books also contain numerous notes on the weather and the direction of the wind.

loyally greeted as "the finest of modern tragedies". "If Pott says so," commented Johnson, "Pott lies."

On one of her rare absences from her daughter, Mrs. Price sent Hertfordshire gossip.

"I never heard anything like the manner of living at Hatfield — 500 fed every Tuesday and Friday for six weeks at Christmas, the House full of company, eating and drinking all day long: Doctor, Parson, and Montilarie (I have not spelt his name right, but you will understand who I mean). The latter did not dine at their table.

Lady Salisbury[1] goes a fox hunting in the morning, or in her open carriage, and to all the balls in the county at night. She had a chase last week that brought them to Cain Wood. Her Ladyship, Mr. Hale and Mr. Wesley[2] got into a hack chaise at Barnet and went home. Another day she went in her chariot, four horses in hand, eleven miles before they threw off. In short, she does anything and everything, all day long."[3]

Her ladyship's young companion and cousin, was in fact, already Member for Trim and a major in the 33rd regiment. But he was so unimportant still that when a choice had to be made as to who should be told he must ride home after a good picnic outside Dublin in a hackney coach with the musicians, poor Arthur Wellesley[4] was thought to be the least qualified to object.

[1] Mary Amelia, daughter of the 1st Marquess of Downshire (1748–1835), wife of 1st Marquess of Salisbury. Future mother-in-law of the Gascoyne Heiress.

[2] Arthur Wellesley (1769–1852), afterwards Duke of Wellington. "Father-figure" of the Gascoyne Heiress.

[3] Cecil Papers: Price Correspondence, I, 175.

[4] Anecdote related to the 2nd Marchioness of Salisbury by Lady Glenfall. Diaries, under date Oct. 2nd, 1835.

III

Bamber (1758–1824)

Father

On July 24th, 1794, Lady Susan Bathurst wrote to Bamber Gascoyne, Esq., M.P. at Bifrons, Barking, Essex.

"I cannot enclose my first letter to *Mrs. Gascoyne* without adding my congratulations to you, Sir, on her bearing that name. None can be a better judge than I of the happiness you have in store. I have known her from seven years of age and have often seen her fine temper tried, without being ruffled, and her good sense and fine disposition constantly acting to make her a comfort to her friends. Loving her as I do, I cannot but feel very much on this day tho' the principal sensation is that of pleasure, at her prospect being so peculiarly unclouded. Allow me to add my thanks for the flattering manner in which you received *Miss Price's Friend* during our short acquaintance in London, and believe me to be, with great regard,

"Sir, your obedient and faithful humble servt:

"Susan Bathurst.

"I hope Mrs. G. has not disappointed you by falling in love with Byfrons." [sic][1]

Mrs. Price's paragon amongst daughters had married. It was high time, for she was eight and twenty. Daughters who are inseparable companions of widowed mothers tend not to marry. Mrs. Price had realized this and resolutely determined to retire utterly, even if it broke her heart, and to love her son-in-law as if he were her own son. There are no doubts that he loved her Fanny. A postscript to one of her daughter's first letters after the wedding was blessedly reassuring.

"My dearest Madam,

"God bless you. I will take care of Fanny.

"B.G."

[1] Price Correspondence, II, 221.

24

"Think how your latter days are gilded by such a Son," wrote Fanny. "Mr. G.", she soon pronounced, was an excellent man. He treated her with uncommon tenderness, and really doted upon her mother. He was not happy because his mother-in-law was not with them (also, surely, rather uncommon). "Lady Selina likes him *vastly*," replied Mrs Price, "so cheerful, so pleasant; she approves much of your choice." He played a good hand at whist, and appreciated wild, solitary romantic mountain scenery. He was of a suitable age, thirty-six, brisk, efficient, and, as Lady Susan had delicately put it, the situation of his bride was peculiarly unclouded. His father had died three years past and he had inherited not only an old Liverpool fortune, still expanding, which had come with his mother, but that of his grandfather, Sir Crisp, the brewer, and his grandmother, the Lord Mayor's lady, heiress also of Dr. John Bamber. By a happy chance, Mr. Gascoyne's properties included land on the estuaries of the Mersey and the Thames. Childwall was as yet unknown to his bride; his widowed mother lived there; but he had made no bones about providing as fine a house as could be found in London, just round the corner from Mrs. Price. Number 10 Great Stanhope Street had belonged to the Burrells, one of the few families known to both the Prices and the Gascoynes (there had been a Barking business connection). Bamber had bought, with the house, the best of Sir Peter Burrell's furniture. And just outside London there was Bifrons, with which she had fallen in love.

Bamber's taste was always for the best, be it in India silk handkerchiefs, fowling pieces, a box at the Opera or a seat in the Curzon Chapel. His library was remarkable for so young a man: he collected Old Masters: he was a friend of authors. Indeed, the only flaw in this piece of perfection seemed to be a slight tendency to gout, an affliction very common at this date. His first attack, in October 1794, shook his wife. He looked terrible. "One of his worst kind of headaches." Her nerve broke and she sent a note and a carriage to South Audley Street to fetch Mrs. Price. When her mother did not come in it she could hardly believe her eyes. "You have but this one child, and can you refuse her?" Even Mr. G. had been thoroughly vexed. It was only thirteen miles. "How can you give me such pangs as those I felt yesterday when the man returned?" But Mrs. Price was not going to come between man and wife, perhaps in their first

25

tiff, and she was perfectly right, for although her unnatural conduct gave her dear daughter sickness and headache for three days, there was quite a normal reason for such symptoms, and in another few days Mr. G. was seated with his Fanny, looking through her mother's books with delight, and she had quite forgotten *"mes souffrances"*.

"This is a true picture of a hum drum November country fireside." By Christmas all was merriment at Bifrons and Great Stanhope Street, and young Mrs. Bamber Gascoyne made careful lists of what she had chosen from her mother's house, and her immediate need for a little of every shade of pink, down to ye deepest pompadour, for her bell-ropes and tassels. She had settled on the Chantilly dinner set, Dresden tea set, three Japan china bowls, two blue jars and a Japan chamber pot. In 1795 Bamber paid Jasper Archer, picture-cleaner, for work on a Teniers and other pictures. In 1800 he added a Breughel to his gallery and gave £4 14s. 6d. for having it cleaned. He had a volume of plays dedicated to him by Sir Henry Bate Dudley in 1791.[1]

"I trust my sweet mother e'er this has been so kind as to write to me. I doat on your letters. Pray tell me all the News. No letter as yet from Mrs. Gascoyne. As I went through Bond Street I met Lady Fitzwilliam, looking very ill and full of care. She dislikes going.[2] Her Boy with her, one of the finest I ever saw. I also met a very *smart* woman walking in Bond Street in a scarlet habit, with very short petticoats, much rouged, with many feathers, arm in arm between two men. She was laughing and talking very fast. What I took for a - - - - - - - - proved to be Mrs. Bertie, and one of the men was her foolish husband . . ."

Mother and child met often in London.

"My dearest Mother,

"Here I am, safe; and of all the days that poor Christians ever travelled in, this has been the completest. I had no idea of it. I got into what the French call *rase Campagne*. In South Street it was perfect stillness. A tempest blows this night that does indeed remind me of King Lear upon the Heath, and although we don't boast of being

[1] Cecil Papers: Price Correspondence, II, 220, 233–5.
[2] Lady Fitzwilliam's husband had just been appointed Lord Lieutenant in Ireland. He misunderstood his instructions and stayed three weeks.

situate either on *Hills or Mountains*, yet here it now blows a complete hurricane. The River seemed by daylight quite wild, from the tossing of the Vessels. What then must be the state of the foaming Ocean? and the Nore too? — not *quite* so smooth as when we shook hands with it last August. My poor head ached ready to split by the time that I got here. I was then grown so desperate that I resolved to take to the Bottle. I ate roast veal for dinner, and drank to the amount of three glasses of Port Wine, which have entirely and completely relieved and cured me . . . I am writing in my dressing room, perfectly in comfort, where Mary dawdles me every minute. I trust this will find you happy, well and very good at Rosedale, my sweet Mother. Pray pen me a usual, inimitably agreeable long letter. Your Son-in-law is busy examining your Book, and I am delighted to think you dine with me on Tuesday next, anywhere."[1]

Bifrons[2] had been built by Dr. Bamber, who had died in 1753 and had been enlarged and improved by his son-in-law, the first Bamber Gascoyne. It faced south and had everything handsome about it — park, flower garden, melon ground. It was just outside Barking, to the south-west and overlooked the levels and Gallions Reach, above Woolwich. The river-scene was always picturesque, whether in a storm or shine. With its slow-moving cattle and sails and dykes, it had a Dutch look. There was a tributary of the Thames, the Roding, running through the grounds, and the Kentish left bank was muffled in high summer by heat-haze and elms. The country names around it were romantic — Beehive, Clay Berry, Little Geries, Windelands. Some of the houses were antique. Malmeynes had frescoed walls and panelling and gay elaborate chimneys, Valentines had carvings by Gibbons.

Barking had once been much more important. There had been a Benedictine abbey, the first for females in Britain. Its Saxon abbesses had been of the blood-royal. But this had been demolished at the Reformation, there was scarcely a vestige left. Sir Crisp had sold the site, including a gateway with a chapel of the Holy Rood. But

[1] Price Correspondence, II, 258–9.
[2] In the summer of 1967 the author was just in time to see the last of Bifrons Street coming down to give place to a block of multi-storey flats. Salisbury, Cecil, Gascoigne [sic] and Cranborne roads still speak of the Gascoyne heiress but the area is now that of dockland and by-pass, cranes, pylons and gasometers.

he had bought land in Essex – the buildings and grounds of an ancient hospital and chapel at Ilford, close by. The parish church of St. Margaret, Barking, had been spared and its monuments presented practically a history of the neighbourhood. There were massive Norman columns. Bamber's father had had all except three, and all the arches and ceilings, encased in plaster. There was a rather humble little fishermen's chapel. A plaque commemorating a sea-captain had a horrific likeness of a ship in a storm at sea and that of a Jacobean military man showed him brooding in a profusely tented field. There was an Elizabethian font and a walnut pulpit. Captain Cook had stood at the altar here with his bride. There had been many residents with resounding names – Berties, Fanshawes, Hobarts, Sir Orlando Humphry. A peal of eight good bells sounded from the stout curfew tower.

The Bamber family were buried in the north aisle. There was a marble bust of that eminent chemist of Mincing Lane, Dr. John Bamber, in what was evidently a characteristic enquiring attitude. He had fine features, an open-necked shirt and flowing locks. He might have been a poet. An inscription told that the death of the doctor's daughter had early left Sir Crisp a disconsolate widower. Sir Crisp was here too, and his mother-in-law and his son, Bamber's father.

The Gascoynes were first recorded in York in 1663, but there was a missing link before John, who had died in 1682, and whose tablet in Chiswick churchyard said he had come from Gawthorpe. He had certainly been the great-grandfather of Sir Crisp, who had been born and baptized in Chiswick. The Gascoyne coat of arms had humour – argent on a pale sable, a conger's head with an ermine tail upon the neck.

Bamber Gascoyne I had been a worthy son of a genial and benevolent sire. He had gone to Queen's College, Oxford, and had qualified as a barrister of Lincoln's Inn; he had been Member of Parliament for five constituencies, Receiver-General of Customs and a Lord of the Admiralty.

The accounts of Bamber Gascoyne II, for 1795 showed bills for "great repairs at Bifrons". But the domestic scene was to be clouded by disappointment. In August of that year his wife bravely pronounced herself "Restored to health". She had been tenderly nursed through a shattering experience by her darling "Mam". She was tearfully

THE BAMBER HOME

Bifrons, Barking, 1794

Reproduced by permission from a sketch in the Guildhall Library copy of Lyson's Environs, *iv.i.88*

y

conscious of "the unremitting never-ceasing kind attentions of one of the best of husbands". It was an unfortunate date for a patient whom the medical men would have liked to send to a warmer clime. Revolutionary France had declared war on England in February 1793 and this war was to last, with a short uneasy interval, for twenty-one years. Bamber, who would gladly have bought a yacht or a *palazzo* for his ailing Fanny, had to take her to Ramsgate. She went willingly. "I am in terror lest my journey to the Sea should be delayed, for indeed London disagrees with me sadly." A personal physician attended the invalid and even so she sent enquiries to Sir Lucas Pepys,[1] Physician Extraordinary to His Majesty. "Ask Sir L.P. whether I am to wet my head when I go into the Sea. Tell him I always wear an Oil Skin Cap, in general. Ask him also whether I may not eat a crust of bread, or something of that sort, before I go into the Water."

They had a somewhat chilly reception from the William Evelyns at St. Clere. Bamber had to be tactful about a host not by nature hospitable. Sarah Price's birthplace was, she knew, much run down. "Mr. G. says it is in some measure due to his never having cultivated his understanding and being insensible to intellectual pleasures."

Ramsgate was an unqualified success. "This place suits a moon." By day it was basking in sunshine. Bamber sat out for hours watching the fashionable world go by. He said that Ramsgate Pier was the finest thing imaginable. It had cost half a million. He regaled himself watching the West India Fleet under sail and the Russian Fleet lying off. "We see the White Cliffs of France very plain, I can't bear even to contemplate the Shores — a Country drowned in its own Blood and teeming with every species of iniquity, torn into a thousand pieces by the outrages of its diabolical inhabitants. Pray God may still avert from this once happy land the calamities that seem to be coming upon it." A rich harvest was lying in the fields, waiting labour to carry it.

"Lady Burrell rides on a donkey, which she finds much benefit from." There was an incomparable telescope and a very agreeable

[1] Mrs. Boscawen had been chagrined when Lady Jane Evelyn had "thrown herself away" on a young doctor. Mrs. Price's brother, George, had married the heiress of the house of Leslie, Countess in her own right. But their daughter's love-match was accepted when Pepys ended a baronet and President of the Royal College of Physicians.

library. Bamber took one of the best marine residences available—
The Cloisters, Kingsgate. They had a phaeton. They begged their
dearest sweet Mammy to add to their bliss by joining them. But
calling herself "Old Sally", the mother-in-law said she would not
quit her bow window in South Street. "The Sea Breezes will in-
vigorate you beyond measure, though you dislike the Element itself.
You cannot conceive," pleaded Fanny, "how bracing and congenial
the Air is." She was pregnant again, and hopes ran high as the winter
passed. But Bamber's accounts for 1796 included a pathetic entry —
"Bill for interment of a stillborn child, April. £1 15s. od."

With the dash and decision which was an outstanding feature of
his character, and perhaps advised by the sympathetic but ineffectual
doctors, he took his wife away from Bifrons. They were going to his
northern property — Childwall. His mother still lived there — Old
Madam Bamber, born Mary Greene, heiress. It had been her home,
and she had not so far shown herself very friendly. There was an
epistle darkly alluded to in correspondence between Mrs. Price and
her daughter, "The letter she wrote to you at Barking". It had
promised a present, perhaps a legacy, which had never materialized.
But from the moment she set eyes upon it in October 1795, Fanny
was enchanted by her Lancashire property. Old Sally heard with un-
bounded relief that Mrs. Bamber senior, was showing herself "so
kind, so civil". "Mrs. Gascoyne must love you because you are so
affectionate and dutiful to me." "I see Mrs. Gascoyne by your
description; and the view; a fine view is my delight. If it please God
I should ever reach Childwall, how I shall sit and work and talk and
delight in the shade of that fine Hill, and looking at the glorious
prospect." They had taken a London *chef* north. "How does Mr.
Warde do? I hope he will not make you sick with his good dishes.
Do not, my dear Fanny, trouble yourself about writing to me when
it is inconvenient. I confess I live upon your letters, yet I would not
have you put yourself to any trouble about them. When Mrs.
Gascoyne wants you, set aside every occupation and business to
attend upon her . . ." It appeared Mrs. Gascoyne had said flattering
things to her son about his choice. "Always say pretty things from
me to Mrs. Gascoyne, and Allen: lay them on with a trowel to
Mrs. Allen; she is the sort of woman to like it, and one secret in
Life is to please people as much as one can and in their own way."

30

". . . My precious Child, take care of yourself, enjoy yourself for you are in a delightful place . . ." The most delicate probing as to her daughter's health brought tender reassurance. Mr Pitt's taxes were pressing hard even on people who had never known what it was to be short of money. "You would be ruined if you had a Nursery. I never heard anything like the Nurse's demands – for only a few days 5 guineas was asked and obliged to be given." "My Fanny is well, My Fanny is happy. What can I wish for? Nothing."

The eighteenth century waned and Mrs. Bamber Gascoyne II was still at Childwall. Mrs. Boscawen wrote that she had stuck up a great "N" in brilliant lamps to decorate her London house in honour of Lord Nelson's Glorious Victory of the Nile. Abuse of the blood-stained revolutionaries of godless France had shifted to the figure of Buonaparte – General, First Consul, Emperor to be. Bamber gave his wife a "Green House for you to puddle in". His mother died in 1799, aged seventy, and Fanny began to make Childwall "comfortable and pretty". Bamber took out shooting parties amongst the beautiful hills and commons trembling with silver frost or yellow with gorse. He had cut off the entail on his Essex and Lancashire estates and let Bifrons.

In the autumn in 1801, when they had been nearly eight years married, it appeared that he was perhaps, after all, to have an heir. Fanny, brought safe to London, was going her full time. But she had done that before, and the result had been tragedy. As the season advanced in extreme cold Mrs. Price's "indescribable trepidation" communicated itself so painfully to her circle of well-wishers that they hardly dared ask if Mrs. Gascoyne was still awaiting what they coyly called "the little stranger". With the New Year the heavens opened and snow descended upon England. To the delight of the ladies of the West Country the drifts were so deep that they halted the Duchess of Gordon, a natural bully, on her road to Haldon and Exmouth. Fanny Gascoyne waxed majestic, serene. Lady Curzon who saw her one morning before hurrying north to Rugeley thought she had never seen her looking so handsome. In the end, Dr. Clarke or Dr. Croft or Sir Lucas seemed to have made a miscalculation; Bamber had to hurry his wife home from an Assembly at Dorset House. Though she had no children, it was not Fanny Gascoyne's first experience of childbirth, and it soon became evident that she was advanced in labour. Monday, January 25th, 1802, was a day which made history in the meteorological calendar. A tremendous hurricane from the north-west struck winter-bound Britain. Several sloops were sunk at anchor in the Mersey, and a row of new-built houses in the Vauxhall road were levelled to the ground. In Mayfair, to the sound of shattering glass and falling tiles, the Gascoyne heiress suddenly and easily made her entrance into a wild world. Dr. John Clarke, who attended Mrs. Gascoyne as *accoucheur*, was a very old friend of the family, and at the top of his profession. He lectured on midwifery at Dr. William Hunter's Medical School and at Bart's. Dr., afterwards Sir Richard, Croft committed suicide in despair after the death in childbed of the Princess Charlotte, heiress to the throne.

The house in which the heiress was born, and from which she was married, still stands, a comfortable red-brick mansion, facing south on the north side of Great Stanhope Street, almost on the corner of Park Lane. The South Audley Street houses of her mother and great-aunt have been demolished and their sites are occupied by offices and flats.

William Evelyn, as head of the family, shook himself out of his accustomed gloom to bid Grandmama, "be sure YOU don't spoil Miss Gascoyne". The Duchesses of Beaufort and Devonshire wrote congratulations to "the lady in the straw", and Ladies Sefton and Mount Edgcumbe and de Clifford and Bathurst and Bulkeley and Scarsdale and Rothes . . . Bamber even got a letter from an unknown neighbour in Great Stanhope Street to beg that if he "would wish my knocker to be taken off, lest it should disturb, I hope he will let me know". The best-phrased good wishes came, as might be expected, from Mrs. Boscawen.

"Thus my curtains were drawn — 'Good News! Mrs. Gascoyne is safely delivered of a fine child! A Girl! And had a Good Time! At 4 this morning!' "

Poor Mrs. Price had already been round herself in the dark, but had retreated hearing that her half-sister was still asleep.

"Put your hand gently on Miss's head and say, Her Great-Great-Aunt sends her blessing."[1,2]

[1] Cecil Papers, V, 233–245.
[2] Mrs. Boscawen surely added a generation. She was the step-great-aunt only of the Gascoyne Heiress.

Mr Gascoigne

London Pub. by Rich.d W.ons 26 Haymarket 1826

Drawn Etch.d & Pub.d by Richard Dighton 1826 Aug.t

An Exotick at the Green House Leadenhall Street
"I do begin to fear 'tis you,
Not by your individual whiskers,
But by your dialect and discourse"

FATHER OF THE GASCOYNE HEIRESS

"Mr. Gascoigne — An Exotick at the Green House Leadenhall Street
  'I do begin to fear 'tis you,
  Not by your individual whiskers,
  But by your dialogue and discourse'."

Drawn, etched and published by Richard Dighton, 1820

IV

Fanny Gascoyne

The Gascoyne Heiress

The Gascoyne heiress, so long looked for, would certainly have been considered wonderful by her nearest and dearest even if she had been a very ordinary child. But from the first it was clear that she was going to be lovely and spirited. From the first also it was accepted that she was going to be the Gascoyne Heiress. Only one of the many letters of congratulations on her birth suggested that beginning with "only a girl" was no bad thing. No subsequent letters showed any signs of hopes of a successor in her nursery.

Dr. Jenner received £10 10s od. for "the vaccine inoculations" and one horror of the Georgian nursery was banished. The infant prospered. A family pattern began to repeat itself — of loving mother and daughter. But this time the correspondence was triangular. Her mother and grandmother wrote to one another torrentially, and when the precious child was left for the first time alone with her grandmother, but for a nurse, Mrs. Price wrote every day. The excellent never-failing Dr. Clarke who had brought her into the world also called weekly, though the little girl was in perfect health.

Frances Mary Gascoyne received her unexplained, ugly, beloved little pet names "Pokey" and "Souls". She was unusually observant. "Papa's horses have a yellow rose on the side of their forehead. Dr. Clarke's have none." The grandmother's letters provided a score of pretty *vignettes* — "Souls" not quite three yet, gone in her blue hat and brown shoes to visit the Ladies Keppel, Lady Albemarle's children. Lady Elizabeth, aged seven, said something of her Mama. "Your little one answered in haste, 'I have a Mama and a Papa too, and a Grandmama'." "I go in a barouche," said Lady Elizabeth. "And I go in a Sociable," countered Miss Gascoyne. Her hostess showed her all over the house and she followed with much dignity, missing nothing. That night, having seen how Lady Elizabeth put away her hat and gloves and handkerchief, she folded up everything within reach. It was the prettiest sight to see her in Lady de Clifford's garden. "She puts her dear nose to every flower, without presuming to gather them." She loved to watch her grandmother saying her prayers. "If you could have seen with what piety and exactness she mimicked me you would have been much diverted."

At this age she signed "with her Mark", but gradually there came half-sentences. "Duty to Father and Mother", "Send 10 kisses to Papa and Mama" and whole sentences, "I have been walking with Uncle", "I want a Donkey". (Thomas, the footman was sent to stalk behind her when she went out in the green fields.) "I am a very good girl" ("written by the heiress", noted Mrs. Price fondly). The child seemed to have an unusual memory. She could not really read yet, but she liked to pretend to be reading, "in her own way", and as to singing, her voice raised echoes on the staircase as she retired for the night at seven p.m. She early showed a preference for Bamber. When choosing houses in books, the best one was always for Papa. The grandmother listened awestruck to the uncanny sound of an only child making conversation with imaginary callers. "When it is dusk we tell stories; when candles come we get round the table and teach the dolls to read." A grand-daughter who never saw her believed that the Gascoyne Heiress had been a shadowy character, "incapable of any self-assertion in public"[1] but she was never shy, and as a little girl "as wild as anything out of the woods". "I don't like you!" she would announce to any one who had crossed her in a favourite project. ("This will have to be corrected, for it is very disagreeable to hear.") Mrs. Price's recipe was to tell her that she was a fool for saying so, followed by a kiss. "She is the best and most agreeable creature I ever saw, and I expect of her all I want her to be." Her temper was excellent; she hardly ever cried and never sulked. She could always be led, but it must be by a silken string. "She is very desirous of doing Right and being a Young Lady, as she calls it." She wondered if Miss More would approve of her . . . "Your child has slept all night and is now playing with the cat and very gay." A letter had to be interrupted, "Souls" in her blue hat and feather, saying "Come Grandmama". The couple went for some long country drives.

Dr. John Clarke found them with Lord Clarendon and reported to

[1] Lady Gwendolen Cecil, *Life of Robert, Marquis of Salisbury*, Vol. I, p. 7.

Childwall from Watford that he could answer for the health and good looks of "Grandmama and Missy, both of whom I saw at The Grove yesterday, where also I met Lady Downshire, who came to Town for two days with the young Lords on their way to Eton." Mrs. Price had told him that Childwall was "environed with enclosure plans and likely to be sunk in Coalmines" but the heiress was rosy and a romp. "Will Liverpool like a Spanish War?" wondered Mrs. Price in 1804. "I shall not: It will be-devil our pockets." The destruction of the Spanish Fleet at Trafalgar solved the problem and "smiling Childwall" became more beautiful every season. When his daughter was about seven years old Bamber let his wife loose upon his old home. Mr. Nash was called in. He had already re-built Hale Hall for the Blackburnes. Childwall was transformed into a yellow sandstone sham mediaeval castle. Young Mrs. Bamber ordered Grecian lamps, and an Octagon Room, and a billiard board, and an oak Gothic sarcophagus. Lord Stafford, who had been Ambassador in Paris, was her guide as to French elegance. Lord Sefton[1] knew the latest devices in lighting.

While the home was being altered Bamber took several houses outside London for his wife and child and her mother. There was one on Putney Hill in 1802, and one in Paddington two years later, rented from Lord Dudley, and in 1809 Lady Anne Barnard's Gothic cottage at Wimbledon and in 1810, 14 The Steyne, Worthing. But his child's heart was in the north. She wrote of "nasty London" and "Darling Childwall". Mrs. Price accepted this philosophically. "The air is fine and the child delights in the place." She had Blackburne cousins at Hale and Gascoyne cousins at Roby. Neither family really pleased her mother. Mrs. Blackburne appeared to have quite lost her head running after the Prince of Wales and his associates when he was in their neighbourhood. She dragged her poor pale girls miles after such company and gave an impossible ball. ("The Member's lady will offend half the County by not asking the Chaperones.") At Roby Hall General Isaac Gascoyne,[2] also a

---

[1] William Molyneux, 2nd Earl of Sefton (1772–1838) of Croxteth Hall, Liverpool, m. Maria, daughter of 2nd Baron Craven.

[2] General Isaac Gascoyne (1770–1841), m. Mary Williamson of Liverpool, 3 sons, 3 daughters. One of the girls, born in February 1802 at 71 South Audley Street, was almost a twin of Fanny Gascoyne, born in the same week at 10 Great Stanhope Street.

Member of Parliament (he had succeeded to Bamber's Liverpool seat in 1802), loathed parting with sixpence. Fortunately, his lady seemed to share his taste. The couple appeared to live in imminent danger of being dashed to eternity owing to their refusal to invest in new harness. "She is always getting into carriage scrapes." Outside the family there were other neighbours, more or less approved – Woods, Corbetts, Pitts, Leighs. When Grandmama Price heard that her bachelor nephew was staying with "my beloved trio" at Childwall, she pooh-poohed the idea of a short stay and plea of posting expenses. "Tell him all the Fine Men travel in the Mail. Mr. Jenkinson, with £20,000 per annum comes up in the Mail. I believe it is *bon ton*."[1]

The child was eleven and her nurse, Mrs. Levett had retired. She had Mlle. Audibert and Mme. Piot, and her personal maid, Lizzy, who was to stay in her service for twenty-five years. She collected seashells and Anglesey marbles. When a letter arrived in October 1814 to Lord Bulkeley at Beaumaris, to announce the marriage of his niece Miss Milbanke to Lord Byron, Mrs. Gascoyne told her daughter, "We all pity her." But every romantic young lady in England envied her, and the heiress was certainly romantic. At fifteen she began her first Commonplace Book. Her signature "F. Gascoyne, 1817", was inscribed within, and on the flyleaf an appropriate couplet:

"From Grave to gay
From lively to severe!"

The book contained impromptus, epitaphs, verses, riddles, programmes, and recipes. The family were very fond of recipes, both genuine and humorous. Miss Gascoyne's recipe "To make a fashionable Assembly or Rout" was satirical. "Take all the ladies and gentlemen you can get. Place them in a room with a slow fire. Have ready a Harp or Pianoforte . . ." Her grandmother's were serious and included Sir William Hamilton's directions "How to Dress Macaroni", and cures for the bite of a mad dog, wasp sting, easy

[1] Charles Cecil Jenkinson, succeeded his half-brother in 1829 as Earl of Liverpool. Born in 1784, he went to sea in 1794, to Christ Church, Oxford, in 1797, and to Vienna as Secretary to Legation in 1804. He served in the Austrian forces at Austerlitz and married Julia Evelyn Medley, cousin of Mrs. Price, a short-lived heiress, known in their family as "The Golden Fleece".

delivery, against plague, and how to make pickles, raspberry, goose-berry and currant wine, and poppy cordial. The heiress had the most momentous – "Dr. Samuel Johnson's Cure for indigestion".

She was still considered too young to perform in private theatricals, but she preserved the programme of *The Midnight Hour*, performed at The Theatre Royal, Hale – where a long range of lighted windows looked out from a gallery, filled with young people, in Christmas week 1814, over the enthralling view of sails bending up and down the Mersey estuary. The West India trade encouraged by Parliament had been abolished. Five-sixths of it had centred in Liverpool, where spectacular fortunes had been made. In March 1817, Bamber's agent was distressed that a Liverpool captain was being brought to trial for traffic in slaves. Mr. Leigh was sure that Mr. Bold could not, as malice affirmed, have been a party to it. He got a worse shock that November, when a highwayman who had been apprehended and taken to Lancaster gaol was said to be "a descendant of the Brettarghs of the Holt, in Little Woolton, which is a family of as much antiquity, I believe, as any in this country". The Gascoyne heiress would inherit it – bought by her great-grandsire Isaac Greene. Curiously enough, her mother and grandmother who were so proud of her talents, never mentioned her sketches, which were proficient. Her "Views at Childwall" were drawn with a loving hand. A fine scene of rural greenery was simply entitled "Near Manchester". She garnished her Album with occasional little decorative water-colour designs of a pack of cards flung down on a table . . . a guitar . . .

She was sixteen, and a Patroness of the True Blue Club of Liver-pool. She was seventeen and Mr. John Leigh was dutifully impressed to see her name amongst those who had attended the Duke of Gloucester's Ball, and even more pleased to find she was not in the least spoilt by her first taste of London gaiety. She was quite delighted to be back in Lancashire in September, where her mother was plan-ning an ice-house. Of course Mrs. Price, who had announced that she never expected to see a place so distant as Childwall, had done so long ago, and was able to appreciate references to every tree in her daughter's letters. An active and resourceful son-in-law had taken all her travel-troubles upon him. She even grew less delicate: "My Back" made only intermittent appearances in her letters, as her grand-daughter became at last A Young Lady. There was a clever charming Young Lady called Olivia De Ros[1] whose caricatures enlivened later Albums treasured at Hatfield. Olivia De Ros gave Fanny Gascoyne an appropriate sketch of a débutante in bed (surmounted by inset scenes of a Chiswick Breakfast and a Ball at Almacks), repelling a coronet, jewellery, invitations and a milliner. The poems of Byron lay upon the floor,

"Visions of Glory, spare my aching sight!
Ye unbought bonnets, crowd not on my view!"

The Gascoyne heiress had already received her first proposal of marriage at seventeen and three months.

"I deem it to be the most manly and the most honourable mode, for one who feels as I do, to make a frank and full avowal of his sentiments, for which, though I entreat your indulgence, I cannot confess myself to be ashamed. And when I declare to you, as I hereby do, that I entertain the strongest attachment and love for you, I am confident that this confession is made to One possessed of qualities which, whatever Her decision, will not suffer Her to treat otherwise than with tenderness, the most anxious and the most dear communications which a Man can make to a Woman. Having thus undisguisedly stated to you my feelings, I entreat and I implore of you to make me happy by consenting to become united with me, and I do so with the ardour and with the humility to which you are eminently entitled, and with which every Man of spirit must feel himself impressed when he solicits the Lady whom he loves.

"For myself, I have nothing to plead except my sincere devotion to you, for I seek nor desire no other boon than but yourself and with you I should be supremely happy. And should you bless me with a favourable reception, the study of my life should be to make you happy by every constant attention and kindness that the fondest affection can inspire. As I perceive that the first avowal of attachment is due, in the first instance to Her who has inspired it, I have

[1] Olivia, daughter of Charlotte, Baroness De Ros, and Lord H. Fitzgerald (1808–1885), m. 1833 Henry Wellesley, 1st Earl Cowley, and became a connection by marriage of Fanny.
The Baroness and her husband had six sons. There were also five De Ros girls, Charlotte, Henrietta, Olivia, Geraldine and Cecilia.

THE DEBUTANTE'S DREAM

"Visions of glory spare my aching sight,
Ye unbought bonnets crowd not on my view."

Sketch by Olivia Wellesley, née De Ros, in an Album belonging to the 2nd Marchioness of Salisbury addressed this letter to you without any previous communication with your Parents, but that I might not, by thus approaching you, appear guilty of indelicacy towards a Young Lady, for whom I feel every tenderness and every respect, I have enclosed it unsealed to your Father. Should you deem its contents or its author worthy of your consideration my next happiness would be to be permitted by you to address each of your Parents and to implore their consent whom it would ever be my delight as well as my duty, constantly to cultivate and to respect.

"With repeated sentiments of attachment and of affection I conclude this letter, by again imploring your consent and favour and I subscribe myself as I feel

"Your most sincere and most devoted

"GARVAGH.

"Hertford St. 25th June, 1819."

George Canning, Baron Garvagh, came from Ireland, and was a first cousin of his namesake the statesman. He had been a widower for fifteen years. He was forty-one.[1] Apparently her father dealt with Fanny's first offer, for though she kept drafts of important letters nothing further about this one survived. It simply dropped into the files that went to Hatfield with her on her marriage.

Her particular friend in the south since they were both eight years old, had been Charlotte Beauclerk,[2] a daughter of the Duke and Duchess of St. Albans. There was continual visiting between the Gascoyne house in Great Stanhope Street and the Beauclerk family mansion in St. James's Square. The Duchess was a good mother, and her plans had been fixed long before the day in 1816 when she had heard by an express from London that her explosive ex-naval husband had unexpectedly succeeded an infant nephew. She had sent on the news directly to her dear Mrs. Gascoyne. Her admiration for "Fanny", "Fanchette", "Fanchon" was sugary. She wanted the Gascoyne heiress for her eldest son, Lord Burford,[3] and

[1] Cecil Papers, VI, 290. In 1824 Lord Garvagh married Miss Rosabelle Bonham of Titness Park, Berks, and got an heir.
[2] Charlotte, second daughter of William, 8th Duke of St. Albans, and Maria Jeanetta Nelthorpe, b. 1802, d. unmarried 1842.
[3] William Beauclerk, Earl of Burford, afterwards 9th Duke of St. Albans (1801–1849).

Lord Cranborne,[1] the heir of the house of Cecil, for her Charlotte. She made Charlotte send her dearest friend an enthusiastic account of the peculiar good conduct of Burford in the Rebellion at Eton, November 26th, 1818, with an attached copy of Dr. Drury's commendatory letter. People were very unkind about Burford. Mrs. Arbuthnot, confidante of the Duke of Wellington, said that he was all but an idiot and had been confined: Lady Cowper said, "The fact is, he is not an innocent or an idiot, but a very raw uncultivated strange Cub, but I believe not a bad kind of person." Charlotte was not without humour.

"We have had a good deal of company here this week. I think you will smile when you hear I tell you that Lady Stepney[2] has brought with her a maid, two dogs and ten birds, Amelius [destined for the Navy and three years old] is quite distracted: he is so delighted with all the animals." Burford was now finishing his education on the continent, with a tutor. A necklace from Italy was sent by him for Fanny, said his sister, who presented it. The Duchess was disturbed. She had heard and seen with her own eyes that Lord Cranborne was at least attracted by Fanny. There was to be "the usual Grand Ball" given at Hatfield in honour of Cranborne's birthday. Charlotte sent to her dear Fanny, who was up at Childwall, a tantalizing description. She had stayed for the occasion at Kimpton with her uncle Lord Frederick Beauclerk, who was the fox-hunting non-resident vicar of St. Michael's, St. Albans. Lord Frederick Beauclerk and Mr. John Knight, the Rector of Welwyn, hunted with the Hatfield Hounds, of which Lady Salisbury was mistress and whose uniform was unique — sky blue with black collar and cuffs and silver buttons. Lord Frederick rode regularly in the Hunt steeplechases and won at St. Albans with "The Poet", a horse that had been third in the St. Leger.

"Lady Caroline Lamb[3] kindly gave us a dinner and bed on the

[1] James Brownlow William Cecil, Viscount Cranborne, afterwards 2nd Marquess of Salisbury (1791–1868).
[2] Lady (Catherine) Stepney, daughter of Rev. Thomas Pollok and wife of Sir Thomas Stepney, Bart., authoress of *Castle Nuovier or Henry and Adelaide*, 1806, and *The Lords of Erith*, 1809. She d. 1845.
[3] Caroline Ponsonby, daughter of Frederick, 3rd Earl of Bessborough(1785–1828), and wife of William Lamb, afterwards 2nd Viscount Melbourne (1779–1848) and Prime Minister. Augustus, whom they took to the Hatfield Ball, was their mentally

26th of September at Brocket Hall. We all set off from her door about nine o'clock in two carriages, Lady C. Lamb, Lady F. Beauclerk, Cousin Lamb's tutor and myself occupied one carriage, F. Beauclerk, Mr. Lamb and Augustus, the other. You cannot have an idea of the excessive foolish conduct Lady C. exhibited during the whole of the 15 miles to Hatfield House. First exclaiming they would all be robbed and murdered, then, if they escaped that death, they should be decidedly all overturned coming home, as she was sure that Lady Salisbury made it a regular system of giving the servants too much liquor. However, we arrived in perfect safety, and after dancing with six separate partners, Lord Cranborne at their head, we retired at half past four o'clock in the morning. The supper was much complained of by all the gentlemen, there being a great scarcity of wine and chickens."

Fanny had sent, with some spirit, cheerful descriptions of the country balls she was enjoying in Lancashire. Charlotte and her mother repeated how beautifully the tall and graceful dark girl performed her dancing steps. The Duchess had sent acid sympathy when the débutante had suffered a social set-back. "I regret poor Fanny's disappointment over Almacks." The girls had paid one another country-house visits. Fanny went to Upper Gatton, near Reigate, and Charlotte came to the villa at Richmond. But when the Gascoynes returned to London for the winter season of 1819–20 the Duchess suddenly regretted that as it was Charlotte's last year "in the study" (i.e. that she was not really out yet in spite of the Hatfield Ball) it was with reluctance that her mother must refuse to permit further distractions.[1]

---

deficient only child, then aged thirteen. Charlotte must have been thinking of Kimpton when she said Brocket was fifteen miles from Hatfield. It is nearer three.
[1] Cecil Papers: VI, 263, 285, 298, 303, 312, 319; VII, 60–75.

V

Cranborne

Suitor

James Walter Grimston, 1st Earl of Verulam, lived in Gorhambury House, built for his father by Sir Robert Taylor. It had a Grand Corinthian portico. The old Elizabethan family house was represented only by picturesque ruins and a gatehouse in the park. It stood two and a half miles north of St. Albans. He was a benevolent Hertfordshire landowner, with a big nose, full lips and bushy brows, a devoted father of an increasing family, and amongst his virtues was keeping a diary. Lord Verulam's *Daily Register or Complete Remembrances* (five inches by eight inches) with marbled covers provided, as well as space for daily entries, tables and lists of bankers, Army agents, lawyers, public holidays and hackney coach regulations. He always gave his headaches and digestive disorders pride of place, but also recalled meticulously the visits of his neighbours. His handwriting was very legible.[1] On January 17, 1820, he entered. "Mrs. and Miss Gascoigne [sic] arrived, and Lord Cranborne, *per* special request." The Cecil heir often stayed at Gorhambury for shooting. It was a well known discovery amongst young gentlemen in love that a beauty who one met in a London ballroom was not always the same when you got her in the country. Miss Gascoyne was tried hard at Gorhambury. There had been a very severe frost since Christmas. On the evening of her arrival the party played Commerce. Next morning Lord Cranborne sat next to her at breakfast. It was "a very dark miserable looking day", and the whole household, with the exception of the host, rose late. That night, incredible as it might seem, they all bundled into carriages and drove off over the slippery roads to Lady Salisbury's Tuesday ball at Hatfield House. "Lord Cranborne paid proper attention to Miss Gascoigne."

The Grimston children, who had enjoyed fireworks, snowballing and high diet during the festive season, were fast falling victims to

[1] Gorhambury MSS, Herts County Record Office.

Childwall Hall, near Liverpool, her early home, by Fanny Gascoyne

Two sketches from an Album of the 2nd Marchioness of Salisbury

Gorhambury, St. Albans, by "Katty" Grimston: scene of the courtship of the Gascoyne Heiress by Lord Cranborne the measles. Lady Verulam had become what her husband described as "sillily violent" when their neighbour Lord Dacre had attempted to turn a joke on the sacred subject of the measles. She was an anxious parent with a house full of guests — "Codrington, the Hothams, the Rous [sic], Cranborne and the Beauclerks" (from Kimpton). They had come for shooting and it was obvious that if it snowed again they might be boxed-up here. Lady Verulam's connection with the Gascoynes was long-standing. "In swam my Lady Liverpool," happily recorded Mrs. Price on a September evening in 1810. Lady Verulam was a connection by marriage, not very close, but invaluable to an intending suitor. She had been born Charlotte Jenkinson, daughter of the 1st Earl of Liverpool, and her brother Charles had married Julia Evelyn Medley. She was generally considered the most beautiful of the Jenkinson sisters. Her husband recorded on January 19th that the Gascoynes, taking advantage of a sudden downpour of rain which had cleared the snow, had returned to London, but Cranborne had stayed on. The Duchess of St. Albans soon came into action again.

"My dear Mrs. Gascoyne,

"Manoeuvring, I see, is not confined to the imagination of the Edgworth family. I am curious to discover Lady Salisbury's *But* in asking for an interview with you, unless it is to ingratiate her little agreeable Mattadore into your dear daughter's graces. But, if I know her well, she requires more personal as well as mental qualifications before she bestows her hand and heart on so prompt a predeliction, as the Palais de Verité must take precedence of the Palais de Hatfield."

The fateful interview of which she had got wind had, in fact, already taken place, and the heiress had sent her grandmother Price a breathless account, of which she kept a draft.[1] She did not mention whether it had been staged at Hatfield or in the Salisburys' house in Arlington Street. Lady Salisbury had desired to make the better acquaintance of Mrs. and Miss Gascoyne, but Bamber, a foeman worthy of her steel, had appointed himself to attend his darling.

"I have had my audience and am fully satisfied; nothing could be kinder than Papa; and I think his conversation with Lady Salisbury

1 Cecil Papers: Family Correspondence, IV, 291.

exactly what one should have *wished*. She began by praising her son's character and disposition; and adding that he was the last of a very noble and ancient house, and the heir of a very large property, which perhaps though in some degree embarrassed, must eventually be considerable. 'Under these circumstances, Mr. Gascoyne,' she said, 'you cannot be surprised that we wish to see him settled in life; we have often proposed to him several persons with that view, but (until he had the good fortune to meet your daughter at Gorhambury) not one that appeared to meet his inclination.'

"Papa replied by alluding to the extreme shortness of the acquaintance. 'Very true,' said she, 'and therefore I should only look forward to it in the course of *a year or two*. In the meantime might Cranborne be permitted to endeavour to render himself agreeable to Miss G.? In which attempt, if he should succeed, perhaps your consent might then be obtained for their union?'

"Papa replied that such a proposal, from her Ladyship, must be considered in a *worldly* point of view, as an honour by any family in the kingdom, and that for her to wish to further it he had to return her thanks. But as to Lord C.'s attentions, the authorizing them might put both parties in a very awkward predicament; that they would be immediately marked by the world for each other, driven like *stricken deer* from the herd, and find themselves implicated – each other without having any . . . of the sort. That I was very young . . . my ideas of the world and . . . me, might alter materially. That *marked* attentions from . . . one person would prevent any other from coming forward, and consequently preclude me from forming new acquaintances – that Lord C.'s acquaintance with me had been so short that his sentiments might also undergo a change. That therefore he was sure Lady S. would agree with him that the whole thing had better rest where it was and if it should again come forward at any future time, might then be discussed more at large. Lady S. acquiesced . . . parted very good friends . . . is the substance of what he told . . . we will talk it over tonight . . . burn this . . . wished my behaviour to Lord C. to [be?] exactly as if nothing had happened."

Bamber had discerned, with the eye of love, that his daughter's affections were deeply engaged, and it must be allowed that the suitor seemed in every respect created to catch the fancy of a

44

romantic girl whose head was full of Walter Scott, or even of Byronic heroes. He was the heir of a family which had provided successive chief ministers for Queen Elizabeth and James I. The Virgin Queen had long been kept a prisoner in his ancestral home. Tradition pointed out an oak under which she had been sitting when messengers brought her the news of her accession to the throne. For several generations the Cecils had not distinguished themselves, but the present (first) Marquess was a stately figure. A guest at Hatfield recently had described him as "seventy years old but well preserved, and a specimen of the gentlemen of the last generation, with easy and elegant manners and a proud graceful courtesy".[1] He looked ill. His dashing, Irish, fox-hunting lady was a leader of fashion and of the high Tory political world. A lady-in-waiting to the Princess of Wales reported in September 1820.[2] "Her assemblies are certainly the best of their class in London. The house is like a nobleman's, and the hostess herself has such dignified manners that they cannot fail to be courtly receptions." There were two daughters, both married, the elder to a brother of the Duke of Wellington, the father-figure of Great Britain, indeed of Europe, the younger to an Irish marquess. The Palais de Hatfield, as the Duchess of St. Albans somewhat ill-naturedly styled it, had in fact been originally a royal palace, a relic of which still existed, couched at a little distance under the protective shadows of the much larger red-brick E-shaped house in which the family now lived. Hatfield, with its gently-swelling park, and long misty avenues embosomed in ancient woods, was something unusual amongst great houses. It had all been built within five years, when the first Earl of Salisbury at the suggestion of his sovereign, had exchanged his property in the east of Hertfordshire, Theobalds, for the royal estate of Hatfield. It had a maze, a terraced flower-garden, a lake, a Great Hall, a Long Gallery, a Grand Staircase, an Adam and Eve staircase, many more lesser staircases, some very steep, and a myriad of chambers panelled in various woods. The flags hanging from the minstrels gallery in the dining hall were Napoleonic trophies, sent by the Duke of Wellington to his cousins . . .

To come to the suitor himself, the Duchess of St. Albans had

[1] *Life, Letters and Journals*, George Ticknor, 2 Vols, 1876, I, 268.
[2] *Diary of a Lady-in-waiting*, Lady Charlotte Bury, ed. f. Steuart, 2 Vols., 1908, II, 263.

called him a Mattadore. The matador is the bull-fighter who gives the quietus. It was not a kind nick-name and it had some significance. His manner and even appearance could be a little combative. The fact was that he had yearned for a martial career. He had been born in 1791, therefore he was now nine and twenty. He had been fourteen when Trafalgar had been won, twenty-one to twenty-four when many of his contemporaries were distinguishing themselves on the sun-baked *sierras* of the Peninsula and the wet woods and cobbles leading to Waterloo. But he had been a precious only son and could not be allowed to join the army. He had been an officer in the Hertfordshire militia for ten years and now commanded the regiment. But the militia was not raised for foreign service, and since Trafalgar there had been little fear of invasion. His country was not going to engage in a major war again while he was of fighting age. He had tried to serve it in diplomacy, had written to the Duke of Wellington, begging to be allowed to join his staff at the Congress of Vienna. His parents, particularly his mother, had soon stopped that. (When he was fifty he wrote to the Duke, "The object I have sighed after all my life, from the time when I asked you to take me as *attaché* to Vienna, to the present, has been employment.")[1] He wanted to serve his country. He had been Member for Hertford for three years. He was debonair, quite fearless, already slightly eccentric, high-handed and passionate. His French was perfect. He often corresponded for choice with his younger sister in French. In 1836 he told the Rev. Henry Lyte, tutor to his eldest son, "Having derived throughout life the greatest advantage from considering French as my native tongue, I have in consequence made my children speak it even before they could speak English."[2] He charmed Mrs. Gascoyne. But the Duchess had not yet lost hope. Mrs. Gascoyne, whose simplicity was pitiful, had said with dignity that she thought well of Lord Cranborne. She must be undeceived.

"I fear you are a little cross about what I named about our friend Cranborne, who I think very delightful in most respects, but we all know him to be so great a SWAIN that the sooner he gets married the better and since their last *éclaircissement* which has so much amused

[1] Cecil Papers: Letters of the Duke of Wellington to the Second Marquess and Marchioness of Salisbury, draft dated Sept. 9th, 1841.
[2] Cecil Papers, XII, 338.

the world where Lord Camden is concerned, I could not help laughing at your standing up for his Chastity as I daresay Lady Salisbury would be glad to break up the little French Establishment he now keeps."

The next news was that the Duke of St. Albans had beheld the Gascoynes at Almacks, and the Swain very happy in attendance. Lord Verulam had noted in his diary on May 17th that his wife had introduced "Miss Gascoyne the Heiress" to Almacks, "where she was much *répandue*", and after that it seemed both she and her mother went there frequently. But the Duchess's shafts had frightened Mrs. Gascoyne more than she allowed to appear. Lord Verulam had an unexpected caller on June 23rd. "Mrs. Gascoyne come in a pucker about Cranborne." The Duchess fought on gallantly.

"I hear so good an account of you all from the Duke who says he saw you last night at Almacks that I hope YOU did not suffer, or Franchette either, whose dancing is divided by *l'Amour et les Graces*. Her little Chevalier Cranborne we hear much of, as when he comes to devote his *soirées* to Almacks, his *matinées* are passed *chez* Lady May Dewhurst, who is an OLD love, I trust a Platonick one, but she will not allow us Aunts to dictate his Liaisons."

It was at this most unsuitable moment that the heiress received another proposal of marriage by letter, and from quite another quarter.

"May 26th, 1820.
"The Earl of Erroll to Miss Gascoyne.
"6 Duke St. St. James's.

"My dear Miss Gascoyne,
"I have just received a letter from General Sir Hussey Vivian, in which he requests me to acquaint him immediately whether it is my intention or not to proceed to Ireland to join Sir Colquhon Grant as it is absolutely necessary for me to decide.

"Previous to making this decision I most anxiously wish to see you particularly after what passed between us on that subject the other evening.

"May I entreat you to send me word as to what hour I may call tomorrow?

"I would have left this myself but am confined to the house with a wretched cold which prevents me from personally enquiring after Mrs. Gascoyne and yourself.

"I remain, my dear Miss Gascoyne, yours most sincerely,

"Erroll."[1]

He was too late. He married six months later, Elizabeth Fitz-clarence, one of the children of William IV by Mrs. Jordan. She was two years older than the Gascoyne heiress and a complete contrast in appearance and character. "What a handsome, spanking creature Lady Erroll is, and how like her mother," commented Mr. Creevey. "She looks as if she was quite uncomfortable in her fine clothes and wanted them off."[2]

Mrs. Gascoyne wrote her last letter to her beloved mother or at any rate the last to survive from these hurried and worried weeks. Her Price nephew was leaving London for Wales and she took the opportunity of asking Mrs. Price to break to him news which she had been too much disturbed to divulge in person. "I wish him to be informed that my Daughter's marriage with Lord Cranborne will take place, tho' not perhaps for many months to come; that it meets with mine and Mr. Gascoyne's most cordial and entire approbation; that it is my Daughter's decided choice, and that the more I see of Lord Cranborne, the more I like his manners, character, mind and conduct. I should wish Mr. Price not to mention this event as coming officially from me, because Mr. G. has named it to no one, not even to his Brother, and I shall get in a scrape tho' I know it is talked of everywhere."

She was dying, and like a good many women who in their prime continually complain of their sufferings, when she had realized that her end was indeed near she had carried the secret in her heart. Bamber was the invalid after whom the Beauclerk family had enquired with solicitude for some months past. Within a few weeks, perhaps days, of her sudden death Mrs. Gascoyne had been bravely attending her admired daughter to London entertainments. She had even given a ball at Stanhope Street. But she had left with good Mr. John Leigh, her husband's agent, a letter to be delivered to Bamber. Before the

[1] Cecil Papers, VII, 3.
[2] On the accession of William IV Erroll became Master of the Horse to Queen Adelaide. There are several beautiful sketches of Lady Erroll in the Sneyd collection at Keele University.

HUSBAND OF THE GASCOYNE HEIRESS

James Brownlow William, Viscount Cranborne, afterwards 2nd Marquess of Salisbury, aged twenty-eight

By T. Bone. From the collection at Hatfield House

loss of her mother Fanny had confided her romance to her dearest friend and Charlotte had replied sadly, "My heart had chosen you for my sister, but since fate decides otherwise, may you be happy." The engagement had not yet been announced. Charlotte signed herself "Your FRIEND" and added "May I address you some day by a dearer name *Oh que je serais contente!* For I acknowledge I do not yet lose ALL hope."

As gossip about the match spread in London she had to warn her amiable Fanny, "The *Froid acceuil* you received this morn on our steps is I fear a prelude to some coolness between our parents," but she remembered that Fanny had always said that nothing could alter their love and friendship for life. The letter of congratulation which the Duchess sent to "My dear Miss Gascoyne, preferred friend of my Charlotte" on her "projected alliance with the pleasing prepossessing and, by all accounts, amiable Lord Cranborne" could hardly have been more distant. "I condole with Mrs. Gascoyne on the loss she will sustain." Within the week she was having to write to condole with Mr. Gascoyne as a widower. It was still possible that the girl's choice had been directed by her mother. Burford was on his way home. After the shortest possible decent interval Charlotte wrote to say that the traveller had arrived "everything our brightest hopes could have wished".

It was October 4th and Lord Verulam entered in his diary. "Lord Cranborne, Miss Gascoyne and Lady Westmeath arrived at Gorhambury." Since she no longer had a mother to chaperone her, Cranborne had called in his younger and favourite married sister. On October 5th their host thought "Lord Cranborne and Miss Gascoyne appear to suit one another exactly. They make love quite as they ought. I like her very much."

It was November 5th, and Lord Clarendon wrote with his usual benevolence from The Grove to his old friend Lord Salisbury that he did not know Mr. Gascoyne even by sight but was told by those who did that he was gentlemanlike in his manner and obliging to those who had any common transaction with him. Lord Clarendon had, actually entertained the Gascoyne Heiress once, at The Grove, in 1804, when she was two, brought by her grandmother, Mrs. Price. Lord Clarendon had been into the question of his debts with the intending bridegroom and thought Lord Salisbury was very kind and liberal in his suggestion for their payment. Lord Cranborne had said he owed not more than £4000 and paid interest on £3000. Were there any straggling debts? There usually were. And most probably the young heir had borrowed on very high terms the money which he had given to help his younger sister. Was this another outside sum?[1]

It was December 12th, and Mr. Leigh who was drawing up the marriage settlement wondered if he might offer a word of warning. "Men in high ranks of life have of late shown such a turn for licentiousness that too much care cannot be taken to guard against it. I never knew a clause providing against a divorce for misconduct in the husband. I think I have heard of such a thing. If such an unpleasant event should happen it is only right that the husband's life interest in the wife's estate should thenceforth cease, and she to have it for life."[2]

The New Year came in with "Siberian weather" and the heiress had received two more extraordinary epistles, the result of the announcement of her forthcoming alliance. The first beginning "My dear Fanny" signed simply "M. J. Eden" was full of self-pity and spoke quite wildly of the breaking of a tie "which was the chief pride and joy of my existence. But that is past and over — alone as I now stand . . . I am now looking forward to our country visit, not, God knows, for the satisfaction of retrospect, but for the relief of absence from scenes which have now lost half their charm and must become insipid, joyless and lonely. Affectionately your . . ." If this unhappy writer was, as seems probable, a neighbour, playmate of her earliest years, Morton John Eden, fifth son of the 1st Lord Auckland, he died in the same year, aged twenty-six. His sister, Emily Eden, authoress, always wrote of the 2nd Marchioness of Salisbury with acidity.

The bride's second strange letter was a proposal from Burford. Poor Charlotte, who was not to be allowed to be a bridesmaid, had to ask that her dear Fanny would "oblige Burford and myself" by returning "the inconsiderate exposé". The Duchess also wrote to apologize for her son's "declaration of his long-concealed tendresse. Pray excuse this Boyish ebullition. Love will hope where reason despairs." She could only trust that in time friendship might blossom again. As Burford's proposal is not filed with the apposite letters it would seem that it was returned. Burford, intent on an heiress, got

[1] Cecil Papers, VII, 19.   [2] Ibid., under date Dec. 12th, 1820.

one, but not for five years. His bride was the widow of Thomas Coutts, banker, *née* Harriet Mellon, the actress. She was fifty and he was twenty-four. After her death he married Elizabeth, daughter of General Gubbins of Limerick, who brought him an heir.

VI

Fanny Gascoyne-Cecil

The Bride

The Gascoyne Heiress was married from the house in which she
had been born on Friday, February 2nd, 1821. *John Bull* commented
unctuously.

"MARRIAGE IN HIGH LIFE

"Yesterday evening, at eight o'clock, Lord Viscount Cranborne,
the only son of the Marquess of Salisbury, led to the Hymeneal altar
the accomplished daughter of Mr. Bamber Gascoyne, in the presence
of the Duke of Wellington, Marquess and Marchioness of Salisbury,
Countess of Westmeath, Marchioness Dowager of Downshire, the
Ladies Hill, Lord Arthur Hill, General and the two Misses Gascoyne, Mr. and Mrs. Evelyn, Mrs. and Miss Stewart and the Earl
of Clarendon.

"The ceremony was performed in the Great Saloon of Mr. Gas-
coyne's house by the Hon. and Rev. Gerald Wellesley. The Duke of
Wellington gave the Lady away. The bridesmaids were the Misses
Gascoyne, her cousins. The bride was habited in a superb dress of
Valenciennes lace and looked most lovely. After the ceremony the
happy pair left town for Mr. Daniel Giles's beautiful seat called
Youngsbury in Hertfordshire, there to pass the honeymoon."

The *County Chronicle* with local patriotism added that the Rector
of Hatfield, the Rev. Mr. Faithfull, had assisted Dr. Wellesley, that
both Lord Cranborne's married sisters had been present, and that the
splendid emblazoned chariot in which the bride and bridegroom had
left Great Stanhope Street had been "launched specially for the
occasion".

The principal officiating clergyman was the youngest brother of
the Duke of Wellington. The Ladies Hill were nieces of the
1st Marchioness of Salisbury, and Lord Arthur, who had been an
aide-de-camp to his cousin, the Duke, at Waterloo, was their

brother. There were actually three Gascoyne sisters as well as three sons, but, according to John Leigh, Miss Charlotte Gascoyne was already betrothed.

The signatures to the marriage settlement, dated February 2nd, were Salisbury, E. M. Salisbury, Cranborne, Bamber Gascoyne, F. M. Gascoyne, Clarendon, Gerald Wellesley, Wellington and Dacre. Nothing need be deduced from *John Bull's* failure to note the bride's grandmother Mrs. Chase Price, as one of those present. She was in cheerful correspondence six weeks later.

To ask the Duke of Wellington to give away the bride was not unprecedented. In 1819 he had given away the Vane-Tempest heiress on her marriage to the widower Lord Stewart, afterwards 3rd Marquess of Londonderry. But in that case the bride had no father and the bridegroom had served under the Duke in the Peninsula as Adjutant-General.

The Giles family were Huguenot refugees from Normandy, and Daniel Giles's father, a Governor of the Bank of England, had bought Youngsbury in 1796 and employed Bird to re-build it, incorporating an earlier Elizabethan house.

Mrs. Arbuthnot (popularly but incorrectly believed to be a mistress of the Duke) entered in her journal, "Feb. 2nd. The Duke of Wellington spent the evening with us, having previously been at the marriage of Lord Cranborne and Miss Gascoine [sic] a very pretty girl who has £12,000 a year. They say he has married her for her money."[1] Amongst the provisions of the marriage settlement had been one that the bridegroom should take his wife's surname and their descendants should be called Gascoyne-Cecil.[2] Mrs. Christopher Pullar was a niece of the owner of Youngsbury, and an habituée at the Saturday-night card parties at Hatfield. Daniel Giles was a Member of Parliament for St. Albans, and on the Sunday before the wedding, the bridegroom's mother had written to him,[3] "The infernal Lawyers cannot be ready so the infernal ceremony cannot be

[1] *The Journal of Mrs Arbuthnot*, ed. F. Bamford and the Duke of Wellington, 2 vols., 1950, I, 68.
[2] The marriage settlement was witnessed on the day of the wedding, but in October 1823, some months after the death of Bamber Gascoyne, John Leigh was still writing about it to the two trustees, both clergymen, Gerald Wellesley and Mr. Faithfull. Cecil Papers, XII, 15.
[3] Giles-Pullar, MSS., County Record Office, Hertford.

till Tuesday." But there was not the slightest sign on the surface that accepting the heiress had been a bitter pill. "Hatfield," continued the *County Chronicle*, "and its immediate neighbourhood was one continued scene of festivity throughout the day in honour of the event. Among other hospitalities, the noble Marquess caused three fat oxen to be distributed together with a proportionate quantity of strong ale. The Marchioness of Salisbury intends giving a grand ball and supper in honour of the nuptials on the 12th inst. at Hatfield."

Youngsbury was a typically comfortable English country house, in the best Regency style, about two miles north of Ware on the south side of the river Rib. A library with an Adam fireplace overlooked parkland and valley. On Monday, February 5th, the bridegroom wrote cheerfully to his absent host.

"My dear Giles,

"Your house is delightful but your pens odious. In consequence of the former I want to ask your leave to come here again on Wednesday, to stay till Friday. The fact is that my good constituents choose that we should make an entrée to Hertford. The devil take them. And we really must make a pretence for going through the town. I find that you have made arrangements for not coming back this week, and therefore have no hesitation in asking your leave. We shall come to Hatfield tomorrow."[1]

On Saturday, 10th, Lady Verulam "took a carriage to Hatfield to pay a visit to the new-married Pair". Lady Salisbury's party was in the end, on Tuesday, 13th, and both Verulams went. "Lady Cranborne, the Bride and lion of the party, looked exceedingly well." The Duke of Wellington was present, and Lord Verulam who had stayed the night breakfasted with him. Lady Verulam had been obliged to go home to her nursery. Friendship between two families, already close (and in a degree historic, since Hatfield and Gorhambury had been linked since the days of Burghley and Bacon), became dynastic.

The young newly-married couple from the first saw much of the neighbours who had provided Gorhambury as a background for their courtship. "Katty" Grimston, the gentle eldest daughter, like Lady Verulam a gifted amateur artist, became a bosom friend of Fanny Cranborne. In May Lord Verulam entered happily that he had dined

[1] Giles-Pullar MSS.

54

with Cranborne in London and found his *ménage* extremely comfortable.[1] In August the Cranbornes came for the Boys Cricket Match to Gorhambury. On January 1st, 1822, Lord Verulam triumphantly chronicled an expedition to Hatfield to see "the little Heir to the House of Cecil" christened in King James's Room by Mr. Faithfull. "Lord Salisbury appeared anxious and fatigued. Lady Salisbury had an excellent party in the evening."

[1] Gorhambury MSS.

PART II
1822–33

Arthur George Villiers Gascoyne-Cecil, 1823–5

TWO CHILD PICTURES

both by Lady De Ros; from an Album of the 2nd Marchioness

Mildred Arabella Charlotte Gascoyne-Cecil, afterwards Lady Mildred Beresford-Hope, 1822–81

I

On Sunday, March 25th, 1827, Frances Mary Gascoyne-Cecil, Marchioness of Salisbury, began to keep a diary. It was not at all on the same scale as the nine volumes produced by her later, which she continued up to the months when she was taken mortally ill. Her first effort covered only six days and was little more than a jotting of social activities, but it forms an essential link in her story.

The six years since her wedding had been years of shadow and shine. On January 21st, 1823, joybells had been rung at Childwall and the tenantry had been given a feast of beef and pudding, ale and tea. She had only just attained the age of twenty-one, although already a mother.

She had been Lady Cranborne for twenty-eight months. Then her father-in-law had died and her husband had become second Marquess. He missed the Commons and hoped for office. She had lost her father in 1823 but he had been long ill, and made very happy by being invited to be god-parent to her first child. The *Gentleman's Magazine* announced that Mr. Gascoyne, a frequent speaker in the Commons before his retirement, had always addressed the House with a thorough knowledge of his subject. He was interred with much solemnity in the Bamber family vault at Barking. The Marquess of Salisbury and General Isaac Gascoyne were chief mourners and the funeral was attended by numerous and respectable tenantry by whom the squire of Bifrons had been much beloved.

His daughter had borne four children in the first six years of her marriage and was now four months pregnant with her fifth. She had lost one. This was no deviation from the pattern usual at the date, but she and her husband had been grief-stricken by the death, at the age of sixteen months, of Arthur George Villiers, a lovely boy to whom the Iron Duke had stood god-parent. Lady de Ros had performed one of her attractive sketches of him. Chantrey was summoned to create a bust, to form an abiding memorial of their grief.[1] This also was quite in the fashion of the day. The childless Adelaide of Saxe-Meiningen, Duchess of Clarence, possessed a life-size full-length

[1] Now at Hatfield House.

59

likeness of the infant Princess Elizabeth of Clarence, lying in her last sleep on a sofa of Empire design. It was marble and had to be carted from place to place whenever the Duchess moved. The death of Arthur had been particularly grievous for his parents, for the first Gascoyne-Cecil son, James William Emilius Evelyn, Viscount Cranborne, was delicate. He too was a beautiful golden-haired child, but he had been slightly premature. The two daughters, Mildred Arabella Charlotte Henrietta and Blanche Mary Harriet, did not ail. The young family had not moved into the London house made famous by the assemblies and routs of the first marchioness. That had been left to her by will, by her husband. It was now known as 21 Arlington Street, but when built for Lord Arlington in the days of Charles II had been called by his name and had stood alone. It had always had a private entrance from the royal park of St. James's, and the present monarch had extended it to the widow who had charmed so many of the royal family there in their hey-day and hers. George IV, once "Florizel" and "Prince Prettyman", was a dreadful complaining invalid nowadays. He did not rise till six p.m. But the Dowager Lady Salisbury had remarkable powers of survival. She continued to entertain in her old style. When they were in London her son and daughter-in-law visited her almost daily. On their marriage they had taken a house in St. James's — 8 Park Place. In 1826 they had moved to 21 Hanover Square, previously inhabited by their aunt-by-marriage Lady Downshire. The other grandmother, Mrs. Price, had died in her sleep while on a visit to them at Hatfield early in the New Year of 1826. She had bestowed the highest token of regard possible for an elderly widow upon the agents of her late son-in-law. She had employed John Leigh, junior, to draw up her Will. *"She leaves the portrait of her dear daughter by Sir Joshua Reynolds to be carried to Childwall Hall and there to remain, as she was the chief designer and director of that house. Her tortoise-shell cabinet believed to have been the property of Queen Elizabeth she leaves to Lord Salisbury.*[1] She had desired to be buried at Childwall and a pompous *cortège* set off from Hatfield for Lancashire in the depths of winter.

Diary of the 2nd Marchioness of Salisbury March 25th to 31st, 1827
   Sunday Not very well — breakfasted a little after ten — not well

[1] Both of these bequests are now at Hatfield House.

enough to go to church — read *John Bull*, tolerably good. Sat talking with Lord S. till near twelve — went and read the prayers in my own room. [The second marchioness always wrote of her husband as "Lord S." No trace of any *petit-nom* is to be found. His sisters confusingly continued to call him "Cranborne". He called his wife "dear Fanny" during her life and "poor Fanny" thereafter.] At one o'clock Mr. Drummond[1] called; nothing to tell one: when he was gone read *Vivian Grey*[2] I had some luncheon and went to eveng [?] church. Dreadfully cold, and a tiresome sermon — caught cold there. Finished *Vivian Grey* before I dressed — mad, but clever and interesting. At six, dressed, got to dinner at half past seven at Mr. Peel's.

[First appearance in the diaries of Robert Peel (1788–1850). He had just resigned on the question of Catholic Emancipation from Canning's ministry, in which he had been Home Secretary.]

Dinner dull enough in itself — a set of men I did not know — but Mr. P. very agreeable and full of anecdote. Got home at eleven and went to bed.

Monday A bad cold, determined to nurse myself for the eveng. Breakfasted between ten and eleven, read the gossip in the *Morning Post* — I seldom go beyond. Wrote some notes, wrote a page of large letters for my little boy, went on with my drawing for Lady Londonderry.

[Frances Anne Stewart, Lady Londonderry (1800–65) was an even greater heiress than the Gascoyne. The Vane-Tempest fortune was based upon coal mines in Co. Durham. The Londonderrys, however, were often in financial difficulties. The 3rd Marquess was twenty-two years senior to his second wife, who was ebullient, and unintellectual. The couple, who were inevitably continually in company with the Gascoyne-Cecils, were rather a life-sentence than close friends.]

Three o'clock some luncheon — laid on the sofa till dinner time — read some new travels in Lapland[3] and a scene in Steven's *Macbeth*.[4] Nobody visited me but Col. Walpole. Dinner at seven. Sat

[1] Henry Drummond M.P. (1786–1800), banker and leading Irvingite.

[2] *Vivian Grey*, first novel of Benjamin Disraeli, published 1826–7.

[3] *Travels through Sweden, Finland and Lapland to the North Cape*, Giuseppi Acerbi, 2 vols., 1802.

[4] George Steevens was employed by Garrick to transform several Shakespeare plays.

with Ld. S. till he went to sleep, then went to dress a little after nine. A quarter after ten went to Ly. Belfast's party, rather dull, saw nobody I wanted to see, did not hit at Écarté, came home at twelve.

Tuesday Better: at breakfast before ten. Finished my letters for the children and sent them, wrote some notes and spent the rest of the morning in reading and making extracts from the *History of George III*[1] for Lord S. At half past two luncheon and went to Arlington St. Staid there a good while . . . Came home. Went on with my drawing. Saw Mme Dévy and ruined myself in caps and flowers. Read a little of Lord Bacon's *Essays*. Dinner at seven. Ld. S. went to the opera immediately after. Finished my drawing and read Ld. Bacon till ten o'clock. Went to bed.

Wednesday Got up with the headache from going to bed too soon after dinner. Breakfasted as usual, daudled, not inclined to do any-thing . . . Wrote to Williams, the Gardener. Felt very unwell, could not set about anything — tried to read and fell asleep. Woke by Ld. Lothian[2] coming in. When he went away went out in the car-riage — inquired after Pss. Polignac.

[The French Ambassadress was Maria *née* Parkyns, daughter of 1st Baron Radcliffe, and had married secondly Jules Arman, Prince de Polignac, son of Marie-Antoinette's disastrous bosom-friends. He had been pardoned by the intercession of the Empress Josephine after Cadoudal's conspiracy to assassinate the Emperor Napoleon; on the flight of Charles X in 1830 he was arrested, but eventually merely exiled and spent many years in England.]

Called upon Lady Shelley,[3] and Lady Harriet Clive;[4] had a great deal of trouble to find the latter out and after all was unsuccessful for she was at home. The wind so intolerable that I came home: had some Arrow Root, and took a variety of messes for my head. Read a little of Shakespeare and went on with my drawing. At six

[1] *History of the reign of George III*, R. Macfarlan (1770–96), 4 vols.
[2] John, 7th Marquess of Lothian (1794–1841). He was about to become a relation, by marriage to a great-niece of the Dowager Lady Salisbury, Lady Cecil Talbot, daughter of Charles, 2nd Earl Talbot.
[3] Frances, daughter and heiress of Thomas Winckley, m. Sir John Shelley, Bart., 1807, d. 1869. Described indulgently by her husband as "my old goose": authoress of lively gossiping diaries, edited 1912 and 1913 by her grandson R. Edgcombe.
[4] Harriet, Baroness Windsor, m. 1819 Robert Clive, second son of the 1st Earl of Powys, d. 1869.

dressed — went to dine at Ld. Gwydyr's, got there about twenty minutes after seven, and waited at least a quarter of an hour before anyone of the rest of the company came. Got ill placed at dinner, consequently bored. The evening tolerably pleasant, a small party came home at twelve.

Thursday One of my *well* days. Breakfast as usual. The newspapers get stupider every day. Wrote some notes. Sat with Ld. S. during his breakfast; saw a woman who was come after the place of House-keeper; wrote to Blondel [The children's Swiss *bonne*.] to give directions about the children. Went on very prosperously with my new drawing. Luncheon at two. Went out in the carriage: found Lady Aberdeen at home staid with her some time, from thence to Lady Hampden's and Mrs. Gascoyne,[1] the latter at home — then to Broadwoods about a piano, and home. Ly. Delawar,[2] Lord Exeter and Lady Verulam came and nearly took up the time till dressing. Lord S. not well enough to go out to dinner. I dined in Arlington St., left it at ten to go to Ly. Charlotte Greville's[3] — so hot I could not stay — went on to Mme. de Lieven's,[4] a dull party, innumerable unknown foreigners — very few men. Came home a little after twelve.

Friday Not so well as yesterday. Breakfasted at half past ten; assisted at the ordering of the dinner for tomorrow, saw another Housekeeper, dressed, as my hair had been *en papillottes* all morning. At one went to ye D. of Wellington's by appointment to see his china etc. Staid there near an hour, returned home, had some luncheon, wrote to Henrietta de Ros; finished a story that interested me in Richmond. Went on with my drawing; tried a new composition for fixing drawings. Read a little of the *Annals of George 3rd*. Ld. S. staid to hear Mr. Tierney's[5] motion in the H. of Commons, did not come home till past seven. Dinner: Ld. S. would not go out — sat with

[1] Wife of General Isaac Gascoyne, M.P., her uncle, b. Mary Williams of Liverpool.

[2] Lady Elizabeth Sackville, daughter of Duke of Dorset, m. 1813, George, 5th Earl De La Warr.

[3] Lady Charlotte Greville, daughter of 4th Duke of Portland, m. 1793 Charles Greville: parents of Fulke Greville, diarist.

[4] Dorothea Christoforovna, Princesse de Lieven (1785–1857), daughter of Count Benckendorff, m. 1800 Russian Ambassador to London 1812–34. Reputed mistress of Metternich and Guizot. A dreaded patroness of Almacks.

[5] George Tierney (1761–1830), Master of the Mint 1828.

him till a little after nine, then went to dress. A quarter after ten went to Mrs. Hope's — less dull than expected — rather amused with what I saw going on there. Came home about twelve.

Saturday Quite well today, but not very early at breakfast. Wrote some notes, sat with Ld. S. during his breakfast then went on with my drawing and almost finished it. Saw a *Coiffeur* recommended by Ly. Gwydyr. Bought some gold beads of a man who came with things. Fastened some drawings in my album. At two had some luncheon and went out in the carriage. Found nobody at home except Ly. Londonderry: my own fault for I know she goes out late. Came home soon after three — read nearly a volume of Richmond — arranged my drawing-room.

II

May 1827–July 1833

George IV had not made a public appearance in London for four years. He generally arrived at King's Cottage, Windsor Park, after dark, for fear, it was said, that people should remark his changed and ghastly looks.

Most unwillingly, when Lord Goderich resigned with profuse tears, in the New Year of 1828, he sent for the Duke of Wellington. "Arthur! the Cabinet is defunct." The Duke, with military promptitude, agreed to become Prime Minister to a man whom he could not respect but must acknowledge could be a fascinating companion. The King's imitation of his various ministers handing in their resignations was in the first order of burlesque. It was not so agreeable when he had to tussle with the King for five and a half hours before he won his point that Catholic Emancipation must come. The Duke was not himself enthusiastic but he knew his duty to his country.

The house of Cecil had not ceased to entertain the royal family. Frederick, Duke of York, had been to shoot at Hatfield in April 1826 and wrote kindly afterwards to promise support, though not attendance, at one of his young hostess's philanthropic fund-raising occasions (a Ball for the Assistance of the Spitalfields Weavers). "I am strongly cautioned not to frequent any hot rooms." He offered his box at the theatre.

He died in January 1827 and Lord S. supported William, Duke of Clarence, at an ill-managed funeral in dreadful weather. The sailor Prince was considered to have behaved with great indecency. He was in high glee that he had outlived his elder brother and must soon become William IV. But his wife, although she had been pregnant no less than four times, and had twice borne a daughter, was now childless. She too had been to Hatfield, for the day, accompanied by "*votre Belle-Sœur*" (Lady Westmeath, lady-in-waiting) and Augustus Fitzclarence, the one of her husband's illegitimate sons to take holy orders. The significance of the widow and daughter of the late Duke of Kent increased annually. On Wednesday, May 2nd, 1828, a little note arrived from Kensington Palace.[1]

"My dear Lady Salisbury,

"It will give me great pleasure to see you here some morning with your children that my little girl may have the pleasure also. If on Tuesday next at half past two would suit you I would propose that day."

It was almost a birthday party. The Princess Victoria would be nine on May 24th. The Cecil children were rather young for her — six and a half, five and a half, three years and eight months. Another infant had been born and died — Evelyn Georgiana Geraldine, aged ten months.

On July 19th, 1828, the Salisburys set out for a continental tour. Fanny had never been abroad before: Lord S. had been to Switzerland in 1814. They went by Paris, Strasbourg, Constance and Como to Milan, Verona, Innsbruck and Salzburg. In Vienna, Lord Cowley, the brother of the Duke of Wellington who had married the elder sister of Lord S., was Ambassador. This was practically the only place in which Fanny's travel diary recorded receiving hospitality from local aristocracy, or indeed any residents. She collected a beautiful little album there in which to stick her sketches and those given her by friends. It was bound in soft green leather and mother-of-pearl which formed a frame for a delicate miniature of the palace at Schönbrunn. Her three travel diaries, illustrated by her own pencil and water-colour sketches, would fill a volume for readers interested in Europe at a difficult time. The continent was still licking its wounds after a French Revolution followed by the Napoleonic wars.

The first Salisbury tour occupied six months and they suffered some hardships. They never were actually reduced to sleeping in their coach, but their accounts of smells of garlic, gnats, foul food, blackguard inns, starving peasantry, discontented tradesfolk and rapacious landlords were enough to daunt a beginner. The roads were often swimming in mud, and accidents to their second vehicle, the *fourgon* carrying their luggage, were frequent. Fortunately they were both compulsive sightseers. Lord S. was splendid. He did not jib at re-visiting a rewarding gallery four times. His lady modestly

[1] Cecil Papers, XII, 47.

insisted that she did not understand pictures, but she had lively powers of criticism and her views were all her own. "As I am no connoisseur the Venus de Medicis had no extraordinary charms for me; a very pretty woman certainly, of a fairy size, *et voilà tout!*"

They came home by Venice and Bologna (where they found *nouveaux riches* living like princes) to Florence, where again an English diplomat showed them some local gaiety. (In Milan, their Italian lacquey and Fanny's maid were the lucky ones. An exiled nobleman of Ravenna, recognizing an old acquaintance, invited himself to dine with the pair.) It shocked the owners of Hatfield that the heads of three of the most important Roman families lived in Naples or Florence. The British Minister at Florence was John Fane, Baron Burghersh, heir of the Earl of Westmorland. He had married a niece of the Duke of Wellington, Lady Priscilla Wellesley-Pole, and had been one of the Duke's aides-de-camp at Waterloo. The Salisburys returned to Florence after visiting Rome and Naples, had a very easy passage over the Mont Cenis from flourishing Turin and were in Paris again with December. Here they found many letters, including one from the Duke of Wellington. ("My dear Lady Salisbury: I enclose a letter from Roschilds at Frankfort who you may rely upon it will be very happy to render you every service in his power. Don't forget to let me know how you go on. Ever yours most sincerely W."[1]) His kindness had also prompted him to go down to Hatfield specially to see how their children were getting on.

A Parisian correspondent wrote apologetically to Hatfield in February 1829 that he feared Lady Salisbury must have found his capital dull. On the contrary, they had arrived to find election riots, barricades and several persons slain in the streets. Paris was, in fact, blowing up for another, but only a Three Days', revolution.

They had brought home unforgettable memories — Lord S. coming safe back to the little inn at Hinterrhein after five hours' hard walking to view the *glacier du Rhin* ("out of the question for me"); Lake Garda at sunset, the Alps purple, the water a clear blue and every object on the distant shore glowing with the brilliant distinctness of an enamel picture; Venice, and the soft transparency of Italian moonlight, floating in at the windows of their good silk-hung hotel (the old Nanni Palace), together with the weird calls of

[1] Letters of the Duke of Wellington, July 22nd, 1828.

the gondoliers; a Festa in Florence, crowds moving in every direction, dressed in gay colours, talking and gesticulating with the utmost animation; entering Rome very early on an October morning by the *Porta del Popolo:* Mass at St. Peter's, with graceful women carrying infants, dropping down on their knees simultaneously on the marble floor: the frescoes at Pompeii, "by far the most curious and interesting thing I saw".

A large example of modern art was awaiting them at Hanover Square. Before they went abroad Fanny had given sittings to Sir Thomas Lawrence for a full-length portrait of the 2nd Marchioness for the family picture gallery. It was one of those sent by the President to the Exhibition of 1829 and, in his opinion, tied with another command performance, that of the Duchess of Richmond, as the best he had ever painted. Critics did not agree that he was as good as ever, and his likeness of Southey was severely satirized. He died in the following January.

The Salisburys resettled happily to the annual round in London and Hertfordshire. They went to Ascot from London in June. In August always came the *Fête Champêtre* of the St. Albans Cricket Club, "a little Vauxhall, with twenty thousand variegated lamps in the hall, and trees, and the Hertfordshire militia band playing enlivening strains". Partridge shooting came next, and Sir John Sebright losing his bet to Lord S. who had promised him that he would find four gentlemen to kill one hundred wild brace in one hour. (Mr. Delmé-Radcliffe, one of the best shots in England, saved the day by despatching eighteen brace in twenty-five minutes.)

At Hatfield they had summer and winter sitting-rooms and dining-rooms and bedrooms. Fanny had principally mahogany furniture, and chintzes, and both her four-poster beds were painted. Lord S. had in his dressing-room a fowling piece and two blunderbusses (one used by poachers), four fishing rods and a framed survey of the park taken in 1786. The summer breakfast-room had japanned furniture and the summer drawing-room a mahogany pianoforte.

In September 1829 the Duke of Wellington said he was glad to hear they were in Scotland very happy and well amused. They stayed at Hawick on their way south and Lord Grey[1] told Princess Lieven,

---

[1] Charles Grey, 2nd Earl Grey (1764–1845), Whig statesman, Prime Minister 1830. Carried the Reform Bill, 1832.

Frances Mary Gascoyne-Cecil, 1829

From a pastel portrait by C. Bartonford, in the collection at Hatfield House

"I found their visit a very agreeable one. She is much more so than I expected, and I think clever."

The owner of a great house which got innumerable enquiries spent many hours in his study. Lord S. was an indefatigable correspondent. Sir Gore Ouseley, a new neighbour, who was turning Woolmer's Park into something remarkable, had heard that a box of treasures — hitherto unknown Burghley papers — had been found at Hatfield. Was it true? He was a Fellow of the Society of Antiquaries and had been Ambassador to Persia, and had given Fanny a sketch of a very ancient church in Georgia. He merited a reply, although he had to be told that the story was most untrue. It must stem from facilities given to a constant correspondent, the Rev. Dr. Nares of Biddenden, Kent, who was writing a life of the great ancestor. Lord S. also covered pages with the result of his enquiries into the condition of the Hatfield poor.

In October, always, came the Berkhamsted Ball which the Dowager never failed to attend. She was still indefatigable. Mr. Thomas Creevey, writing to his step-daughter from Stoke Farm near Egham,[1] was not charitable — "old Salisbury arrived yesterday . . . in her accustomed manner, in a phaeton drawn by four long-tail Flanders mares — she driving the wheel horses, and a postilion on the leaders, with two outriders on corresponding long-tailed blacks. Her man and maid were in her chaise behind; her groom and saddle horses arrived some time after her. It is impossible to do justice to the antiquity of her face. If, as alleged, she is only 74 years old, it is the most cracked, or rather furrowed piece of mosaic you ever saw; but her dress, in the colours of it at least, is absolutely infantile . . . Sefton says she is very clever and he ought to know. I wish you just saw her as I do now. She thinks she is alone, and I am writing at the end of the adjoining room, the folding doors being open. She is reclining on a sofa, reading the *Edinboro' Review* without spectacles or glass of any kind. Her dress is white muslin, properly loaded with garniture, and she has just put off a very large bonnet, profusely tufted with bright lilac ribbons, leaving on her head a very nice lace cap not less adorned with the brightest yellow ribbon."

Yet her grace and charm were extolled as unchanged when she visited her native land in August 1829. Her nephew, Lord

[1] *The Creevey Papers*, ed. Sir H. Maxwell, 1912, pp. 508–9.

Downshire, had kindly invited the old lady to Hillsborough and his tenants presented her with an address of welcome which covered several pages. Her reply was brief but very warmly and elegantly expressed. She preserved many results of her visit in her Album which was somewhat more ambitious than those of her daughter-in-law, and included a letter from George, Prince of Wales, brilliant sketches of Italy from two Hill nephews, and one from the Duchess of Wellington, in sepia, "of La Gitana and El Jovenato, of Spanish origin", with a note in a tiny hand explaining that if it was too large the borders could be removed. The Dowager's Album also contained many pictures and programmes of the theatricals at Hatfield.

Lord S. did not himself perform, but he had no objection to filling his house with talented amateurs, some drawn from quite the opposite political camp. Fanny had loved theatricals since her childhood at Hale Hall. In "A short Reign and a Merry One", she was "The Countess de Rosière".

Lord Morpeth spoke the prologue which had been written by Hertfordshire's leading female literary figure, Lady Dacre[1] and showed a great sense of occasion.

The Duke of Wellington sat in the front row. Fanny acted extremely well in the opinion of everyone except Lord Auckland's sharp-tongued sister, clever Miss Emily Eden who was staying with a brother, the Rector of Hertingfordbury. "Lady Salisbury, whom I thought the least good, was only objectionable because she was like an actress on the real stage . . . Her dress disfigured her cruelly." Fanny handsomely asked the whole party from Hertingfordbury to dine in the following November but Lord Brougham had invited Miss Eden to the Lord Mayor's banquet that day.[2] The two little one-act plays produced in the winter after the Salisburys first continental tour were so successful that a much larger affair was planned for the following April, after the next baby, in February, but before the christening, on May Day. Fanny had lost her last

[1] Barbarina *née* Ogle, Lady Dacre (1768–1854). She was mother-in-law of the Rev. Frederick Sullivan who succeeded Lord Frederick Beauclerk as Vicar of Kimpton. See *A Family Chronicle derived from notes and letters selected by Barbarina, the Hon. Lady Grey*, ed. G. Lyster.

[2] *Miss Eden's Letters*, ed. V. Dickinson, 1919, pp. 176 *et seq.*

infant, a girl. As her sixth child was a son[1] he got an exceptionally warm welcome.

He had a very grand London christening, reported by the press. The Salisburys had moved again, to a handsome house, 4 Grafton Street. The Princess Mary, Duchess of Gloucester, was a god-parent, but she wrote in a flutter to say that owing to the precarious condition of her dear brother, the King, she must ask the Dowager Lady Salisbury to represent her. The remaining sponsors, the Duke of Wellington (Prime Minister), Lady Aberdeen[2] and Lord Talbot[3] were present. Robert Arthur Talbot was baptized by Dr. Wellesley who had married his parents, and a dinner described as sumptuous was followed in the evening by a rout to which came two princes and princesses (Esterhazy and Lieven), nine dukes (Wellington, Newcastle, de Laval, de Montmorency, Devonshire, Argyll, Montrose, Rutland and Richmond) and even more duchesses. By an ironical chance, the son to get the largest attendance of aristocracy at his baptism was the one whom his father came to regard as a dangerous Red.

Throughout the spring bets were being offered in the clubs that the Duke of Clarence would be in a strait-jacket before his brother died, but George IV was gathered at last on June 26th, 1830, and William IV, obviously delighted at his elevation, having startled his first council by opening "This is a damned bad pen you have given me", proceeded "to preside very decently, and looked like a respectable old admiral".[4] The Duke reported that he had done more business with his new monarch in ten minutes than with the last in as many days.

The Salisburys departed for their second continental tour – the Low Countries and the Rhine. The Duke met them in Brussels and showed them the field of Waterloo. Fanny brought back a large annotated collection of fine pencil and sepia-and-wash sketches. She presented one of the best to her mother-in-law. It was fortunate that they had not chosen France, for in August Charles X suddenly

---

[1] He was born on February 3rd, 1830, and his birthplace still stands.

[2] Harriet Douglas, m. 1815 George, 4th Earl of Aberdeen, Prime Minister 1852–5.

[3] Charles Chetwynd-Talbot, Earl Talbot (1777–1849). First cousin of Lord S.

[4] *The Greville Diary*, ed. P. W. Wilson, 1927, 2 vols, I, 262.

appeared in an American frigate off Spithead asking for asylum for himself and his family. He was desired to reside in Scotland – the royal palace of Holyrood House. He was familiar with it, as it had been assigned to him after his first flight from a French Revolution in 1795. As the Comte d'Artois and a noted breeder of bloodstock he had been well known in English sporting circles. The Dowager Lady Salisbury sent him a letter of welcome. He replied, very touched, in a small niggling hand asking to be remembered to the Seftons, and the Dowager stuck this in her Album next but one to George IV as Prince of Wales. England, after very little hesitation, acknowledged his successor, of the Orleans branch, and Louis-Philippe ascended the throne as a Citizen-King.

Fanny was experiencing the great happiness of seeing the Duke of Wellington under her own roof. He had come to stay at Childwall for the opening of the Liverpool and Manchester railway. He was attended by his secretary Charles Arbuthnot, and Mrs. Arbuthnot recorded in her journal how September 15th which started off so brilliantly was shattered by the fatal accident. Mr. Huskisson M.P. fell under an engine and died of his injuries.

The Dowager's next important additions to her Album were all connected with the impending Reform Bill and a caricature dated November 5th, 1830, happened to combine portraits of many of the political figures about to make continual appearances in Fanny's Diaries, and comment on the Duke dated a few days before her first recorded intimate political conversation with him.

He was depicted instructing his Cabinet: "Having been obliged to recognize the King of the French, we must— as a set off, acknow-ledge our friend Miguel.[1] The Belgians — poor people! not knowing how to take care of themselves, must be protected from the evils of independence! So much for foreign affairs — now for domestic. I say that our present system is the very perfection of systems, and con-sequently admits of no improvement. *I will go further and say that while I have power no species of Reform shall take place!* And now, having

[1] The King's Speech had mentioned the approaching recognition of Dom Miguel, third son of John VI, of Portugal. He had agreed to marry his niece, Maria de Gloria, heiress of his elder brother, Pedro of Brazil, but had seized the crown as an independent sovereign. A revolution in Belgium following that in France had been repressed.

said it, if P[eel] will but manage the new Police, and H[ardinge] go to Ireland, G[oulburn] abstain from projects of finance and Ell[e]nb[orou]gh hold his Tongue, we may manage to keep our seats for another session."

It was a satire on the Duke's sudden and unexpected declaration against Reform which had shocked even his adherents on November 2nd. A peer arriving late in the House, and becoming conscious of an unusual atmosphere, had whispered to ask Lord Aberdeen (Foreign Secretary), what the Duke had said. "He said we're going out," whispered back Aberdeen, whose sense of humour was deep-hidden and Caledonian: and so it had to be. On November 23rd Fanny wrote down carefully, "Conversation with the D. of W." He had been out of office eight days: "The Duke told me that at 4 o'clock on the Monday preceding the 15th he had been warned that the Ultra Tories were determined to oppose the Government on Reform, and turn them out. He had determined to abide the storm. Lord Stormont had wanted to raise a question of the Committee on the Civil List. The Duke had been entirely taken by surprise by the result of the Division.[1] Peel thought they must resign. The Duke very unwilling in view of the consequences. 'He had said he would sleep on it, but next day the Cabinet thought it would be best to resign in time to prevent the Reform question being brought on that evening, so he had asked for an audience with His Majesty.' The King behaved admirably — cried very much, and was so much agitated that the Duke feared for his senses."

The consequences were, as the Duke had foreseen, very unpleasant and 1831 and 1832 were gloomy years. Peel and he were burned in effigy at Carlisle with copies of the Duke's fatal speech crammed in their mouths. On the night of March 1st when Lord John Russell[2] was due to introduce the Bill a mob marched across the Green Park to attack Apsley House, but drew back when they found it shuttered and dark, with veterans standing beside cannon which had been in action at Waterloo. The first Bill had passed its second reading and was carried, but by only one vote. Lord Grey's ministry resigned after nine months. The Bill was abandoned. On April 27th the mob

---

[1] The Government had been defeated by twenty-nine votes.

[2] John Russell, 1st Earl Russell (1792–1878), third son of 5th Duke of Bedford. Whig statesman.

73

smashed the windows of Apsley House facing Piccadilly. The Duchess had died two days before and her corpse was still lying in the house. The Duke ordered new iron shutters and did not replace the windows.

The King, horrified by the accounts of the vast expenditure on the coronation of George IV, wanted to forego this ceremony altogether and was persuaded with difficulty to have a very small quiet one, in September. Lord S. bore *Curtana*, the pointless sword of Mercy. Fanny asked the advice of the Duke who was now established as her father-figure. He did not think it was necessary for her to go, but he thought she was right in considering it desirable. Things had been so badly arranged that he had to inform her at the last moment that ladies who did attend were to be received in their robes and coronets at the next Drawing-Room. This would create an effect and cost nothing.

His subjects did not appreciate the King's well-meant economy. The country was becoming exasperated. There had been rick-burning and smashing of the new machinery in the industrial north. In Bristol, half of a most beautiful square was demolished and the Mayor reading the Riot Act was very nearly murdered. Troops received the order to fire and charged, killing sixteen persons, soon magnified by press accounts to five hundred. The King implored the Duke to form another administration, pledged to some measure of reform. The Duke tried to obey his royal master but failed. Peel had refused to lead in the Commons. Lord Grey was sent for again. Lord S. had become Lieutenant-Colonel of the South Hertfordshire Yeomanry, and his lady rallied to address the assembled regiment on their duty to their country on a July day of 1831.

Last November news of an outbreak of *cholera morbus* had reached England from Russia. Eleven months had passed and now reports of the first deaths from this new and awful plague had arrived from Sunderland.

Lord S. had an interview with the King in January 1832, attending Lord Verulam, Lord Lieutenant, to present an Address from the County which deposed that the Bill would place the whole power of the State in the hands of political adventurers. On July 7th, 1832, the Bill received the Royal Assent and became law. The Dowager's

Album was enriched by a satire named "The Pill, the Whole Pill, and Nothing but the Pill", and a riddle card in which the converging letters spelt the word REFORM in four hundred and eighty-four ways. She had seen something of violence in Hertfordshire. Stones and mud had been cast in at the windows of her coach as it had followed that of her son and daughter-in-law into the county town. "I heard of the row at Hertford," wrote the Duke to Fanny on November 23rd, "but I did not know that you had been assailed. The miscreants ought to be swept from the face of the earth!" Lord S. had been warned not to venture in again but had gone, quite alone, on horseback. A friendly deputation greeted him at the Cross. The Duke had advised him not to go to a Hertford meeting of Whigs and Moderate Reformers. He had gone, nevertheless to one in March, and according to Mrs. Sullivan of Kimpton Vicarage, would not have got a hearing but for Lord Dacre. "Poor dear little Lord Salisbury in a large drab grey coat" had looked wretched. However, "though the people disliked every word he uttered, he was liked the better for his spunk". It was well for him that he had his matador streak, for his actions for slander and libel and assault against Mr. Duncombe were swelling his files in the offices of Messrs. Nicholson and Longmore of Hertford. Thomas Duncombe (1766–1861), a Yorkshire Whig landowner of fine physique and flamboyant address, had contested Hertford unsuccessfully in 1823, successfully in 1826 and 1830, but lost the seat in 1832. This election, however, was declared void. Duncombe's candidatures were said to have cost him £40,000. From July 1835 until his death he sat for Finsbury borough. He was distinguished as the best-dressed man in the House. Lord S. had experienced the greatest difficulty in getting suitable prospective candidates for the Election. Only the Verulam heir had been ready and successful. Baron Dimsdale[1] was "not inclined to enter Parliament at present on account of the expense, trouble and uncertainty", Abel Smith of Woodhall[2] did not wish to stand at present. He had "neither the time, inclination nor courage". His

[1] Thomas, 4th Baron Dimsdale (1796–1865), descendant of Dr. Thomas Dimsdale who was created a baron of the Russian Empire by the Empress Catherine for inoculating her and her family against the smallpox, 1768.
[2] Abel Smith of Woodhall (1788–1859) changed his mind and represented the county of Hertford for many years.

relative Lord Mahon[1] and Lord S.'s own Talbot relative Lord Ingestre had been elected and unseated, after investigation, for bribery and intimidation. Lord S. had paid the election expenses for all.

Lord Ingestre, a gay young sailor, had gone off cheerfully for Malta, promising to send two donkeys for the children by the *Britannia*, and carpets for Hatfield House from Smyrna. He hoped for "one of Lady Salisbury's entertaining letters". To comfort Lord Mahon, who was a more serious type, she lent a volume of the works of Miss Edgeworth. She had been lending books to the Duke of Wellington (of whom she now wrote simply as "the Duke") for years, and he sent her solemn enough stuff in return — "Have you read Ward upon Mexico?" For a general notion of the Turkish government and system, Tuckereau and Green would serve, but he was sending also Blaquiere's narrative of a second visit to Greece, "I send you back your Rousseau who is a terrible fellow certainly." The Gascoyne heiress was likely to be well supplied with the works of Rousseau. Her grandfather Chase Price had offered the author asylum on his Welsh estates in 1766.[2] She still kept up her Commonplace books, but had progressed considerably since 1817 and "Lines addressed by a Father to his only daughter who had eloped at the age of 16 with an officer." She filled pages with passages from Rousseau, and La Bruyère and Bossuet and Montesquieu, and, nearer home, Mason and Cowper, and Clare and Coleridge and Scott and Byron and Miss Bowdler and C. J. Fox and Dr Johnson and Pope and Swift. She loved the dramatic — Lady Jane Grey and Queen Elizabeth at Tilbury; and useful information about trees, and ship-building and products of the Orient. She kept up to date. Her last English entry (1838) was from Macaulay.

[1] Philip Henry Stanhope (1804–75), afterwards 5th Earl Stanhope. Under-Sec. of State for Foreign Department; President of the Society of Antiquaries.
[2] Cecil Papers: VII, 229–245; and XII, 171, 183. Letters of the Duke of Wellington, 18, 48, 65.

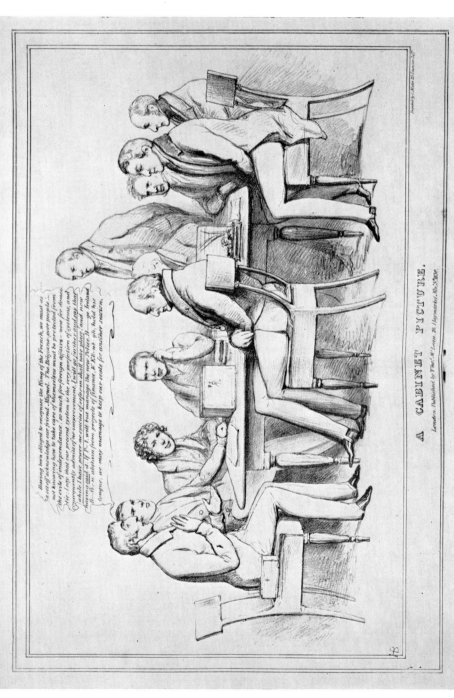

Having been obliged to recognize the King of the French, we must as a sort of acknowledge our friend, Miguel. The Belgians, poor people — not knowing how to take care of themselves must be protected from the evils of independance, so much for foreign affairs — now for home.— I say that our present system is the very perfection of systems, and consequently admits of no improvement. I will go to the length of saying that whilst I have power no species of reform shall take place, and now hearing said of W. P. I with his manage the new Police.H——ys Ireland B——n obtain from projects of finance, &c. &c. &c. &c. hold his tongue, we may manage to keep our seats for another session.

A CABINET PICTURE.

London, Published by Thos. M. Lean, 26 Haymarket, Nov. 3, 1830.

Printed by Motte D'Oisson Lith.

"A CABINET PICTURE"

The Ministers from left to right are: the Duke of Wellington, Lords Aberdeen, Ellenborough, Lyndhurst and Bathurst, Sir George Murray (hidden), Lord Melville (standing), Lord Rosslyn, Sir Robert Peel and Henry Goulburn. Nearly all the figures in the caricature appear constantly in the Diaries.

Sketch from the Album of the 1st Marchioness of Salisbury; published by T. McLean, 26 Haymarket, November 5th, 1830

PART III
The Diaries
1833: July–December

[The first Ambassador to be sent to London from the Citizen-King of the French had arrived — the Marquis de Talleyrand-Périgord, Prince of Benevento. He was seventy-eight and had been Bishop of Autun, and married to a disgraceful woman ("The times were very disturbed"). He had heard the Du Barry screaming in a tumbril and Josephine upbraiding Bonaparte for the murder of the Duc d'Enghien. He had turned his coat again and again. "That wicked old man!" exclaimed Mr. Creevey. He had brought with him as Ambassadress the Duchess of Dino,[1] wife of a nephew. (Her mother, a Princess of Courland, had been Talleyrand's mistress and it was said that her own third child, Pauline, of whom Talleyrand was very fond, was his child and not that of his nephew, from whom she was separated.) She was more beautiful, according to current taste, than her rival Ambassadress the Princess Lieven because she was plumper. The Duke of Wellington represented to William IV that Madame de Dino had been received at the Austrian court and by all the royalties present at the Congress of Vienna. "Oh! very well," said the King. "I will tell the Queen. And you had better tell her too."

The Prince had always had a club-foot and was now very lame. He seemed sometimes, sunken in his neckcloth, almost immoveable; but his old eyes moving quick as a lizard in a countenance of unearthly pallor appeared to the Duke of Cumberland to miss nothing. His voice sounded as if it came from the bottom of a well, but few people believed it spoke truth. In an extraordinarily short time he was generally accepted. He had his own chair in the bow window at White's, and the Travellers' Club courteously installed a rail for him to haul himself up the main staircase.]

The Diary

Saturday, July 6th, 1833 Dined at Talleyrand's, and sat next him at dinner. He was in great force. According to the régime of the *ancienne cour* he seemed to make a point of carving and helping every dish placed opposite to him which he did slowly and with difficulty; even the ice he distributed. He spoke little in the early part of dinner,

---

[1] Dorothea, third daughter of the Duke of Courland (1792–1862).

the pleasure of eating being the supreme attraction, but was afterwards more communicative. He seldom joins in general conversation, but occasionally deliveres an opinion in a short epigrammatic sentence which is never forgotten. Speaking of George IV he said, "*C'était un Roi grand seigneur — il n'y en a plus. Les Rois recherchent aujourdhui la popularité — elle ne mène à rien. Elle ne sauroit durer, il n'y en a rien dans ce siècle qui dure.*" Speaking of the first French revolution he remarked the similarity between the events now in progress in this country and those of that day. I asked him at what epoch of the revolution he conceived us to have arrived — he replied "*Le 4 Août — la nuit des sacrifices: quand tout a été donné abandonné, par celui même qui étoit chargé de tous défendre. L'indécision de Louis XVI a causé la révolution: il a voulu plus faire qu'il n'en a fait.*" With reference to the measures to be taken upon the Irish Church Bill, which is to come up in a few days in the House of Lords, he seemed to recommend some decisive step. "*Le retard c'est l'indécision. L'indécision perd tout. Votre noblesse voudroit se retirer des affaires pour reparôitre ensuite avec plus d'effet. L'émigration a perdu la France. La retraite c'est une espèce d'émigration.*" He conceived that the Princes of the blood in France might have done much if they had remained in their country. "*Voilà votre Ministre,*" he said, "*assis à cette table* (the Duke was opposite) *C'est l'homme du monde qui a le plus de droiture dans les sentimens et dans la conduite: j'ai souvent eu des affaires a conduire avec lui, et je peut l'attester.*" Of the approaching discussion on the Irish Church Bill he said, "*Les destinées de l'Europe en dependent.*" He reminded me also of an expression he had once made use of "*L'expérience ne sent à rien — on apprend jamais rien*", and added "*Parce que l'expérience ne fait que prouver l'idée qu'on possède déjà — il faut d'abord la posséder cetté idée — et voilà ce qui manque à la plupart des personnes.*"

After dinner the Duke told me a curious incident he had had from Talleyrand, of Charles X. When the Martignac ministry were forced upon him he sent to the Pope to ask a dispensation from the oath he had taken at his coronation to observe the charter: the Cardinals dissuaded the Pope from acceding to this application, but about a year after it was renewed, and by the influence of Maffei, the nuncio at Paris, finally granted. "*Voilà,*" said Talleyrand, looking at the picture of the dethroned monarch. "*Le meilleur homme qui fût jamais, et cependant il est cause de tous les malheurs de l'Europe.*" A striking coincidence is observable in this anecdote between his conduct and that of James II whose history already affords so many parallel circumstances to that of Charles X.

When the news of Napoleon's death reached Paris, the Duke was at some evening party in company with Talleyrand, and upon someone exclaiming *"Quel évènement!"* the latter replied with his usual imperturbability, *"Ce n'est plus un évènement: c'est une nouvelle."*

July 7th Dined at the Duke of Wellington's; several officers and persons connected with the West Indies chiefly composed the party.

[The first mention in the diaries of Apsley House, Hyde Park Corner. Its appearance was majestic, as when the Duke had bought the freehold he had faced it with Bath-stone ashlar of a golden colour. It owed its name to having been built for the second Earl Bathurst when he was still Lord Apsley; the original Adam house was red-brick. It occupied an L-shaped site facing west and south, with wide views through very large windows of eternally changing London skies, and of traffic, with vistas in three directions, down Constitution Hill and over the Green Park and Hyde Park. Its contents were famous and included a colossal Canova nude, a statue of Napoleon (in the staircase vestibule), a vast array of presentation plate and porcelain, medals and decorations, and pictures, some bought by or presented to the Duke, but the most important being the collection of the Spanish royal family, looted by Joseph Bonaparte and recovered from his carriage on his flight after the Battle of Vittoria. The restored King of Spain asked the Duke to keep them, and some of the best, mainly Spanish, Dutch and Italian old masters, decorated the walls of the Waterloo Gallery, ninety feet long and hung with yellow brocade. It was in this gallery that the Duke and the Gascoyne heiress paced together, on many recorded occasions. From 1830 to 1852 the Duke held an annual Waterloo Banquet. An engraving of that held in 1836 shows all the generals mentioned by Fanny, including one who makes most frequent appearances in the Diaries — Field-Marshal Sir Henry, afterwards 1st Viscount Hardinge (1785–1856): Peninsular and Waterloo veteran; Governor General of India, 1844–7: Commander-in-Chief British Army, 1852–5.]

The Duke, in great force, talked of his campaign in Zealand, and told us an anecdote of himself and Sir Willoughby Cotton who were dining and passing the evening at a country house in Zealand and went up with the rest of the company to enjoy the freshness of the evening at the top of the house, when suddenly a blaze of light appeared in the horizon — Copenhagen in flames. "We were glad enough to get off!" he added, "our reception became quite another thing after that discovery."

After dinner he showed us some of his pictures, one of the great Duke of Marlborough on horseback, one of Schomberg, and a famous one by Le Fèvre of Napoleon. It was observed to him that he would soon assemble all the celebrated Generals of European History except the greatest: it is indeed much to be regretted that he does not seem likely to leave to his descendants any portrait of himself. One room is principally fitted with modern portraits of those his own friends and companions in arms, taken about the year 1814: how much altered since then! The only one which retains its resemblance is that magnificent picture of Lord Beresford by Lawrence. The Duke gave £1200 for Wilkie's[1] celebrated "Chelsea pensioners" . . .

[Talleyrand's gloomy prophecies were not fulfilled. The Duke annoyed the Ultra-Tories by speaking and voting for the second reading of the Government's Bill for regulating the Protestant Church of Ireland. Lord Falmouth, although a connection by marriage (grandson of Fanny Boscawen) entirely lost the good opinion of Fanny by saying that if the Duke did not oppose the second reading he would retire into the country and interest himself no more in politics. "He had always been a Church and King man etc. etc." . . . "He is a pompous fool." About Lord Londonderry she had long ago made up her mind, "Open to the highest bidder."]

July 27th I was not sorry to leave town for the season. It has been a very dull one, as is universally acknowledged. The excitement which attended the first burst of the Reform bill has passed away, and yet politics and the anxiety inseparable from the present state of things continue to spoil the pleasure of society: our situation is no better but we have lost the animation and the novelty which prevented our feeling the depressing effect of it at first . . .

---

[1] Sir David Wilkie (1785–1841). Painted "The Scotch or Penny Wedding" bought by the Prince Regent for the Royal Collection and "The Blind Fiddler" presented by Sir George Beaumont to the National Gallery: a valued guest at Hatfield.

August 6th Ld. S. who had been to town brought back the Duke who came to dine and pass the evening. He was in great force and very amusing about the Dukes of Gloucester[1] and Cumberland,[2] describing their sitting on each side of him in the House suggesting their own ideas into each ear (one of which is stone deaf), and totally preventing his attending to the Speaker opposite: the Duke of Gloucester especially always proposing some impossible situation. "And what would your Grace do under *such* a circumstance?" "For heaven's sake, Sir, let me just hear one word of the speech that is going on, for I have to reply to it." He told me that the Ultras were behaving better and anxious to make it up with him: but he was determined to have no explanations, no *lovers' quarrels* — it would all come right. He seemed to wish Lord S. to remain within reach of London till the end of the Session: on that account he has put off his journey to Scotland for the present.

[Lord S. made frequent fishing holidays to Scotland. Judging by a letter in French from Fanny to her daughter Blanche, dated simply "Wynyard, 21 Septre." she accompanied Lord S. to Drumlanrig in that month, probably in 1832. They had come via Carlisle and Newcastle to stay with the Londonderrys. A water-colour sketch of Loch Vennacher in Album 3.W.60/16 may date from this trip. It has stanzas from *The Lady of the Lake* opposite.]

The Duke is deserted by almost all his friends already, the Session is so late — and it would be too bad to leave him to fight his battles with nothing but empty benches to back him.

7th The Duke went to town at eight o'clock this morning. Lord and Lady Mansfield and their daughters came down for one night. A pretty affair this of Don Key's!

[Sir John Key (1794–1858), Lord Mayor of London 1830, one of the leading supporters of the Reform Bill in the City, and re-elected for 1831, had advised the King not to come to open London Bridge attended by ministers, owing to the unpopularity of the Duke of Wellington. The visit to the City took place in August 1831. Wellington accompanied the King who created Key a baronet.

[1] H.R.H. Duke of Gloucester (1776–1841), "Silly Billy", m. his first cousin the Princess Mary, fourth daughter of George II: no issue.

[2] H.R.H. Ernest, Duke of Cumberland (1771–1851), fifth son of George III, King of Hanover 1851.

Amongst the young men who had recently stayed at Hatfield had been Henry Wellesley, son of the Duke's youngest brother, Lord Cowley. Fanny, who had written down Olivia De Ros on August 3rd as "delightful, so gay, so unaffected and kind hearted", received an unpleasant shock on the 13th.]

Olivia left us. I discovered by some hints she gave that she had accepted a proposal from Henry Wellesley. I never was more surprised or I may say disappointed. Disappointed in her fickleness, and her want of proper feeling in placing me in such a disagreeable position with the Cowleys who must suppose it is my doing.

[Lord Cowley had married Lady Georgiana Cecil, elder sister of Lord S., but Henry was not their child. He was a son of Lord Cowley by a first wife who had bolted with Lord Anglesey in 1809. Olivia was twenty-six and saw no future in continuing as maid of honour to the gentle Queen Adelaide. She had two younger unmarried sisters, no mother and six brothers. Henry, who had lost his mother when he was six and received a step-mother when he was twelve, was now twenty-nine, in the foreign service and disappointingly diffident. Fanny could not forget that he was an offspring of a bolter.]

17th Politics are very dead just now: a few peers remain in town, about thirty, including the two sides, and occasionally a little good is done by the Conservatives in the way of amendments, but every lady that can get away is gone.

19th Went to town. Lady Charlotte Berkeley dead of the cholera. It shows the force of novelty in everything. Last year when Mrs. Smith died the consternation was general, from one end of England to the other: this year poor Lady Charlotte's fate has scarcely made a sensation. London is a perfect desert: the cholera full as bad, in fact, I fancy, as last year.

20th I hear from Shepperton the Cowleys are furious and the blame of course laid upon us. Henry and O. determined to marry in spite of all opposition . . .

21st The Duke told me a curious anecdote of Lord Liverpool, who went to him and expressed his earnest desire of adhering to his politics notwithstanding that he had for some reason been prevented from voting in a Portuguese debate a few nights before. But he had also had a conversation, he said, with the Duchess of Kent, who had told him that he (Ld. L.) was the person of all others from his station, friendship for her, etc. etc.; whom she should eventually look to: and as she put it to him whether he would think it advisable, *considering the present circumstances of the King's health*, to attach himself to a line of politics that might be an objection to his holding office hereafter. A pretty clear declaration of H.R.H.'s Whiggish intentions! She does not like, it seems, that the Duchess of Northumberland[1] should interfere too much with Victoria's education which appears after all to have been very inferior up to the appointment of the Duchess of Northumberland . . . Conroy[2] is all powerful. The Duchess of Kent applied some time ago to the Duke of Wellington for promotion for his sons: the style of the letter was very peculiar – she did not name Conroy, but merely said "My protégé, you will know to whom I allude . . ." Some years ago she met Princess Esterhazy at Cheltenham. *"Ma chère"*, she said, "don't let us make formal visits here or be in each other's way. You go your way, I go mine; we will each amuse ourselves according to our own taste." Both of course were equally well provided.

The Duke is as despairing as ever about the country – so is Lord Rosslyn. They agree in thinking there will be no blow-up, no bloodshed, that all our ancient institutions will be destroyed by due course of law, that the property of the rich will be attacked in various ways and that till tradesmen and manufacturers and those who live on the production of luxuries find the consumption of their goods ruinously diminished, there will not be any danger of commotion. At the same time the Duke thinks there is nothing to be done; that long experience only can disgust the nation and change its feeling, and that till that is the case we cannot move.

22nd The Duke went to town at 8 o'clock. This day I heard of the death of Lady Aberdeen: she was one of those few people I really valued and esteemed: I felt it accordingly. For herself, a happy release from suffering. Lord A. is wretched.

23rd The account proved unfounded: but she is despaired of. Ld. S. in town for the House but came back at night.

24th Quite alone this, and the succeeding days; I hope the Cowleys begin to believe our innocence of Henry's affair.

[1] Wife of Hugh Percy, 3rd Duke of Northumberland, *née* Lady Charlotte Herbert, grand-daughter of Clive of India.
[2] Sir John Conroy (1786–1854), private secretary to the Duchess of Kent.

25th Ld. S. ill: he attempted to go to town but was forced to turn back.

27th A positive account of poor Lady Aberdeen's death.

28th Ld. S. very unwell in the night. I was rather alarmed. Everything is awkward in these days of cholera.

[By Sunday, September 1st, Ld. S. was sufficiently recovered to entertain the Duke of Cumberland and a large party at Hatfield, for four days. The Duke of Cumberland's influence upon George IV had been held to be pernicious: he was the most unpopular of the sons of George III. He was obliged to go to law to defend himself against slanders. The stories that he had murdered his valet and had a child by his sister, the Princess Sophia, persisted. A letter from him to Lord Salisbury (Cecil Papers, XII/209), dated September 13th, 1833, explains that "I stood charged with such atrocious and heinous crimes that I had no other means left me but to prosecute."]

September 5th They all left us today. I must say he has made himself very amiable in this house – endeavoured to be civil to everybody, said nothing disagreeable and swore very little, comparatively. He is completely at his ease and puts everyone else so – in that respect much superior to the Duke of Gloucester . . . I suppose he wishes to make himself a footing in good company. The Duke of Wellington would not come to Hatfield, he cannot stand the bore of either of the Royal Dukes, G. and C. I am very glad to find there are hopes that Prince George may recover his sight: a celebrated oculist from Berlin is arrived and takes a new view of his case. What a blessing it would be for the country.

He is certainly anxious to please, and is by no means a bore. There is a story that the other day he was heard to say à propos to Whitehall Chapel which is to be applied to some secular purpose "By G--, it's so d--d irreligious."

[The Duke of Cumberland had a blind only son, and it had gradually dawned upon the Salisburys that their beloved eldest son, Cranborne, was only partially sighted and going deaf. He was not mentally deficient; rather bright for his age. If evidence could be found that his mother had had measles during the early stages of her pregnancy the problem would be solved. He was a classic case. But no such theories were current at this date. "A short history of my mother as derived from such papers and letters as we

86

have,[1] records a family legend, known by two Balfour grand-daughters."

"My grandmother died when my mother was between fourteen and fifteen, in October 1839. I have been told, probably by Miss E. G. Faithfull, daughter of the Rector of Hatfield and a life-long friend of my mother, who was a few years the younger of the two, that the eldest child of my grandfather, whom we called Uncle Cranborne, who became blind while still a boy (or was he born blind?) and was otherwise imperfectly developed physically, was said to have been injured by an accident to his mother before his birth. In those days and I suppose still, when they rode side-saddle, women were helped to mount their horses by a man making a sort of stirrup of his two hands into which the would-be rider put her foot. On this particular occasion, according to the story, as the story is remembered by Alice, my grandfather, when helping his wife to mount, made too violent a lifting movement and she fell over the other side of the horse."

The Duke of Cumberland offered to look after Cranborne if his parents thought fit to send him to Berlin for treatment by Baron Graefe but they did not immediately accept the offer. The handsome invalid boy was said by his travelling tutor-companion to have been taken by other tourists for a member of the English royal family — perhaps the blind Cumberland heir.]

6th Left Hatfield for Ingestre at ½ past nine and arrived there at the same hour at night. We found only a family party.

7th I am delighted with the place which far exceeds my expectations. The house handsome and comfortable — the grounds very pretty, with magnificent timber . . . We all assemble at prayers at nine in the morning, then breakfast. After luncheon we generally rode — dinner late, and the evening ended early. Altogether I passed a pleasant quiet time; it is a house of perfect liberty and ease.

11th Came from Ingestre to Childwall, where the children met us.

12th Devoted this day to going over the place. The foliage is so much damaged this year by the dry weather and high winds that I never saw it in less beauty.

13th and succeeding days Nothing worth writing down. We lived here quite alone, fully occupied with visiting the tenants, putting the plantations in order etc. I think the former were still glad to see

[1] Cecil Papers: Transcribed E. M. Sedgwick, 1933.

us, but our long and almost constant absence must make a difference in their feelings. I feel more and more the impossibility of making Childwall a residence.

22nd Had a letter from Olivia de Ros announcing Lord Cowley's consent to their marriage.

October 3rd I left Childwall with the children. After all I cannot but regret leaving it: it is always a painful moment: — so beautiful, so wasted, and as if one's presence is not so much valued there as it may have been . . .

[Lord S. had not had his fishing this year but to Hatfield now came visitors from the land of the mountain and the flood. John Gibson Lockhart (1794–1854), acidulated literary critic, had married in 1820 Sophia, elder daughter of Sir Walter Scott, and was to become famous as the biographer of his father-in-law, who had died in September 1832.

Wilkie's extraordinary appearance was attested by many contemporaries: he was unusually tall, raw-boned and sandy-haired and had "a strange, feeble, tottering pale look" — evidently a perfect "Dominie Samson" type.]

19th The Lockharts, Clanwilliams, Capt. Percy, Ed. Drummond and Wilkie, the painter, here. Mr. Lockhart is very agreeable, not the less so for his bitterness — a Tory Rogers. Mrs. L. simple and natural with plenty of Scotch shrewdness: her manner is totally unformed but pleases from the utter absence of all affectation. Wilkie, with the looks of a clown, and the manners of a "Brancas" appears to have a good deal of sense and observation concealed beneath his oddities and shyness, independant of his talent in his art.

21st Wilkie went to see the pictures at Panshanger — and returned apparently much pleased: though he pronounced many to be copies that bear the reputation of originals.

[Panshanger, a Whig stronghold, was the Hertfordshire seat of Peter, 5th Earl Cowper, drastically altered by him in 1808, and provided with battlements and towers faced with Atkinson's patent cement. The park was one of Humphry Repton's most admired efforts. It was demolished in 1954. Lady Cowper, born Emily Lamb, daughter of the 1st Viscount Melbourne, married as her second husband in 1839, Henry, 1st Viscount Palmerston.]

I think Mr. Lockhart is of the despairing order of politicians – with too much reason, I fear.

22nd They all left us. Today Olivia is married at Windsor.

[The visit of Sir Walter Scott's daughter and son-in-law was the natural sequel to Hatfield's most successful theatrical entertainment performed in January of this year – the Waverley Novels *Tableaux Vivants*. The elder Gascoyne-Cecil children and Grimstons took part, and sketches were produced by Wilkie and Lady Verulam. Lady Salisbury was Edith Plantaganet: Lady "Katty" Grimston,[1] Rowena. Several contemporary diarists and letter-writers mention the event and amongst the most enthusiastic was Miss Charlotte Augusta Sneyd. Charlotte was one of the six daughters of Colonel Walter Sneyd of Keele Hall, Staffs. and Louisa, daughter of 1st Lord Bagot. She was an erudite woman and edited in 1847 Vol. 37 of the Camden Society publications from a MS. in sixteenth-century Italian. She performed many sketches at Hatfield and was a constant visitor till her death in 1882. Keele Hall is now the University of Keele and owns the Sneyd MSS. "There was a sort of fellowship in the concern which made everybody intimate directly and I never was in company with so many people in such good humour and disposed to be pleased. The Duke quite as eager as a child . . . There was a most beautiful collection of heroes and heroines, but the most beautiful was universally allowed to be Miss Mary Ames as Isabelle de Croy.[2] Lady Robert Grosvenor looked very lovely as Berengaria[3] . . . Lord Hillsborough was the most perfect Coeur de Lion[4] . . . I am quite pénétrée at the excessive kindness of the Salisburys to me. I am lodged in the State Dressing Room and Lady Salisbury had the good nature to come to fetch me every day before dinner to go in with her."[5]

The Duke of Wellington had been appointed Warden of the

---

[1] Lady Katherine Grimston (1810–74), eldest daughter of 1st Earl of Verulam.

[2] Mary (1814–77), daughter of Levi Ames of Ayot. St Lawrence, Herts, and The Hyde, near Luton, m. 1836 Sir William Codrington, Commander-in-Chief in the Crimea.

[3] Charlotte Wellesley, sister of the 1st Baron Cowley, and a niece of the Duke of Wellington, m. Lord Robert Grosvenor, afterwards 1st Baron Ebury, 1731.

[4] Arthur Hill, Earl of Hillsborough (1812–68), afterwards 4th Marquess of Downshire; nephew of the Dowager Lady Salisbury.

[5] Sneyd MSS: Charlotte's letter of Jan. 18th, 1833 is S(RS/CAS/)16.

Cinque Ports in 1829 and nothing pleased him more than to entertain favoured guests in "the most charming marine residence I have ever seen". Walmer Castle was a massive, circular keep, built of Kentish rag. The only visible entrance to it was by a drawbridge with a portcullis, above a deep moat now filled with his Grace's vegetable garden. Opinions varied as to comfort at Walmer. The study of William Pitt, occupied by the Duke as bed-sitting-room, was singularly austere, with a north aspect, but the quarters designed for entertainment and visitors had been revolutionized by the late Duke of Dorset during his tenure of office. From the dining-room and adjoining drawing-room it was possible to step out directly onto a small terrace overlooking the Straits of Dover. The white cliffs of France could be easily discerned.]

October 24th Went to Walmer. We got there about ten at night, and found the Duke sitting with Lord Mahon and Sir John Keane. He is looking as well as I ever saw him.

25th Delicious weather. Walked with the Duke to Deal Castle and afterwards drove out with him in the carriage. He told me Peel was going abroad to winter at Rome: I observed I could not comprehend what game he was playing. "Nothing but weakness," he replied. "He is afraid – afraid of everything" . . . He repeated his opinion that the country was doomed to revolution, revolution in due course of law; should it, however, terminate in a contest of arms he thinks that Napier (of the Peninsular War) is the only man who has military talent for a leader of the democrats. "He is twelve or fifteen years younger than I am," said the Duke, "but he has no health."

[General Sir Charles Napier became the conqueror of Scinde (1843). He suffered such agonies from head-wounds got at Bussaco and Corunna that he kept a light burning to help him through sleepless nights.]

26th This morning the Duke gave us some amusing anecdotes at breakfast: one in particular of Mr. Canning relative to the statue of the Duke of York at the United Service Club. Some months previous to his death, the Duke of York wrote to the King warning him against Canning. George IV immediately showed the letter to Canning himself. It was, as the Duke observed, written either too soon or too late for the Duke of York to follow it up by any other step, on account of the state of his health, and too soon to have the effect of a dying

request. Canning attended the funeral, where he in fact caught his death, and at the dinner on that occasion, took the opportunity of animadverting on the intended statue, expressed his surprise that a set of military men should take upon them to decide what personages deserved to be commemorated by monuments and statues, and his opinion that they were *too highly paid* . . .

Speaking of poets, the Duke said, "I hate the whole race. I have the worst opinion of them. There is no believing a word they say — your professional poets, I mean — there never existed a more worthless set than Byron and his friends for example. Poets praise fine sentiments and never practise them, their praise of virtue and fine feeling is entirely from the imagination: if they describe a fine action they quote some other author from whom they have taken the idea, to prove it was nature. There was no blemish in Scott's character but his reserving from his creditors a settlement for his children when he entered into the bookselling speculation: nothing else can be said against him, but he was not a professional poet. The column erected to the Duke of York would never have been completed had not the architect Sloane subscribed £3000 . . ."

Speaking of the Duchesse de Berry, "a curious character, of which folly is the prominent feature. She is one of those foolish people who imagine that to *will* a thing is sufficient. No such nonsense! You may *will* to go to the moon. She once said to me, *"On peut tout faire, il n'y [a] qu'à le vouloir."* *"Oui, Madame,"* I replied, *"mais il faut avoir aussi les moyens."*

She sent Chateaubriand to Charles Xth to know if he would receive her; his answer was that nobody had less right than he had to visit the frailties of human nature with severity, as no one had given way to them more. "I pity and feel for the Duchesse de Berry," he added "but I must consider myself as the guardian of her children; if she chuses to go and live with this avowed husband for a time, I may then present her to them as a respectable *mère de famille en secondes noces.* At present it is impossible."

[Caroline de Bourbon, Princess of Naples (1798–1870), as widow of Charles, Duc de Berri, son of Charles X, attempted to arouse an insurrection in Britanny in 1832 to secure the throne of France for her posthumous son. She had borne a further son in May 1833 to Comte de Lucchesi-Patti, the marriage had been announced in February.]

The King [William IV] has desired both Prince George of Cambridge and the Duke of Cumberland to avoid passing thro' Belgium in their way to Hanover; thereby shewing his dislike of Leopold, the very prince whom his Ministers have in his name placed and supported on the throne.

This day we drove to Dover and saw the new Quay proceeding under the Duke's direction. We were less edified by meeting the Speaker and his wife[1] whose acquaintance I however succeeded in avoiding. It appears that she is the pest of the neighbourhood from her eagerness to be admitted into Society and anger against all those who decline receiving her. She scarcely allows him to go to any house where she is not invited.

28th The William De Ros's[2] and Henry and Olivia Wellesley came. The weather like summer. Walked with the Duke upon the beach. Mr. Gleig dined here.[3]

29th Went again to Dover to see the Castle.

30th Went over to Ramsgate, saw the pier etc. The children were out walking with their tutors and nurses, anxious to shake hands with the Duke; they pressed round him and seemed much gratified with the notice he took of them.

This, and the preceding days the Duke told me several curious anecdotes, and others to Lord S.

The Duke has been occupied with some papers of Mrs. Fitzherbert's which came into his possession as executor to the late King. She wished to have them restored to her; the Duke refused to return those which regarded the King. Lord Stourton, a Catholic, and Lord Albemarle, were appointed on her part to arrange it with the Duke and they met at her house a short time ago. Lord Stourton was desirous to detain the certificate of her marriage with the King, or at least, if it were destroyed, to have its destruction recorded. To the latter the Duke objected, as he conceived it would imply that he considered the document to a certain degree valid, and of some

[1] Charles Manners Sutton, first Viscount Canterbury (1786–1845). Speaker 1817–35: m. as his second wife, 1828, Ellen, daughter of Edmond Power of County Waterford, widow of John Purves of Purves, N.B.

[2] William De Ros (1797–1874) succeeded his brother Henry as 23rd Baron; m. 1824 Lady Georgiana Gordon-Lennox (1795–1891) daughter of 4th Duke of Richmond, who published recollections of her mother's famous ball.

[3] Rev. George Gleig (1796–1888) published a life of the Duke, 1862.

THE CECILS AT THE SEASIDE

The 2nd Marchioness reading aloud to Lord Cranborne, Lady Mildred and Lady Blanche Gascoyne-Cecil

Sketch by Miss Charlotte Augusta Sneyd of Keele; from an Album of the 2nd Marchioness of Salisbury

importance; but he agreed to restore it to Mrs. F. as a paper of no real consequence — since the marriage could never be esteemed good in the eye of the law. Lord Stourton observed that in every other country *it would be valid* . . . Another paper was sought for in which the Pope transmitted his commands to Mrs. F. to live again with the Prince after he had deserted her for Lady Jersey and subsequently married Caroline of Brunswick. He was seized with a desire of returning to her and implored her in the most passionate terms to receive him. She referred it, as a case of conscience, to the Pope who after discussing it in full consistory, gave his mandate in favour of the re-union. This paper had however disappeared, Mrs. F. having destroyed it on some alarm of a Popish riot: she proposed to obtain a copy for herself from the Archives at Rome. In the end, the papers with a few insignificant exceptions, were burnt. Among them was a will, written by the Prince at the time of his greatest passion for Mrs. F. and full of the most extravagant expressions, leaving everything to "my own own own wife wife wife, my own dear Maria, my only love".[1]

Lady Jersey,[2] as it is well known, brought about his marriage with Princess Caroline of Brunswick[3] to destroy Mrs. Fitzherbert's influence and place her on the same footing as his other loves . . .

When Princess of Wales, Queen Caroline was one day sitting next to the Duke of Wellington at dinner and praising the Duke of Cumberland. The Duke of Wellington assented, but observed that Her R.H. had chosen the flower of the family: "The Prince is a man of universal accomplishments etc." "Not at all," she replied, before all the company and servants. "He understands how a shoe should be made, or a coat cut, or a dinner dressed and would make an excellent tailor, or shoemaker or hairdresser, but nothing else." In the Duke's opinion Princess Charlotte would have turned out quite as ill as her mother, and her death was a blessing to the country: in addition to her mother's inclinations she had an exceeding bad manner: as an instance of it, she always called the Duke "Arthur", *tout court*.

[1] Maria Smythe (1756–1837), daughter of Walter Smythe, m. 1st Edward Weld, 1775, 2nd Thomas Fitzherbert 1778, 3rd George, Prince of Wales, 1785.
[2] Frances Twysden (1753–1821), m. 1770 George Villiers, 4th Earl of Jersey.
[3] Princess Caroline of Brunswick (1768–1821), m. George, Prince of Wales and was mother of Princess Charlotte (1796–1817).

This day the Wellesleys embarked on their way to Stuttgart.

[Henry Wellesley had been appointed British Minister. Olivia de Ros gave him the self-confidence he had hitherto lacked, and he became an even better Ambassador to Paris than his father.]

Hers is an awful undertaking. I distrust both his temper and principles. I believe her to be perfectly sincere in professing that she did not intend to deceive me, and that her acceptance of him was sudden and unforeseen; but my opinion of her understanding is much lowered tho' that I entertain of her heart remains the same. Lord St. Vincent and Miss Jarvis [sic] dined here; the latter sings very beautifully and looks very mad.

[John, Viscount St. Vincent (born Rickett), was the nephew and heir of Admiral John Jervis, Earl St. Vincent. His daughter, Hon. Mary Anne Jervis, nicknamed "The Syren" by Wellington, took up quarters in Walmer village, and he was relieved when she married (1840) "the Black Prince" Dyce Sombre, a wealthy Nabob.]

31st Left Walmer, to my great regret: reached London in time to go to the play. Farren[1] in *Uncle John*: the best piece of acting of the kind I ever saw.

Friday, November 1st Left town for Hatfield . . .

Nov. 2nd and following days. Nothing particular. We were almost entirely alone. The hot water machinery for warming the house was got ready.

11th Went to Gorhambury to meet Mr. Barham who is coming down *on trial* for Lady Katharine.

[John Foster Barham (1800–38), son of John Foster Barham of Trecwn, Pembroke, and Stockbridge, Hants., by Lady Caroline Tufton, daughter of Sackville, 8th Earl of Thanet. John Barham II was M.P. for Stockbridge till 1831, for Kendal 1834–7.]

12th The lover expected all to-day in vain.

13th He arrived at breakfast having been delayed by the fog the day before — 6 hours between London and Barnet — and obliged to sleep at St. Albans. He acquitted himself very well to-day in his very awkward and difficult position. He is not good-looking, nor the reverse: tall, with small eyes and a reddish face, and rather tigerish

---

[1] William Farren (1786–1861) of an accomplished theatrical family; excelled in a variety of comic characters at Covent Garden, Haymarket Theatre and Drury Lane.

in appearance. I see no fault at present in his manner or conversation: and at least he has the rare merit of being desperately in love.

14th She is favourably disposed, and will not be able to hold out long against the pressing entreaties of her family and the persecution of her mother to give him a final answer.[1]

Today we returned to Hatfield to receive the Miss Blackburnes.[2]

15th A letter from Emily Grimston saying Katty has finally consented. I hope it may be for her happiness: it is a leap in the dark. I regard her as lost to me — he is a Whig, and will probably avoid associating with us as much as possible.

17th–20th A review of the Yeomanry in the Park. They dined afterwards in the hall — nearly 200. A very good spirit appeared among them. The Queen was drank [sic] with more feeling than the King, and the Duke of Wellington with great applause, and Lord Grimston as County Member with enthusiasm. The whole went off very well, Lord S. proposing M. Dedel's[3] health, made some allusions to Holland as our old ally which was extremely well received.

I had a good deal of conversation with Sir H. Hardinge. He thinks the best chance of salvation for the country is some mixed administration that may gradually back out of the violent measures hitherto adopted by the Whigs, and at the same time give an opportunity to the great Whig families who may feel alarmed at the threatened attacks upon property to separate themselves from the Radicals. His wish is to see Peel at the head of the Govt. and the Duke Commander in Chief. He says Peel never contemplated going abroad for more than a fortnight, to buy furniture. He told me he thought Mrs. Arbuthnot did mischief by setting the Duke against Peel, and agreed with me that it is the duty of every friend of either to unite them as much as possible. Peel, Croker and Lord Fitzgerald were anxious to have placed the Speaker at the head of the Tory Administration that was in agitation in May '32, as a temporary Premier, his abilities not being such as qualified him to meet these critical times in a more permanent character, intending that the Duke should succeed him after a space. This was opposed by Lord Lyndhurst and Arbuthnot,

---

[1] Lady Verulam's four daughters eventually married the Earls of Clarendon, Caledon, Craven and Radnor.

[2] The Misses Blackburne were her cousins from Hale.

[3] M. Dedel, Belgian Ambassador.

which occasioned the delay. On the Monday, the day before the Duke resigned his commission to the King, Sir Henry dined at Peels' — only three or four men. W. Peel was strong in his condemnation of the Duke's conduct. As soon as the servants were gone Sir Henry said he could not but be surprised and disappointed at his observations which were evidently intended to prejudice his brother Sir Robert against the Duke, and he regretted to perceive that they had not been without effect: that nothing could be further, he was convinced, from the Duke's intentions than to slight or to throw any reflection upon Sir Robert. Sir Henry then wrote a note privately to the Duke, begging him to write to Sir Robert and invite him to join some others of the party who were to assemble that night at Apsley House. The Duke wrote a very proper note and Sir Robert went. The next day, or a few days after, Sir Henry called upon Peel and told him he was going to call upon the Duke. Peel made no observation in consequence. Sir Henry said, "Come Peel! I cannot manoeuvre, I am no intriguer. I will tell you at once what I came for; it is to take you with me to the Duke. Come along; a week hence will be too late." And he succeeded in preventing at least the appearance of any unpleasant feeling in consequence of the different lines they had taken at that crisis.

Lord Rosslyn, who still keeps up correspondence with his *ci-devant* friends among the Whigs thinks the alarm is spreading amongst them, and that the Duke of Richmond, Graham and Stanley are anxious to adopt a more conservative course — that Lord Grey also is uneasy, but that Brougham opposes any thing that might extricate them from their present difficulties in the hope of forcing Lord Grey to retire, and of succeeding him.

The *general* idea seems to be that the *mouvement* party in the Cabinet will prevail and Lord Durham will become Premier.

A capital story of the Duke of Cumberland — boasting of his attachment to the Church he said, "By G-- I'd be d---d for religion!" I hear the Duchess of Kent is entirely in Lord Durham's hands. A pleasant prospect!

Monday, Dec. 2nd The Duke of Gloucester and a large party here.

3rd H.R.H. did not shoot well and was rather out of humour — contradicted Lord Mahon three times about his Grandfather's age, and asked me if I remembered Mr. Pitt.

[William Pitt had died in 1805; Fanny had been born in 1802.]

However, I must say that if he is not brilliant he is very civil and endeavours to make everybody pleased with him.

5th We followed him to Gorhambury.

6th I never saw anyone happier than Lady K. Mr. Barham seems a good sort of man.

9th A party of five and twenty. Lord Norreys entertained us excessively with taking off the principal speakers in Parliament – the Duke of Wellington, Lord Grey, Lord Lyndhurst, Lord Holland – all excellent. Peel seemed to enjoy it, but looked half shy lest his own turn should come next – which it did – the day after he went away.

10th A Tuesday *Soirée* – very tolerably full. Lady Salisbury had a terrible fall and was bled: she was thrown by some waltzers.

[Lady Salisbury's accident in the ballroom reached the London press under the heading "Flooring a Marchioness". A reporter who supplied the Court Journal was said by colleagues to have been present disguised as an extra waiter. "The female Nestor" apparently tried to cross the floor and came into contact with "the Hon. Mr. Herbert twirling the Lady C. Grimstone (sic) in the mazy dance", and as the old lady was very small and withered and they were young and revolving rapidly, she was flung on her face. "The music ceased, the dancers dispersed, and the splendid *Sal de Bal*, a few minutes before the scene of such general gaiety, became the chamber of mourning." The Hon. Mr. Herbert was Sidney Herbert (1810–1861) son of 11th Earl of Pembroke, afterwards the Secretary for War who invited Florence Nightingale to go to the Crimea. The Dowager had achieved yet another nickname since the 1832 Elections – "Old Sarum". This depopulated area, north of the cathedral city of Salisbury, had been one of the notorious "rotten boroughs". It had seven voters and had returned two members to Parliament since 1295.]

11th Wonderfully recovered to-day, considering she is 84: she came out of her room to dinner.

19th Lady S. left us to go to town, still very weak from the effects of her fall. A tenants' feast . . .

Sunday, December 22nd The Duke came. I never saw him looking better, and in much higher spirits than at Walmer. He remains with us two nights and then proceeds to Woodford. I see he thinks a change of government is approaching: he said the present state of things could not continue, that we must return to the ancient constitution "whether by legal means or by force I cannot tell. If this administration is succeeded by a more radical one, our way will be long and painful before we come to that result, and there will probably be a considerable change in respect to property – but that we *shall* come to that result, I do not doubt. Peel never knows his own mind; he is conscious of that defect and therefore afraid of committing himself; his opinions are only to be gathered from what he accidentally lets fall" . . . The Duke told Peel some time ago that the ancient order of things must be restored. "You must bear in mind," said Peel, "at all events that it must be by *legal* means." Since that conversation another person expressed the same opinion to Peel, adding, "You will see that these military men if they have the settling of affairs, will bring back Old Sarum, Gatton and the whole system." "They must reserve a representation for the large towns," observed Peel, "or I cannot be a party to it" – thereby indicating what the Duke calls "a progress in his ideas" and that the horror he felt at the idea of military interference was much diminished. It is evident that the Duke feels he cannot do without him, tho' he never can entirely depend upon him.

[Peel was the son of a calico manufacturer of large fortune and had the sensitiveness and awkward cold manners of a man socially not quite sure of himself. He was warm hearted. His wife, Julia, daughter of Sir John Floyd, Bart. mother of his seven children, gave him a happy home life, but was in her own phrase "no politician".]

The Duke thinks Lord Holland[1] one of the worst amongst the Whigs, "a bad man," utterly selfish and unprincipled, and popular from the effect of manner only; Lord Londonderry not to be trusted, *wicked* and deceitful in the highest degree. Metternich[2] told the Duke he thought he had more talent than his brother (the late Lord Londonderry)[3] but added, "*Il ne faut pas vous fier à lui.*" "*Je le connais très bien*" was the answer. When the Duke was at Vienna, Lord

---

[1] Henry Richard Fox, 3rd Baron (1773–1840).

[2] Metternich, Prince Clement (1773–1850), Austrian Foreign Minister.

[3] Londonderry, Robert Stewart, Viscount Castlereagh, 2nd Marquess of Londonderry b. 1769. Foreign Secretary; committed suicide 1822. General Charles William (1778–1854), who succeeded him, was his half-brother.

Stewart, as he then was, kept up a private correspondence with his brother, the Minister, unknown to the Duke and contrary to all rules of diplomatic form. The Duke found copies of these letters in the Foreign Office when he returned home. He showed them to Lord Castlereagh "whose affection for his brother was like that of a lover for his mistress, he could think nothing wrong that he did".

Again, when the Duke went to Verona, Lord Stewart resumed the same practice, sending private despatches to Mr. Canning, who returned them to the Duke, hoping to *brouiller* him and Lord Stewart. The Duke called the latter and remonstrated with him, and the scene ended by tears on the part of Lord Stewart.

The Duke is of the opinion that the whole of the present royal family are more or less tinctured with insanity. The late Duke of York [was] the best of them, but with much to condemn. He must have known of the infamous proceedings of Mrs. Clarke — yet such was his infatuation for her that he gave way to them, and swore to a total ignorance of things of which he must have been conscious. The Duke of Cumberland has never been guilty of such reprehensible transactions; the only difficulties he ever fell into about money were in consequence of lending £25,000 to the late Mr. Villiers, to whose wife he was attached.

But the late King was most extraordinary about money. He never could bring himself to part with the most trifling sum for his ordinary expenses. There was often a difficulty about getting money sufficient to leave London, and upon one occasion a sum was required to be paid before five o'clock in the day to enable a favourite horse of his to start for a race. The King was applied to for the money. "Oh yes, by all means," he said. "Pay it; you can get it anywhere, you know, easily." But the money was not forthcoming and at the last moment Colonel Lee applied to him for it again. "I told them to pay it," said the King. "Yes, Sir, but where is it to be got?" "I know nothing about that!" "But I know," returned Lee, "in that little box on the table." "Well then, since you *will* have it, take it," and the King gave him the key. The box held several hundreds.

At his death there was sufficient ready money in guineas and bank notes (some of one pound only) found in his different desks and drawers to pay his physicians about £10,000. It was almost all contained in innumerable perfumed silk pocket-books, of which he had

99

a constant succession, and which were put away as soon as they were full. They were also stuffed with souvenirs of every kind, dirty gloves, locks of hair of ancient date, matted with pomatum and powder, ribbons, notes, etc. etc. of different and various origin. He deceived himself about his danger to the last, yet loved to make a scene with his sisters, and take leave of them.

The Duke thinks the Whigs are very unpopular. I believe they are, but I *fear* not to the extent he thinks. Speaking of men's education, he observed that they learnt nothing at a public school and less at college, but that English public schools were chiefly valuable as forming the habits and feelings of a *gentleman* and giving a knowledge of the world, and an independence and *originality* of character rarely to be met with abroad. "You will find every Frenchman cast in the same mould, but every Englishman has a distinct character."

He thinks men *generally* inferior in real and useful information to women, and that many a young man reads to be fit for the society of women. He spoke much of the abuse of charitable institutions and of the plans for National Education now supposed to be entertained by the Ministry. "I approve of education, but let it be education connected with a system of discipline. The first object of education should be to teach them not to break the laws of God and man. Now, you teach them to read, and then turn them loose into the street to pick pockets . . ."

I repeated to the Duke a saying of the Duke of Gloucester which had entertained us very much — that he "always made it a rule in a campaign to place his troops in the *best possible position*". Whatever other people might do, he thought "*that* the best rule, to take the *best possible position*". The Duke laughed and said, "But I can tell him he's *wrong*, quite *wrong* — that is not the way to win battles: I can tell him how to fail in his plan, tho' I can't tell him how to succeed. I have got a *knack*, to be sure, of winning battles myself, but I don't know how to teach it to other people."

23rd It rained all day. I spent it chiefly in conversation with the Duke. He was in remarkably high spirits, taking great notice of the children, and entering into all their amusements, telling various anecdotes, and making us all laugh excessively . . .

24th The Duke left us for Woodford. A. Hill here. Lady Salisbury is also returned, but much weaker and more unwell than when she left us. Today she was obliged most unwillingly to keep her room.

Xmas Day, Wednesday, December 25th

26th A party of country neighbours came for the Hertford ball next day.

28th Lady S. better. Lady Cowley came down to see her . . .

31st A Tuesday evening. It blew a tremendous storm, but we had a full *soirée* and the New Year was merrily ushered in. What will it produce?

PART IV
1834

I

Thursday January 2nd Lady S. left us for town: quite recovered.

3rd Went to Belvoir. Got there about nine in the evening. Lady Brownlow, Mrs. Arbuthnot, Mlle. Este and Lady A. Manners came to see me in my room. According to their separate accounts there must be rather an amusing *carte du pays* to examine here. Queen Mab's visit to Strathfieldsaye has evidently excited great conjectures, and hopes appear to be universally entertained of the downfall of the *régnante*, who is not popular. I do not believe in a change of dynasty — besides the Duke told me Queen Mab's coming to S. Saye was entirely at her own invitation.

[Belvoir Castle near Grantham, seat of the Dukes of Rutland since the days of Henry VIII; rebuilt by Wyatt 1816. The Salisburys' host in 1834 was John Manners, 5th Duke (1778–1857). His wife, Lady Elizabeth Howard, daughter of Frederick 5th Earl of Carlisle, had died 1825. Lady Brownlow (1791–1872) was a childhood's friend of Fanny Gascoyne— born Lady Emma Edgcumbe. She was the third wife of John Cust, 1st Earl Brownlow (1779–1853). Mlle. Este was Augusta Emma, daughter of the Duke of Sussex (sixth son of George III) by his illegal marriage to Lady Augusta Murray. She was born 1801 and married, 1845, Sir Thomas Wilde, afterwards Lord Truro. The Duke of Sussex's two children took the name of Este as it had belonged to common Italian ancestors of both their parents. Lady Adeliza Manners, fourth and only unmarried daughter of the Duke was acting as his hostess. She married 1848 a clergyman, her cousin, Canon Norman, Rector of Botesford. "Queen Mab", who haunted Strathfieldsaye, had been born Lady Sarah Anne Child Villiers, daughter of John Fane, 10th Earl of Westmorland, and had married 1804 the 5th Earl of Jersey. The mistress of George IV called *"la régnante"* was Lady Conynghan. Strathfieldsaye, a long low house mostly of late Georgian date, previously the seat of Lord Rivers, was chosen by the Iron Duke in 1817 and granted to him and his heirs by the Crown. He had it heated "by 'tubes' of hot water" at the same time that Hatfield was so supplied. The situation, near Reading, was exposed and some guests complained of cold, but not Fanny Salisbury who wrote to her daughter Blanche in 1838 that her room was "so delightfully hot" she dreaded returning to Arlington Street. "The men have been out shooting every day and I do not think Papa has had much time for tennis."]

4th The Duke of Rutland's birthday – ushered in by the firing of cannon corresponding to the years of his Grace's age. A most disagreeable commemoration as it appears to me. The usual ball is not given tonight as it happens to be a Saturday. There is an immense party in the house – 34 at dinner today. Nothing can be more magnificent or better *monté* – but it is almost too numerous a party and on too grand a scale to be agreeable.

We sat in the great drawing-room which I believe is only used on this occasion. The Duke of Wellington was talking of the life in country houses in the winter, and observed upon the immense waste of time in the manner of passing the day, and the inconvenience of it to a man like him who when he was either out or receiving company at home could scarcely find time to answer his letters. "I, who have been engaged in business, commanding armies, *or something of that sort*, all my life, can scarcely conceive how people contrive to pass their time so totally without occupation."

I do not like the statue of the Duchess in the drawing-room: there is something chilling and melancholy in that marble figure standing among her living descendants. The apartments are all magnificent, but ill connected, and after all, no modern Gothic, even on the extensive style of Belvoir, can really give the illusion of antiquity, and is, therefore, so far, a failure. For if you fancy the castle built for purposes of defence, you must fancy it built at a time when defence was necessary, or it becomes absurd.

5th Service in the chapel in the morning: in the afternoon the Duke of Rutland assembled a select society of ladies in his room and read a sermon.

6th We went to see the hounds throw off. They had good sport and the Duke of Wellington seemed highly pleased. No neighbours at dinner to celebrate the day, which surprised me, except Sir W. Welby, and a Mr. and Mrs. Norton, the man a great Radical who distinguished himself disgracefully in the riots at Nottingham. If the Duke of Rutland selects so few of his neighbours, this person ought not to be among the number. A dance of the servants in the evening, in which all the party in the house joined: the Duke of Wellington taking Lady Adeliza, and so on.

7th Left Belvoir for Belton: a number of the party were drafted off there at the same time: the Duke of Wellington among others.

8th I think this is much more comfortable than Belvoir and the diminution of the society makes it more enjoyable.

[Belton House, near Grantham, the home of the Brownlow family; built 1685 and attributed to Sir Christopher Wren, had magnificent carvings by Grinling Gibbons.]

9th Most of the party went to a Musical Festival this morning at Grantham, but I was excused. I am glad to hear the Duke was well received there as it is reckoned rather a Radical population. "Let's see old Wellington," and much applause. He proceeds from thence to town.

10th Left Belton for Apethorpe.

[Apethorpe was the Northamptonshire seat of Lord Westmorland. Fanny refrains from comment. Peel, reported to his wife in January 1833, that a guest did not know what misery could be until he had stayed at Apethorpe — a house the size of a lesser Oxford college, a bedroom a quarter of a mile from the billiard and drawing-rooms, containing no fire (owing to his host's terror of a conflagration), but a closet inhabited by spiders and rats. His candle blew out half-way to this paradise.]

11th Got to Hatfield. The John Talbots here.[1]

14th A Tuesday evening — the last. I was afraid of the fatigue of going up to town in the morning for Lady K. Grimston's marriage which took place to-day.[2]

16th This day and the following we had a party of Verulams, Miss Sneyd and several men, till the beginning of the week.

20th Went to Strathfieldsaye. Not a very large party when we arrived. The Duke of Gloucester, Sir R. Wilson, the Arbuthnots, F. Egertons, Clanwilliams, Lord Mahon, the Duke of Gloucester as usual exceedingly *questionneur* and disputatious — contradicted the

[1] John Charles Talbot, Q.C., fourth son of Charles, 2nd Earl of Shrewsbury (1806–76), m. 1830, Caroline, daughter of 1st Lord Wharncliffe.
[2] The wedding took place at St. George's Hanover Square from the Verulams' London house in Grosvenor Square.

Duke repeatedly about the Peace of Utrecht — but seems vastly delighted at being here. The Duke had a fall the other day; his horse was pushed into a ditch and rolled upon him, but he was not hurt. It makes me shudder to think of such an escape. Lord Mahon told us some curious particulars of Kaspar Hauser — what an irreconcilable and incomprehensible story!

[Amongst the feats attributed to General Sir Robert Wilson (1777–1849) of the British Intelligence, were bringing Canning advance news of the Treaty of Tilsit, obtained in the disguise of a Russian boatman (1807) and conveying Count Lavalette, in the uniform of a British officer, out of Paris in broad daylight, though under sentence of death (1816). Wilson was a prolific author. Lord Mahon was well qualified to expand upon the story of Kaspar Hauser as his father had adopted the mysterious youth in the dress of a German peasant found wandering in Nuremburg in 1812. One of the theories about him was that he was the Crown Prince of Baden, kidnapped from his cradle in Karlsruhe 1812. He died, probably from self-inflicted wounds, 1833.]

The Duke expresses himself confident of his election to the Chancellorship of Oxford; no opposition talked of at present.

[The Duke had been dubious about his qualifications when first approached, "he knew no more of Greek and Latin than an Eton boy in the remove". Too late to withdraw his acceptance he heard that another party in Convocation had invited Peel to accept nomination.]

21st Esterhazy[1] came down here to breakfast, says he is confident Louis-Philippe has no wish to send troops to the Peninsula. The day too wet for shooting. Lord and Lady Bathhurst and Lady Georgiana came to dinner. The Duke has generally some of the neighbours to dine here when there is a large party.

22nd Lord Douro and Holmes and Col. Gurwood came today.

[Arthur Richard Wellesley, Marquess of Douro succeeded his father as second Duke of Wellington. The relations of the Duke with his sons were never satisfactory. He was a stern parent and they suffered from consciousness of inferior abilities. Colonel John Gurwood was private secretary to the Duke for many years. His work as editor of the Duke's despatches was a monument of accuracy

[1] Prince Paul Esterhazy (1786–1866), Austrian Ambassador to London.

and industry. He had been severely wounded in the head at the storming of Ciudad Rodrigo and died by his own hand.]

They were able to get out after luncheon to shoot, otherwise I think the Duke would have died of it. His royal guest is exceedingly tiresome on a wet day and pesters everyone with questions. He is perpetually calling the Duke his brother chancellor, and observed upon the curious coincidence of two Field Marshals being Chancellors of the two Universities — evidently putting their military as well as their literary talents on the same level.

The Duke was speaking to me at dinner of Col. Gurwood's intended work which will contain many of his letters written in India and furnished by the Duke himself. "Upon my word, I was quite surprised on looking over them to see how well they were written. Tho' I was very young then, I could not write them better now. I see that I had at that time all the care and foresight and attention to every detail that could forward the business which I had in charge, which is the only means of ensuring success."

It must be very curious to see such a mind in the beginning of its career, already distinguished by those qualities which were afterwards to lead to such unparallelled glory.

He was speaking afterwards on the subject of the education of the lower classes. "I would have them," he said, "taught morality and religion — the religion of Christianity — taught to do no harm to their neighbours. For that is the essence of all religion; that is the wonderful part of Christianity. It imposes no privations it only requires you to live without doing harm to others."

I suggested to him that in case Lord Londonderry, who is said to be ruined, should part with *all* his pictures, the Duke should become the purchaser of that done of himself by Lawrence, as it is really a shame his family should not possess a single good portrait of him. He promised me he would see about it. He gave me *Marie Tudor* to read today as a curious specimen of the present French literature and morals.

So, Queen Mab not having succeeded in obtaining from him some hairs of Copenhagen's[1] tail, procured them from the groom, and I have no doubt there is some foundation for the story I heard the other day, that she has got a bracelet of Copenhagen's hair, set with jewels, lying at some jewellers, and professing to be given her by the

[1] Copenhagen (1808–36), the chestnut charger ridden by the Duke at Waterloo.

Duke. I hope this woman will not succeed in throwing ridicule upon him by persuading the world he is at her feet.

23rd Lord Charles[1] arrived last night from Berlin. He gives a good account of Prince George who is recovered from his late attack and Graaf [sic] persists in the opinion that he will recover his sight after operation for cataract, which is to be deferred for two years.[2]

The Duke of Gloucester departed this morning, to the general joy — accompanied by his inseparable Sir R. Wilson. The Duke went out hunting and we saw them throw off. Colonel Gurwood showed me some of the papers he is engaged in arranging for publication. What a voluminous writer the Duke has been! No man, I suppose, has written more, and always without a copy; the first sketch of his thoughts upon paper is the last. He revises the whole of Gurwood's book, and the latter speaks of his memory as astonishing, every detail of the time is recollected by him with the most perfect accuracy. This, Gurwood ascribes to his invariable adherence to truth, a hard reflection upon short memories.

It is an extremely agreeable society here, well informed men and great deal of interesting conversation, besides the pleasure of being sure of finding in every room a knot of *fellow* worshippers of the Duke whose favourite subject is his praise.

24th The Duke was up and out this morning at 7: breakfasted at 9, went out with the hounds and had nothing to eat till he returned to dinner at half past 7. He did not appear the least fatigued or sleepy in the evening, played at whist, and I left him in the drawing-room when I went to bed at 12 o'clock, talking with great animation. Lord Rosslyn and Mr. Addington, the late minister at Madrid, came to-day; the latter was talking with the Duke over several anecdotes of his old Spanish friends — especially the Duchess of Bencomte, whom he described as devotedly attached to the Duke and as considering herself indebted to him for everything, having been an exile under the French Government of Spain, from her immense possessions. She had many admirers in her time, some of whom excited the jealousy of the Queen of Charles 6th. One of them, Penän, standing one day near the Duke, the Duchess of B. exclaimed, "*Voilà deux*

[1] Lord Charles Wellesley (1808–58), second son of the Duke.
[2] Prince George of Cumberland, King of Hanover 1851, deposed 1866, died aged sixty-one 1878, totally blind.

grands hommes!" She seems to have been a sort of Charlotte de la Tremouïlle, and stood in the trenches at the siege of Gibraltar.

In the evening the conversation turned upon Kaspar Hauser and the nearest approach made by human nature to the state of brutes. The Duke is of the opinion it is to be found in the isles of Andaman peopled by savages of negro descent and unacquainted with the use of fire.

I never saw a man so relieved by the absence of the Duke of Gloucester. He declares he shall never come into his house again. But this I think is the resolution of the moment while the recollection of the bore is fresh upon him.

25th We went to see Bramshill, a curious old place of Sir John Cope's built originally for Prince Henry, son of James I. The outside is a very handsome specimen of the Elizabethan style, the situation beautiful. The interior has nothing remarkable, though it might be made a very fine thing if properly fitted up. But the present proprietor is said to be very poor and it is evidently going to ruin. We saw the closet where the unfortunate bride is supposed to have been smothered. It is of japan, not very large, and I can hardly imagine any human being shut up in it to fail of making themselves heard.

The Duke told me he had thirty letters to write today.

January 26th, Sunday Went to church — afterwards to the stable to see the Danish pony the Duke is breaking in for Blanche.

[He had written in November 1833 about "A Norwegian . . . red and white, six years old".][1]

Copenhagen begins to look very old and thin. He is in a paddock by himself. I think he is said to be 27 years old.

No neighbours dined today except Mr. Briscall, the clergyman who was the Duke's chaplain abroad, and is constantly here. The Duke has just received an account of a present which is arrived to him from the Emperor of Russia, of models of his artillery etc. — fourteen large packing cases full, and he is in doubt where to put it and talked of its being placed in the hall here. But I do not see the possibility of finding room. This house is too small to hold half the fine things that require it already.

27th Arbuthnot I consider a very prejudiced though an honest man, and I am therefore inclined to receive his statements with

[1] Letters of the Duke of Wellington: 123, 24.

some allowance. But he made an observation upon Peel which is perfectly just — that he was disgusted with the House of Commons "because he could neither bear a supporter in it, nor to be unsupported".

The Duke tells me he has a letter from the Duke of Cumberland since his return, anxious to be active and as *remuant* and troublesome as ever.

This day we left S. Saye . . . I have seldom spent a pleasanter week than this at S. Saye.

28th Went on to London. The children met me there to go to the pantomime.

29th Dined in Arlington St. Lady Sal: quite well. The Duke is elected Chancellor of Oxford . . .

30th Ld. S. joined me and we left town for Hatfield.

31st Ingestre and Frederick De Ros here for the last day's shooting of the year.

Sunday February 2nd Quite alone. This day I have been married 13 years. Few persons can boast as I can that 13 years have only added to my attachment and sense of my husband's worth. I have reason to be thankful.

3rd Lord S. went to town to be present at the Duke of Wellington's dinner at the opening of Parliament.

5th Lord S. returned. The King's speech was extremely conservative, Lord Grey's equally so, especially his expressions with regard to the church. No amendment moved by the Conservatives — the Radicals utterly defeated in their attempt to introduce one. I begin to hope the Conservative party in the Cabinet have got the ascendancy and mean to resist further innovation — the worst is they never can be trusted for a day. No business in either house at present. The King ill received by the mob in going to open Parliament.

The Duke told Lord Salisbury a curious fact respecting his residence in India, that the only two books he had with him on his campaign there were Caesar's *Commentaries* and the Bible. Today he gives a dinner to the deputation from Oxford — his Latin speech in answer to their address was composed by Sir H. Halford.

6th We remained at Hatfield quite alone till the 17th.

17th Came to settle in town.

18th London is very dull, I hear: no houses open but those of the Premier and the two Ambassadors, Talleyrand and Lieven.

28th Lord S. returned. They say the Trade Unions are arming. The workmen employed in the gas works having struck, several streets have been in darkness the last two nights, and on Saturday the Opera was concluded at an earlier hour than usual for the same reason.

Saturday, March 1st A few people to dinner yesterday and today — no news, London very dull. It is said there will be a strike among the workmen throughout England in the course of the month — A regiment is sent for from Ireland to be stationed in Lancashire.

13th Peel and Hardinge and some others dined here: they arrived late from the division upon excluding the Bishops from the House of Lords. Who would have believed, three years ago, that such a motion would have found 58 supporters in the House of Commons? It reminds one strangely of the Long Parliament, some of the arguments of which were indeed quoted, and the intervening 200 years do not seem to have furnished many new ones . . .

Sunday March 30th, Easter Day

Sunday April 6th The weather for some days has been delicious: the spring wonderfully forward.

7th I came to town, leaving Lord S. and the children at Hatfield.

9th The Trades Unions are much talked of as assuming a formidable appearance and some people think a serious disturbance will be the consequence, which is likely to be forwarded by the unsettled state of France.

14th Parliament meets today. I never recollect London so completely at a stand: not a dinner or a party going on except the mere Ministerial ones. I remember the time when after Easter one's table was crowded with invitations. Lord S. came to town today.

15th News of the insurrection at Paris.[1] If the troops succeed in putting it down it will be a great event in favour of government and good order all over Europe: if not, I suppose we may soon expect something of the same kind here.

16th News that the Paris insurrection is put down. I think this will act as a sedative for some time to the Trades Unions. They were

---

[1] Republican and Socialist agitators engineered a series of risings and strengthened the power of Louis-Philippe as defender of the middle class interest.

expected to present a petition today in favour of the Dorchester unionists at the Levée but for some reason or other they did not.

I find the Londonderrys do not mean to sell their portrait of the Duke.

18th The Duke called upon me. Spoke of Col. Gurwood's book which is just come out. His own correctness of recollection being mentioned, the Duke said, "You cannot conceive how every circumstance of a field of battle is impressed upon my mind, every stone, however long the time since the event."

He parted from me not expecting to see me again before my confinement, with the utmost kindness and expressions of friendship and affection that make me too proud.

21st A great procession of Trades Unions to-day, to present a petition through Lord Melbourne for the repeal of the sentence against the Dorchester Unionists. They are said to have amounted to 25,000, marching in perfect order. Lord M. declined accepting the petition and they dispersed peaceably. Great preparations of troops, artillery etc. had been made in case of any disturbance, but their chief object probably was to drill their followers and make an exhibition of their strength. After two or three more of these peaceful parades we shall probably come to something more serious.

Thursday April 24th My little boy was born. Thank God it *is* a boy.[1]

Sunday, May 4th I left my room for the first time.

May 11th The Duke came to see me. He told me he thought there was every reason to believe the King was going mad. His conduct in some respects resembled that of George 3rd before his last illness, and some years ago, when the present King left the Admiralty, he was actually so mad as to be put into a strait waistcoat. Like George 3rd who never forgave Willis, he has never forgiven the man who did it.

[Francis Willis attended George 3rd in his first attack of derangement in 1788 and was much criticized for maintaining that the patient would recover if more gently treated and allowed more freedom.]

He told me that at the Levée the other day Peel passed by all the deputation from the University of Oxford who were attending the Duke without taking the least notice of them, with one exception,

[1] Lord Eustace Brownlow Henry Gascoyne-Cecil (1834–1921).

114

that of the Provost of Merton,[1] a strong Whig, but who happened to be the man who proposed Peel as a candidate for the Chancellorship. If it was an accident it was an odd one, if not it was a curious proof of the *cotton twist*. But it is evident to me that some influence is at work to make the worst of all Peel does in the eyes of the Duke and to persuade him that he intends to slight or neglect him in trifles where I am sure no such intention exists. I suspect it is the Arbuthnots. Hardinge has begged me of us to ask Peel and the Duke to meet one another. But one is so accustomed to being courted, and the other has so much sensitiveness and plebian pride that they are easily led to take mutual offence. However, Peel is daily of more importance in the country and its fate in a great measure must rest in his hands.

17th Went down to Hatfield.

19th I think the air and change have already done me good. Saw Mr. Faithfull this morning: he thinks there is a strong spirit in favour of the Church. The Country is in the greatest beauty and everything promising well for the harvest.

30th Left Hatfield, to my great regret, and came up for the children's ball at St. James's. I was not, however, able to go but sent the children with Lord S. [One of Olivia De Ros's best sketches *"le Bal d'Enfans"* depicts preparations for such an entertainment — little girls prinking, a furious little boy having his hair curled by a French *coiffeur*.]

31st Great preparations making for the Duke's Installation at Oxford and many people going; there is however a considerable dread among his friends of Mrs. Arbuthnot's presence as they think she will place herself in some conspicuous situation with him that will shock the Professors. I hope she has not quite such bad taste. The Duke of Cumberland is going. How he will swear!

Tuesday, June 3rd The christening of my little boy. He was named Eustace Brownlow Henry . . . A large family party dined here afterwards — the Duke, the Cowleys, Downshires, R. Grosvenors etc. The Duke kissed my little boy three times. He may be proud of it in after life. The Duke was in high spirits: he gave me an account of the negotiations that had taken place about the admission of the Duke of Cumberland and Talleyrand to a Doctor's degree at

---

[1] Robert Marsham, D.D.

Oxford. The Duke of Cumberland was determined to go, but upon the University being sounded it was found that there might be some opposition to his taking a degree. The Duke of Wellington then struck out a plausible reason against his soliciting that honour, that the etiquette was contrary to it as he was Chancellor of Dublin: and the Duke of Cumberland, according to his suggestion, wrote him a letter to decline it. A still greater reluctance existed to conferring that honour upon the ex-Bishop of Autun. The Duke of Gloucester discovered this fact and immediately communicated it to his friend the Duchesse de Dino. Talleyrand, upon this, wrote to the Duke of Wellington, assigning his lameness and infirmities as the cause that deprived him of attending the Installation and requesting the Duke to give him the satisfaction of assuring him, by his answer, that he was fully convinced such was the motive of his absence. An incomparably well written letter, the Duke says. He of course wrote in return such an one as Talleyrand wished which will doubtless be published.

II

Oxford

June 8th We went to Hatfield in the evening (it being Sunday) in order to cross the country to Oxford the next day, on account of the expected difficulty of procuring horses on the straightest road: Lord Mahon with us.

9th A beautiful day — got to Oxford about ten in the evening and took up our quarters at the Angel.

[The Angel, in the High Street, on the south side of the sacred bend, almost opposite Queen's College, was evidently by 1834 the best inn. Lord Nelson and family went to the Star, and Garrick, a connoisseur of inns, had a personal friend at the Star.]

10th We were in the theatre by ten o'clock. The reserved seats for the peeresses were already taken, however by the activity and civility of one of the proctors we all got placed except Mme. de Lieven who came in late, and was kept standing for some time until room could be made for her, and after all remained during a great part of the ceremony in the second row. She did not look pleased. The theatre was excessively crowded, and the undergraduates in the gallery amused themselves till the entrance of the Duke of [sic] calling out the names of various public men, and giving political sentiments with suitable hissing or applause. The cry was always unanimous, and the feeling of the most decided Tory kind (even *I* feel almost too liberal for the air of this place); nothing but Ultra Toryism and Ultra Protestantism will go down. It was quite delightful to find oneself in such society. Lord Grey and all the Ministers were furiously hissed: the King's name produced little sensation: the Queen violently applauded, "the Bishops" called forth thunders of applause, and all the Ladies rose to do honor to their name. The name of Wellington of course still more cheered, and again everybody rose. About eleven the Duke of Cumberland entered; his face was pale with agitation, as he probably considered the sort of reception he should meet with very uncertain. But the theatre rang with acclamations, and after he had taken his seat he was repeatedly obliged to rise again to acknowledge them. Then they called out the Duke of Sussex, as if to show the difference, and hissed. The Duchess of Kent's name seemed to elicit little feeling of any sort. But when the Duke entered the very building shook with the applause. It continued for many minutes. He looked gratified, he could not do otherwise — even he must have been flattered by such a reception from such an assembly. When at last it subsided he read the list of those who were to take degrees. He got through it very well — one or two false quantities were scarcely detected — but the names and the form of words were evidently written in a very confused manner, from the difficulty he seemed occasionally to have to make out the writing.

[The Duke had applied to his physician, Sir Henry Halford "as most likely from his prescriptions, to know Latin". Creevey and Greville, both of whom left accounts, were indulgent, but the University was startled by their Chancellor's pronunciation of Jacobus as three short syllables, followed by Carolus with a protracted "o".]

The Vice-Chancellor[1] stood by him, shaking from head to foot and too nervous to be of much assistance. Dr. Phillimore[2] then made

[1] George Rowley, D.D., Master of University College.
[2] Joseph Phillimore (1775–1855), Regius Professor of Civil Law (1809–55).

117

a very good Latin speech and the different candidates for the degree were brought up. The Duke of Newcastle and Lord Winchelsea were most loudly applauded; but all met with approbation. Lord Fitzroy Somerset was also much cheered, and so was the Duke of Buccleuch. When the Duke left the theatre the cheering was renewed.

I went afterwards with most of the other women to a luncheon in All Souls: we walked about the college afterwards and admired the quadrangle and the library: the chapel I think is very inferior. There was a great dinner today at the Vice-Chancellor's for the men: we ladies dined in the Coffee Room at the Angel, a pic-nic. About six or seven men who were not engaged to the Vice-Chancellor sat down with about twenty women, and I have no doubt we afforded much amusement to the people who were dining on the other side of a screen at the farther end of the coffee room. In the evening I had a soirée, according to the Duke's desire, who had bespoken it before we left town. Lady Brownlow lent me her room for the purpose it being much the best in the inn.

There are a great many people here that we know – the Brownlows, Jerseys, Clanwilliams, Wiltons, G. Somersets, Hardinges, Arbuthnots, Buccleuchs, besides innumerable men. London, I hear, is a perfect desert, Oxford and Ascott [sic] have taken everybody away. The dinner, however, lasted so late that the Duke and the Duke of Cumberland and the rest did not get to us till we were just going to bed.

June 11th, Wednesday We were in our places this morning at the same hour. The cries in the Gallery were very entertaining today – "Whigs and Pickpockets", "Tories and Honest Men", "French Allies" (hissing), "French wines" (applause), "A laugh for the Dissenters" (upon this there was a long and universal laugh, the most ludicrous thing I ever heard), "Lord Grey and his return in office", "Parliament as it is" (hissing), "Parliament as it was" (vehement applause), "The present House of Commons" (hisses), "The House of Lords" (great applause), "The memory of George 3rd" (great applause), "Peel with Emancipation – Peel without Emancipation" (very differently received), "The Privileges of the Universities – Non-admission of the Dissenters" (both of course much cheered). And after having exhausted every possible subject at last somebody called out, "The whole human race." There is an unfortunate proctor here of the name of Dyer who seems to excite the wrath of the undergraduates most particularly, and by way of putting two most obnoxious things together, they called out "Dyer and the Dissenters."[1]

The Duke of Cumberland was equally well received today and the cheering at the entrance of the Duke was as gratifying as before.

Another long list of doctors. Everything military is so much in fashion at the University that the mere mention of a man's having served in the army is sufficient to draw down thunders of applause: and upon this principle Lord A. Hill and Sir Hussey Vivian had a most cordial reception. Lord Templemore, the only other Whig, was actually hissed. Lord Encombe advancing to take his degree produced a most touching scene. His name was loudly applauded and when he approached the Duke the cheers redoubled. The Duke shook hands with him and passed him on to a seat beside Lord Eldon[2] who, extending his hand to him, which the young man kissed, was so overcome at this public tribute of approbation that he leant on the desk before him, and covering his face burst into tears. Everyone was affected.

After the degrees had been conferred, the Newdigate Prize poem was recited by its composer, Mr. Arnold.[3] There were some beautiful passages in it, which were applauded, but towards the end, an ingenious and rather sudden transition being made from the subject of the poem to the victories of the Duke, the lines —

> "And the dark soul a world could scarce subdue,
> Bent to *thy* genius, Chief of Waterloo!"

called forth such a burst of enthusiasm as I never witnessed in my life, and even the Duke told me afterwards he had never seen anything like it. The whole theatre seemed one living mass that rose in concert: the Peers, the Bishops, every creature joined to do homage to the Deliverer of Europe: the noise was positively astounding and continued fully quarter of an hour. As to the under-graduates and the occupants of the arena, they scarcely knew how to give vent to their feelings; they roared, they screamed, they waved hats and

---

[1] James Hardwicke Dyer, Fellow of Trinity College.
[2] John Scott, Viscount Encombe (1805–88), afterwards 2nd Earl of Eldon, who succeeded his grandfather, the 1st Earl, 1854, was created D.C.L. Oxford, June 11th, 1834.   [3] Not Arnold—Mr. Joseph Arnould of Wadham College.

handkerchiefs, they actually jumped and danced with delight. It was quite overcoming: such a moment, the witnessing such homage to the greatest man existing, was worth any trouble or any sacrifice! And when one considers that this applause so unanimous and so enthusiastic was not the applause of a common mob, of a horde of ten-pound Reformers, but the tribute of all that is most distinguished for intellect, education and birth, and of all the rising generation of the country, one cannot but think it worthy *even* of that great man who called it forth. The Duke himself was not at the moment aware of what had produced this explosion: Mr. Arnold's rostrum was on his deaf side, and he could scarcely hear a word of the poem, so the allusion to Waterloo was totally lost upon him, and he could not conceive at first what had produced the sensation on all sides, which came upon him like an earthquake. However, in time it *did* subside, and the other compositions were proceeded with, none, however, of the English ones at least, had any striking merits.

I went afterwards to a luncheon at Mr. Sneyd's,[1] one of the Fellows of All Souls.

Today was the great dinner at Christ Church, which took almost all the men away. Lady Clanwilliam and her sisters, Sidney Herbert, Mrs. Arbuthnot, Lady G. Somerset and I dined together in a private room at the Angel. In the evening the Ball at the Star. It was the most frightful crush I ever beheld, the staircase and every place so thronged that it was impossible to move. I got away with great difficulty.

I hear the Duke has given great satisfaction to the heads of the University, and his business-like way of proceeding and rapid decision have surprised and delighted them. Some point having occasioned a discussion at a meeting this morning, he said "Our only business is to find out what it is our duty to do — and to do it!" But there never was anything like the enthusiasm his presence has created here: and I am convinced that if he were to set up his horse, like Caligula, the whole town would pay obeisance to it.

June 12th, Thursday No theatre today. There was a charity sermon at St. Mary's to which I did not go. I went later to the Clarendon Press with Lady Brownlow, to meet the Duke, who came there in state to see the establishment. He looked admirably well in his black

[1] Louis Sneyd, fellow of All Souls 1809 and Warden 1827.

gown walking at the head of the other dignitaries — so dignified, so graceful, as if he had done nothing else all his life.

Afterwards we had luncheon at Exeter College; the hall though not to be compared in size to some others is very beautiful, the roof reminded me of the Old Palace at Hatfield. There is some good carving in the chapel, and the Quadrangle and garden are beautiful. We dined again in the Coffee Room, and had a better attendance of men, as the Duke dined today at St. John's where there are not so many invited. He came, as well as the Duke of Cumberland and many others, in the evening. I never saw the Duke in such spirits, or his countenance so expressive of satisfaction.

June 13th, Friday The theatre at the usual hour. The enthusiasm does not seem the least diminished. There was a long list of Doctors made today — beginning with Lord Dartmouth and Lord Cole, the contrast of whose size produced a most absurd effect. Sir C. Wetherall was much cheered, I should say he was next favourite to the Duke himself. Lockhart and Wilkie took their degree — both were applauded, especially the latter. Dr. Hume, the Duke's physician, narrowly escaped a very different reception, his name having been originally set down as *Joseph*, and it was only by accident discovered and restored to *John Robert*.

[Sir Charles Wetherell (1770–1846) was a local hero. His father had been Master of University College. Wetherell was a violent and indiscreet anti-Reformer, and it was his arrival that sparked off the Bristol Riots. He was Attorney-General in 1826 and 1828. John Robert Hume had been Wellington's surgeon in the Peninsula. He was admitted a Fellow of the College of Physicians in 1836. Joseph Hume, also originally a surgeon, and a Tory, became a leader of the Radical party. He was renowned as having spoken more and worse than any other private member, but was indefatigable in showing up abuses.]

The Duke performs the representation part of his office admirably well, bowing to the "Domini Doctores" and "Magistre" with great grace. His only difficulty is to manage his cap, which he cannot easily get hold of when it is necessary to pull it off, and he occasionally makes a *military* salute instead, putting up his two fingers to the side of his head.

There was nothing remarkable in the recitations today — the

last, a poem by Mr. Graham, was the best, and the various allusions to the Duke were vehemently cheered, and when he left the theatre for the last time, the sensation was only inferior to that produced the other day by the name of Waterloo. The people pressed forwards on all sides to touch his hand. He said to me afterwards, "If I could be spoilt by this sort of thing, they would spoil me here." I think he feels it deeply.

I went after the theatre to see the hall at Christ Church, a magnificent room, I admired the chapel also very much from the extreme antiquity of parts of it. At half past 3 there was a great breakfast at All Souls to which the ladies were admitted. It was given in the library, where they danced afterwards (Scotch reels especially) with a spirit which must have startled all the musty old authors on their shelves. It was really a beautiful scene, the scarlet robes of the Doctors, and the gaudy gowns of the young noblemen adding prodigiously to the effect.

I walked with the Duke over the Chapel and different parts of the College: he could not help exclaiming as he contemplated its magnificence, "And they would destroy all this!" He thinks the mode in which the destruction of the Church will be attempted will be by issuing some sort of Commission of enquiry similar to those that have already been tried with the Corporations.

Our pleasure was rather damped by the news of the loss of the Cambridge election: it is clear that there is no great change among the people, at least in the large towns: and I begin to think, from the strong feeling on both sides, that we must come ere long to a crisis. Perhaps Oxford may again be the headquarters of the Conservatives.

As there was no means of lighting up the Library[1] we repaired when it was dark to the Angel, where a last soirée concluded the most delightful week I ever spent. Besides the excitement and gratification of the public proceedings, we had a most agreeable Society among ourselves, no quarrels, nor jealousies, even among the women. Upon the whole Mrs. Arb. has not been very conspicuous,

[1] Electric lighting was introduced into the Codrington in 1909. The "new" lighting was put in under the librarianship of Professor Ernest Jacob in 1961. The tungsten lights on the South side of the great library were abolished, and that side, and the upper range of the northern side were lit by tubular phosphorescent lights of pink and white.

tho' I am afraid she has occasionally walked about the town with him of a morning, and at All Souls she tried to monopolize him as much as she could, but he did not encourage it.

14th Went to see Magdalen and New College before we started. The Quadrangle, and indeed the whole exterior of the former is beautiful, and the chapel, which is renewed, is remarkably well done. We were so fortunate as to come in during the service, and the organ is excellent. One can never avoid reflecting on such occasions on the immense power the Romish Church must naturally have had over the minds of its votaries by such powerful appeals to the senses — architecture, painting, picturesque effect, music, even perfumes, brought to her assistance: and when one looks at those beautiful and peaceful cloisters, one may for a moment understand the fascination that could induce the choice of a monastic life.

The chapel at New College is still more beautiful, and the modern painted glass almost equal to the ancient. We were shown William of Wykeham's crosier of silver, and though hollow, the weight must be very great. The grounds of this College are beautiful.

Altogether Oxford will remain upon my mind like a fairy vision of beauty and delight. I should almost regret to return there at any future time, lest the illusion should be dissipated.

We left this fairy land to return to the "work day world" about eleven and reached Hatfield to dinner.

III

Wednesday June 18th (Anniversary of Waterloo) Gilt laurels were selling in the streets this morning, which is a mark of feeling in honor of the day which I did not expect. A great number of people of all sorts went to look at the preparations for the Duke's great dinner at Apsley House. There was a dinner also of fifty at the Carlton Club. Peel spoke out in the most satisfactory manner and declared himself the leader of the party. Better late than never. He is pledged to resist all innovations in the Church.

21st The second reading of the bill for the Admission of Dissenters was carried last night. Sidney Herbert made his first speech on the Conservative side and with great success. Peel complimented him.

I hope he is beginning to learn the necessity of *buttering* young men. Stanley, I think, seems to have backed out awkwardly from his former declarations.

We dined at the Lord Mayor's to meet the Duke of Gloucester: a splendid dinner in the Egyptian Hall of from 250 to 300 people, exceedingly well done. There were a great number of Conservative grandees there, and the Duke of Richmond, who, however, in returning thanks for his health carefully avoided all politics. By some unlucky mistake Denman[1] who dined there was forgotten, and the health of the Master of the Rolls given with "The Bar". Denman looked furious, and when the mistake was rectified returned thanks in a very surly speech. I saw Alderman Wood who looks like a grey hyena.

[Sir Matthew Wood, champion of Caroline, Princess of Wales; he gave financial assistance to Lady Hamilton, and to the Duke of Kent. He received a baronetcy from Queen Victoria.]

"Church and King" was given by the Mayor and drunk with great applause, as was also "the Queen" and "the Duke of Wellington". Altogether it was a fine sight and I am glad we went. I think it is right for the aristocracy to cultivate a good feeling with the city.

24th Went with Lord Mahon to see Sir James South's[2] Observatory at Kensington. The night was so cloudy that we were disappointed of our original object of viewing Saturn and the moon through the telescope: but I was very much amused with his conversation and anecdotes: and he very good naturedly took much trouble in showing us his instruments etc.

27th Duke of Gloucester and a party dined here: among them Talleyrand. I sat next him. As usual he talked in a very conservative style; spoke of the change that had taken place in French society, and said that he no longer had any pleasure in Paris. *"Je n'y connois plus personne. Tout est changé: on n'y voit qu'une élégance bourgeoise. Ce qu'il y a de moins curieux pour les étrangers en France c'est Paris. Mais le nord et le midi de la France ceux sont deux pays différens, en morale, en physique, en tout."* He said that if Louis 18th had lived the "Trois

[1] Thomas, 1st Baron Denman (1779–1854), Solicitor-General 1820, Lord Chief Justice 1832.
[2] Sir James South (1785–1867), a founder of the Royal Astronomical Society. He observed with Herschel and Humboldt.

LADY MILDRED AND LADY BLANCHE

With Hatfield House in the background

Sketch by Lady De Ros; from an Album of the 2nd Marchioness of Salisbury

Jours" would never have taken place, *"il avoit de l'esprit et il n'avoit pas de passions. Il n'étoit pas Roi d'un parti."* He agreed in the resemance between Charles X and James II.

29th Cranborne returned from abroad. His eyes are not improved, but I had the satisfaction of hearing from Mr. Urquhart that he was perfectly well pleased with the progress of his mental powers. We must be thankful it is no worse: though assuredly it is a *great* calamity.

[Cranborne now in his thirteenth year had been sent with a tutor, John Urquhart, a retired Naval medical officer, for cruises in the Mediterranean and Adriatic. From Naples, marble paving, lemon trees, statues and classical reliefs were despatched to Hatfield House, followed by Cyprus wine, and Malmsey from Sicily. He had survived a slight attack of smallpox at Naples. In May 1834 his mother wrote to tell him he had a new brother, Eustace, and his sisters added postscripts. Lady Blanche's told him "Bobby is quite well and can write his name by himself," and the document closes with the message, "Sisters have some silk-worms. I am very glad you are coming home soon." "I have held Bobby's hand while he writes. He is now going to write his own name by himself" (in the hand of Lady Mildred) and finally, in large capitals the first recorded signature of the future Prime Minister, aged four, ROBERT.[1]]

The Duke called upon me. He had been to visit Don Carlos at Brompton who is just arrived and gave me a most amusing description of their interview.

[Don Carlos, claimant to the throne of Spain, was the second son of Charles IV. He arrived in England, June 1st, 1834, left for France July 2nd: he remained in Spain till his defeat in 1839. Gloucester Lodge, which gave its name to Gloucester Road, and was demolished in 1852, had been built in 1805 by Maria, Countess Waldegrave, secretly married to William, Duke of Gloucester, brother of George III. It was a two-storey country house on the site of the Old Florida Tea Gardens, Brompton.]

The King, his wife and sister and two sons, and about forty servants are packed into a small villa, Gloucester Lodge which already begins to look very dirty. The Queen, very dark and like a Brazilian, and the princess extremely dirty and ill dressed. "You never saw,"

[1] Cecil papers: XII, 229, 295, 273–82.

the Duke said, "such a couple of wretched devils — neither able to speak a word of French. As to the King, he is a fool, as I always thought him. He began by asking me my advice as to what he should do. I told him I never gave an opinion without having all the circumstances of the case before me — 'And to show you, Sir, how little I know of the state of your affairs pray give me leave to ask you are you in possession of a port in Spain?' (*Don Carlos*) 'No: I don't think we have: but Zumalacarreguy[1] may conquer one for me.' (*Duke of Wellington*) 'But you forget, sir, that in that case Zumalacarreguy must desert the care of the provinces of the interior.' (*Don Carlos*) 'Ah! that is very true, but don't you advise me to go to Spain by sea?' (*Duke of Wellington*) 'You must be aware that every motion of Your Majesty is watched. My visit to you is by this time known to the Government and what I am saying to you at this moment probably will be known to them.' (The door was wide open at the time.) 'The Government of this country is inimical to you, and they have the power by law to prevent your fitting out a ship and embarking for Spain, and in *your* case they will use that power.' (*Don Carlos*) 'Do you advise me to go by land?'

(*Duke of Wellington*) 'In that case the police here would give notice to the police in France, who would stop you on your journey as soon as they thought it convenient.'

(*Don Carlos*) 'Well, and then?'

(*Duke of Wellington*) 'And then "*vous seriez un Prince arrêté*". I cannot advise you; but if your object is to raise recruits here you will easily do it, if you have plenty of money. If the money fails — there is an end. Some people perhaps will tell you that there is a large party in this country ready to take up your cause. It is all nonsense: there is not a man who would walk across the room for you. But if you have money you may do anything.' "

The Duke, after telling me this conversation, added "There is a treaty into which England has entered, contrary to Don Carlos's interests. The King's faith is pledged. There never was a more fatal treaty for England — but it is done. It was in the same way that I succeeded to the Greek treaty — there never was a worse — but the King's faith was pledged and I was bound to see it carried into exe-

[1] General Tomas Zumala-Carregui (1788–1835) defeated the royalists at Alegria, Oct. 1834.

cution. There is no object in this Quadruple treaty but an alliance with France — to have a treaty of any sort with France — and to get rid of the ancient alliance of England with the Northern powers."

"And why?" I said.

"Because *we* went the other way — no other reason."

The Duke seems to think the Government will go on, and is decidedly of the opinion that it hangs entirely upon Lord Althorp.

[John Spencer, Viscount Althorp (1782–1845); a politician of great consequence, somewhat against his will: described by Melbourne as "the tortoise on whose back the world reposes". The death of his father, Earl Spencer, on November 10th, 1834, meant that the Whig Party lost their leader in the Commons.]

"Mind what I say. If that man goes, they cannot last." He told me that he knew from good authority that Lord Althorp is in such distress of mind that he is tempted to destroy himself, and has been heard to say "It is lucky I had no pistols within my reach this morning". A more important fact is that Peel has had an interview with Stanley, but has not as yet at least, communicated it to the Duke.

[Edward Smith Stanley resigned and drifted towards the Conservatives, 1834; he succeeded his father as 14th Earl of Derby Oct. 1851.]

31st Dined at Lord Kinnoull's to meet the Duke of Cumberland — very dull. The interview between Peel and Stanley turns out to have been upon a mere matter of business.

Monday July 1st The Duke of Cumberland dined here. I never can ask the Duke to meet either Cumberland or Gloucester as he has a horror of it, and their surprise at *never* meeting him here increases every time they come. It is difficult sometimes to find an answer to their very pointed questions on the subject.

2nd The Duke's Ball. A very pretty one and not so crowded as the one he gave two years before. No royalty there but Cumberland. I stayed till between three and four. The Cabinet was all asked but I saw none of them except the Chancellor and the little Origin of Evil.[1]

9th The Ministers are out.

At five o'clock I went down to the House. Lord Grey gave his explanation: he was much affected, in appearance at least, on rising,

[1] Lord Althorp, Chancellor of the Exchequer, and Henry, Lord Brougham and Vaux (1778–1868), Lord Chancellor.

and attempted once or twice to proceed but was obliged to sit down and gave way to tears. Lord Holland hobbled to support him on one side and the Duke of Cleveland offered him his salts on the other, and this pathetic scene lasted some minutes. In the meantime the Duke of Wellington, apparently willing to give him leisure to recover himself, went on presenting petitions. At last Lord Grey rose again and in a speech of some length and eloquence delivered with his usual grace and dignity of manner, gave his reasons for resigning, which chiefly resolved themselves into the impossibility of carrying on the Government without Lord Althorp (whose resignation had preceded his own) and his (Lord G's) increasing age and infirmities. He entered into a justification of his Administration on the three points to which it had been pledged from the beginning, Peace, Retrenchment and Reform, and ended by alluding to the imputations cast upon him for providing for his family, to which, he said, *no Minister had ever made himself less liable*. At this part of his speech, his brother, the Bishop of Hereford, cried. Altogether, his age, his manner and eloquence might have produced a very touching effect if one could for a moment have forgotten that the wilful destroyer of his country stood before one, about to relinquish, like a second Necker, that post which his own unprincipled and time-serving measures had made it too difficult to retain. There was a feeling of Remorse ran thro' his speech, I thought, or at least a feeling of *doubt* whether he had pursued the right course. Of Reform he made no boast: that distinguishing feature of his Administration was scarcely touched upon.

The Duke replied, injudiciously, I thought, but the immediate object of his rising was to defend Peel, who had been attacked by Lord Grey. He did not speak so well as I have heard him and I think Lord Grey should have been left unanswered, or else his speech completely cut up and replied to, neither of which was done. Brougham then in an insolent and overbearing speech informed the House that only two Ministers had resigned — Lord Grey and Lord Althorp — upon which Lord Palmerston[1] who was below the bar was heard to observe "It is a d – – – – d lie!"

[1] Henry Temple, Viscount Palmerston (1784–1865). Foreign Secretary in Grey's Ministry, Nov. 1830–Nov. 1834; Melbourne's, 1835–41; Lord John Russell's, 1846–51. First Lord of the Treasury and Prime Minister Feb. 1835–8, June 1859, Oct. 1865.

We had a large party at dinner. The impression is that Brougham is to be the Premier. Our people are very much out of spirits.

10th Nothing known, except that Lord Melbourne was sent for yesterday and, it is believed, nobody else. They say he is moving heaven and earth to bring Lord Althorp back.

11th The Duke called upon me. He thinks their only chance of patching it up is to prevail upon Lords Grey and Althorp to return. How excessively ludicrous it would be, after the last dying speech and confession.

Lady Jersey's party in the evening. Every creature that had a possibility of coming was there in the hope of hearing some news. A report that Lord Melbourne, who was commissioned by the King to make a Ministry upon Lord Grey's principles had been obliged to give it up, and that the King is expected in town this evening.

12th Intensely hot weather: not that it is at all required to make us *hotter than we are.* No news.

Dined at the R. Grosvenors — the subject of politics forbidden — a great bore in these days. Lord S. dined at the Fish Dinner, met the Duke of Wellington who told him that there had been a communication made last night to himself and Peel, but that he was not aware of it at the time I questioned him. It was a proposition for a coalition between the Whigs and Tories which he at once and unhesitatingly denied. Lord Munster says it is a great mistake to suppose the King had a dislike to the Tories. "The only thing my father cares about on earth is a good dinner" . . .

[George Fitzclarence, Earl of Munster, was the eldest son of William IV and Mrs Jordan. The Duke of Wellington told Lady Salisbury that on the death of George IV he had consented to appoint Lord Munster Lieutenant of the Tower instead of his old and tried friend Sir Henry Hardinge. Munster then told William IV that as a Prince of the Blood he should have a high Court appointment at the coronation. The King had asked the Duke to bring him to reason. The Duke spoke in what he described as strong terms, but that autumn Lord Munster came again wanting an estate.[1]]

Dr. Willis, I understand says there is no danger of the King's going mad — for that he would have gone mad long ago if there had been *anything to go mad with.*

[1] Cecil Papers: IV, 335.

14th A new Ministry is said to be formed with Lord Melbourne at its head. I prefer this to a Conservative Ministry at the present moment, and surely such a piece of patchwork cannot last.

16th Dined with the Barhams and went afterwards to Vauxhall.

17th This was the hottest day, almost, I ever felt. We went in the evening down to the Beulah Spa[1] and got a little fresh air and returned late.

18th A dinner at home and some people in the evening. Talleyrand talked to *me* very conservatively and strongly recommended *action* on the part of the Conservatives. *"Il faut agir et non parler. Il faut mettre les Ministres dans une minorité"*. I wonder whether he thinks we ought to do just the reverse? The Duke promised to come and show me the statement he drew up in answer to the King's message respecting a coalition. I hear Talleyrand declares he will not return from France while Lord Palmerston is in office. He was talking of Peel's attack on Lord Palmerston. *"Il avait bien raison!"* he said with more animation than he usually shows . . .

22nd The Duke brought me the papers he promised. Lord Melbourne wrote him a letter on the 11th stating that he had been summoned by the King in consequence of Lord Grey's resignation, on the 9th, when the King detailed to him his views respecting the state of the country and his wish to form a Coalition Ministry. It appeared a Memorandum of these was made and put into Lord Melbourne's hands, but this Memorandum was not communicated to the Duke. Lord Melbourne proceeded to say that having considered of the King's proposition he had returned a written answer to His Majesty which he now, by His Majesty's commands, communicated to the Duke. This answer was enclosed. It began by recapitulating part of what had passed between the King and Lord Melbourne, stating that the King had expressed his wish in the present critical state of the country, and having seen the dangers to which the Ministry were of late exposed by the conflicting opinions of different parties, to form an Administration on an enlarged basis and nommément the Duke, Sir R. Peel and Mr. Stanley. Lord M. then goes on to say that to one part of his Majesty's declarations he can bear witness,

[1] Beulah Spa, Beulah Hill, Upper Norwood, Croydon. The Spa closed in 1855 but there was a hydro and hotel until 1939. In 1939 the Beulah Spa public house was built which is still there.

that no personal feelings or opinions would stand in the King's way in making this arrangement, for he was well aware that no Sovereign could be more free from all predeliction or prejudice, personal or political. The King, he says, had expressed at the same time his sense of the difficulties attending this plan, and the inconveniences of Lord M. personally undertaking it, and these difficulties Lord M. had found upon consideration so *insurmountable* that he was forced to give up all hope of accomplishing it. He states that he has no personal objection to any one, that he has the utmost respect for the individuals mentioned, and for Mr. Stanley great affection, but that these individuals were opposed upon principle to measures which he, in the present state of public opinion "considered essential (instancing particularly the Irish Tithe and Church Commission bills), and that a coalition formed of persons differing in such important particulars could not redound to the good of the King's service or the welfare of the country, and would be the more difficult as the Whigs must demand everything and could concede nothing."

The Duke replied by a letter to the King expressing his grateful sense of His Majesty's consideration for him, but adding that it did not appear to him from Lord M.'s letter that it was the King's wish that he should offer any observations on Lord M.'s statement. This brought a second letter from Lord M. stating it to be the King's wish that The Duke should send him his observations.

The Duke's paper in reply, addressed to the King, was extremely well written. After shortly recapitulating what had passed, he observed that his opposition had been founded upon his views of the constitution of the country and his wish to preserve the just power of the King, the privileges of both Houses of Parliament, the rights of Corporations and of individuals, both here and in the Colonies, in the Church of England as by law established. That he had always advocated the foreign policy which went to preserve those alliances that had enabled the late King to bring the revolutionary war to so triumphant a conclusion, that he had long served His Majesty and his predecessors, and was still willing to serve them wherever he could be useful, but that he agreed with Lord M. that a union between persons entertaining such different views on the most essential points could never produce a Government that would command the respect of the Country, adding that the last three months had afforded sufficient instances of the detriment a Govt. sustained from the difference of opinions among the ministers.

The King's answer was civil but short. He lamented that he could not avail himself of the services of the Duke which he had much wished; but confessed that the reasons offered to him had convinced him that his plan was impracticable. Peel's answer to the King, the Duke told me, went more into detail, especially in the Irish Tithe and Commission of Enquiry bills, and the King's reply to him was nearly on the same words as that to the Duke. The Duke told me that he thought it better the Conservatives should not take the Govt. at present, and that he indeed doubted the possibility at any time of procuring a Conservative House of Commons under the Reform Bill. But more than that, he doubted whether it would be practicable to carry on a Tory Govt. in the House of Lords, at least as long as the Duke of Cumberland lived. "He has a flying squadron of twelve or fifteen who would be ready at any time to thwart or annoy me, besides those who would desert me as soon as they found they were to have no places — such as the Duke of Buckingham and Lord Londonderry. The Duke of Cumberland was playing that game last night upon the Poor Bill, and would thwart us whenever we came in, by a secret cabal, exactly as he used to do in George IV's time."

After the Duke was gone I went on to a party to Greenwich with the Granville Somersets, not without some fear of catching the cholera on the river. It is very much about, and Lady Headfort died of it yesterday, entirely, it is said, in consequence of going on the river.

23rd Left London for the season.

Saturday, August 2nd Lord S. came down with Lords Ellenborough and Rosslyn, the Clanwilliams and the G. Somersets. They had a splendid division last night in the Lords on the Admission of Dissenters bill — majority 102 — greater than any division of the Opposition in this century. At least this, I trust, will put swamping the House of Peers out of question. The Duke came down to dinner in high spirits. He told us Mrs. Arbuthnot had been ill at Woodford with an attack of the nature of cholera — but was better. I was just gone to bed when an express arrived to the Duke with the intelligence of Mrs. Arbuthnot's death! He threw himself in the greatest agitation on the sofa, as Lord S. told me, and the letter on the floor: and then rose and walked a few minutes almost sobbing about the room, after which he retired. In the morning Lord S. got a note from him saying he must go to Mr. Arbuthnot — he left for Woodford about half past eight on Sunday morning.

It is a dreadful loss to him — for whether there is any foundation or not for the stories usually believed about the early part of their *liaison*, she was certainly *now* become to him no more than a tried and valued friend to whom he was sincerely attached — her house was his home, and with all his glory and greatness, he *never had a home!* His nature is domestic and as he advances in years, some female society and some fireside to which he can always resort become necessary to him. On this account I grieve most deeply for her death. I cannot bear to think what a loss it is to *him*. As I knew her more, latterly, my regard for her personally also increased: she was, I really believe sincerely attached to him — a woman of strong understanding, considerable information and perfect discretion, the quality of all others which has most attraction for the Duke. She was particularly strong and never ailed anything, so that her death has something peculiarly awful in it . . .

11th, Monday Went to town to take leave of Lady R. Grosvenor before she sets off for Scotland. London is dreadfully hot and very empty.

12th The Duke called upon me. He looks remarkably well, and upon the whole in good spirits. He talked a great deal of poor Mrs. A.'s death, and gave me all the particulars. It appears the attack was inflammatory. He dwelt particularly and apparently with admiration upon the spirit and vigour of mind she displayed up to the day before her death — reading her letters and newspapers and joking with Sir Henry Halford about her own appearance. The Duke seems more impressed *now* with the affliction of Mr. Arbuthnot, which is extreme, than with her loss, so much is he in the habit of directing his mind to whatever are the exigencies of the present moment, rather than of regretting the past. He thinks the H. of Lords is rising in the estimation of the country and told me he had many applications for his support to bills in the H. of Lords as if he were still a minister, and they depended on him.

Parliament is to be prorogued on Friday next week. I suppose not a creature will be left here: everybody is going off, in steam packets or mail coaches as fast as they can in all directions.

13th Returned to Hatfield.

14th, Thursday A Bazaar for the Infirmary at Hertford.[1] I was obliged to go and sell. Lady Verulam and Lady Cowper had also stalls. The crowd was immense and the bore and fatigue excessive. I think a good deal of money was received.

15th We were left alone. They got near £600 at the Bazaar.

18th The cholera is said to be very prevalent in London.

22nd Lady K. Barham and William Wellesley here for one night. He told me of a letter the Duke wrote to one of the young Arbuthnots on the subject of their father, pointing out religious consolation as his sole resource, and observing that Mr. A. could not hope for happiness from anything in this world. By all acounts Mr. A. is in a most distressing state. The Duke was with him at Woodford last Saturday again.

All this week we were quite alone, except this day. I was out a great deal, sketching views of the place for a set of china etc. etc.[2] It is quite refreshing to enjoy a little solitude and quiet after the hurry of London and the irritation of politics.

29th Mr Ryder and the Grimstons came here to attend a ploughing match and dined afterwards with the farmers at the Salisbury Arms.

30th and following days Some shooters here — Lord Wicklow and the Ashleys. Lord Ashley is as Conservative as ever. He is just come from Panshanger. It is his opinion that Lord Melbourne will go to *any* lengths.

Cranborne left us the 30th for Hamburg, on his way to Berlin: he is to see Graaf there and the Duke of Cumberland has promised to take care of him. But I own I have less and less hope of the ultimate recovery of his sight. The others are all I could wish. Lady Sal. is here: we get on very well: business never mentioned.

Sept. 3rd Heard of Olivia Wellesley having got a boy.

8th I left Hatfield on the way abroad. Lord S. detained there some days longer with his Yeomanry. I dined in Arlington St. which I could not well avoid and slept in town.

[1] Hertford County Hospital, North Road, Hertford stands upon an eminence. The three-bay pediment encloses an allegorical group of figures. It had been opened in 1833.

[2] Cecil Papers: Wellington Letters, 104, 116. In March of the preceding year the Duke had seen a consignment of porcelain plates, ordered by her from Paris, through the customs.

Sept. 9th, Tuesday Went from London to Walmer. Found the Duke with Lord Camden staying in the house. Two naval officers dined there. At dinner the conversation turned upon the heat of different climates. The Duke said he recollected a day in India in one of his campaigns when the thermometer was 135 in the tent. They were marching at one o'clock in the day, and in crossing the sandy bed of a dried-up river six men suddenly fell down dead from the heat.

Sept. 10th, Wednesday The Duke was speaking at breakfast of the line taken by the H. of Lords on passing the Reform Bill. He said, "I have often thought of it, and sometimes had doubts about it, but I am of opinion it was the right one. At least it insures a *gradual* revolution and it is my opinion that a gradual is better than a sudden change.

"There will always be great difficulties while you have a Church with property — the Dissenters are very powerful. It was almost impossible to govern the country before the Reform Bill and now it is far worse" . . . The Duke advised the Queen strongly not to go abroad when he saw her at Sandford College, and told her that she never went away but some mischief happened. The King originally proposed the expedition by way of a favour to her: she disliked it in fact, and there were difficulties about meeting her mother. One day when he was going to town she asked him what she should do about her mother. "It is all settled ma'am," he said, "I have settled it all. Your brother is coming to fetch you, and on such a day you start — and such another day you will be back." However, when the time approached he appeared to be very unhappy, and cried whenever it was mentioned, but never would be induced to make any alteration. Once there was a discussion in the Cabinet respecting the time to dissolve Parliament, especially as it might affect the Catholic Question. The Duke said, "What we ought to do is to try and get such a Parliament as may serve the King and preserve him from being attacked on the Catholic Question." This was heard coldly and Lord Liverpool then produced letters from Lord Lonsdale and the Duke of Rutland stating that it would be very convenient to them if the dissolution were deferred, on account of the expense. "I don't care," said Canning, "for their expense. I am glad of it: all I am anxious for is to obtain a favourable Parliament for the Catholics."

135

I walked almost all day with the Duke on the beach, and afterwards on the ramparts. He was speaking of his voyage to Spain, when he occupied himself in learning the Spanish language, and told me that when he got to Castile he found himself perfectly able to understand the addresses of congratulation made to him *"for some little successes* I had *about Oporto* and so on" . . .

Tuesday, 11th The Duke showed me a Bible and a small Gospel of St. John in a morocco case, like an almanac, which had been sent him by a lady with whose name he was not previously acquainted. In the title page the words "St. John, Chap. 3, verse 5" was written, and many of the texts underlined with pencil marks.

[This is the first appearance of "Miss J." in Lady Salisbury's diaries. Miss A. M. Jenkins of 42 Charlotte St., Portland Place, to whom the Duke eventually addressed 390 letters over the next 17 years, was a perfectly obscure young woman, aged 20, who, having succeeded in converting a condemned criminal, conceived it was her duty to save the Duke's soul. The correspondence was published in 1889 in New York and its authenticity was widely doubted in England, but when Sir Herbert Maxwell saw the original MSS., soon after the publication of the first edition of his *Life of Wellington* in 1899, he pronounced that there was "not a shadow of doubt that they are genuine". Miss J. (whose christian name never emerges) had called at Apsley House in April 1834 to deliver the Bible, having been encouraged by receiving a reply by return of post to a letter which she had addressed to the Duke in January. The Duke did not write again until August 27th, more than a fortnight after he had shown the Bible to Lady Salisbury. He called upon her at her suggestion on November 8th. He addressed her as "Mrs." Jenkins, and when he was undeceived mistakenly concluded that he had been given a *rendez-vous*. He allowed her to shower upon him long screeds of advice, criticism and complaint until the day of his death. Miss J. survived until 1862, having become so eccentric that she could not live under the same roof as her married sister in New York.]

He told me that Peel was now in very good humour with him, but had been several times this year quite the reverse, especially of late, in consequence of the Duke's determination not to permit a second reading of the Irish Tithe Bill in the House of Lords. Peel got Lord

Aberdeen to speak to him on the subject, but finding it was of no use, went out of town without seeing him. However, the Duke wrote to him, and Peel seemed pacified, and asked him to go down to Staffordshire.

The Duke thinks that a *row* in Ireland is our best chance — a dreadful remedy but a sure one. "Still, the Protestants are in a false position when placed in opposition to the English Government, and it is difficult to say what they can do." He thinks the property of this country is coming to its senses, but while the Reform Bill is in force they have no influence. "Formerly," he said, "there were certain places entirely given up to the democratic interest, and it was very proper in a constitution like ours that there should be such. Other places in the hands of the property of the country. But the Reform Bill has brought home democracy to every man's door, it pervades every place, and overwhelms all other interests." He expressed a doubt whether, even if the Reform Bill were repealed, the country could again enjoy its ancient constitution without further changes. "The House of Commons has of late swallowed up all the power of the State. The rotten boroughs moderated this power by the infusion of aristocratic influence. To restore them would be impossible. It would remain to be considered in what manner to re-establish the ancient balance, whether by giving the House of Lords more power, by controlling the money bills and so on, or by giving the King a real and effectual vote." He said, "If there were a revolution in this country it must end by a military dictator: revolutions always have. That dictator would not be me, I am too old; but there would be one."

We went to-day to the Dover Races — Mrs. Ellison and I in the carriage with the Duke — a pair of horses and everything as simple as possible. We took some pieces of dry bread as our luncheon. The Duke asked me if I would have any; I said "a bit of bread", and the request was literally fulfilled. The races indifferent, but the day was very fine and there is a pretty view of the Downs from the course. The Duke extremely civil to everybody and they seemed pleased with his kindness.

Friday 12th Lord Salisbury arrived about half past eight this morning having travelled all night. The Duke was very good natured, writing down all the posts for our road in France and sending over to Dover repeatedly about the packets.

We drove over to see the ruins of Richborough Castle — a curious Roman antiquity. I went on the box with the Duke, the Cowleys and Lord S. inside. The Duke told me that Talleyrand had desired it might be made known to him that he, T., had no intention of returning to this country till the present Ministers were out of office, but that should the Duke come in, and wish for him as Ambassador for France, he should be ready to resume his post. He told the Duke that the Ministers here were pushing forward the revolution so fast that England set a bad example to France, instead of France to England, and that he was decided to retire as he had no wish to be accessory to plunging Europe into another general war, towards which Lord Palmerston's measures tended . . .

After dinner the Duke gave us an amusing account of Thistle-wood's conspiracy. A man of the name of Edwards was the principal informant of the Cabinet and communicated intelligence to them months before the event. At first he was not believed by the greatest part of the Cabinet. The Duke, Lord Melville, Lord Westmorland and Lord Sidmouth were the only members of it who gave him any credit. Edwards continued, however, to transmit such correct information of all that really passed, as reported at the meetings of the conspirators, that it was almost impossible to disbelieve him. At one time he stated that one of the conspirators had followed the Duke from the H. of Lords, had seen him conversing with a gentleman with one arm (Ld. Fitzroy Somerset), that they had stood some time looking at a china shop, and that when Lord F. left him, another gentleman had joined him, upon which this man gave up following him. All this was literally true.

On another occasion, the whole Cabinet dined at Ld. Westmorland's, the Duke and Lord Melville went together, and as they got out of the carriage, the Duke observed to Lord Melville that two ill-looking fellows were watching them. Edwards, in his next communication, stated that there had been an intention to attack the Cabinet that day at Ld. W.'s, and that two of the conspirators were set to watch, that they afterwards repaired to a public house in the neighbourhood where they found the coachmen and servants of the different carriages drinking with a constable, an accidental circumstance, but which alarmed them so much that they gave up their design. Had they persisted in it, the Ministers must have been destroyed, as no preparation was made against it. Still, Edwards's reports were not generally believed and the Cabinet separated upon the dissolution of Parliament. By the time it met again, however, there had been so many confirmations from different quarters of the existence of a plot that it was impossible to doubt it. A day or two before the dinner at Lord Harrowby's, he was stopped by a cow-keeper in the Park, who asked him if he was Lord Londonderry, and being answered in the negative, requested him to transmit a letter. This letter contained the account of the intended attack. Edwards himself was appointed to watch the street door at Lord Harrowby's and when the attack was made in Cato St., and Thistlewood escaped, the first thing he did was to go in search of Edwards and take him to a hiding place in the city, where he was discovered by his means. Had it not been for this last transaction, Thistlewood would have remained in ignorance of Edwards's treachery. The Duke recom-mended to his colleagues that they should lock themselves up in Ld. H.'s dining-room, securing the door so as to render it impossible to break through before the troops should come up by which means the conspirators would be taken in the act. But the rest of the Cabinet having no military vocation, declined. Edwards was afterwards pro-vided for, but the Whigs did all they could to ruin him; as they did before, to those who discovered the Irish rebellion.

[Arthur Thistlewood (1770–1820) was the illegitimate son of a Lincolnshire farmer and had held a commission in the militia. He had been a troublemaker since 1816 when he had organized a mutiny. He had been sent to prison for sending a challenge to Lord Sidmouth, Home Secretary in 1818, and in the next year joined a secret revolutionary society. He was surprised at a *rendez-vous* in Cato St. with about twenty-five confederates as they armed themselves for their expedition to Lord Harrowby's house in Grosvenor Square, but escaped having killed a police-officer. Next day, on Edward's information he was arrested in Moorfields. He was executed with four fellow-conspirators, May 1st, 1820.]

Speaking of the Dissenters, the Duke said, "It is the same party that destroyed the Monarchy in Cromwell's time, and that have been at the bottom of every democratic project since, and the worst feature of the Reform Bill is that it has given power precisely to that class where the Dissenters are prevalent. This cry, or that cry, are equally unmeaning — the real and great object of that party is the destruction of the Church."

The Duke wrote to Lord Roden after that great meeting in Ireland, that he hoped it would not go off in smoke but that the Protestants would form an Association strictly upon defensive principles, having for its object to secure to the Clergy their dues, and to maintain the just execution of the laws. Lord Roden is coming down to Walmer to consult with the Duke on the means of doing it.

At the time of La Valette's escape, when Sir R. Wilson was detained prisoner in Paris, the Duke desired the postmaster to examine the seals of all the letters directed to him. There was one with Lord Grey's coat of arms. Had the Duke taken possession of it, or even suffered it to reach its destination, considerable inconvenience might have arisen to Lord Grey: the Duke did neither but returned it to him in a blank cover. I observed that I thought this very generous conduct. "It was straightforward, it was the right thing to do, depend upon it," the Duke answered. "I had no business from party feeling to bring one of the King's subjects into a scrape with a foreign power if I could prevent it."

[Comte Antoine Lavalette was condemned to death in November 1815. In a letter to Prince Eugène, captured and read aloud to the Congress in Vienna, he had expressed uninhibited joy at the arrival of Napoleon from Elba. His wife rescued him from the Conciergerie prison, and Sir Robert Wilson and two dare-devil companions provided him with the uniform and papers of an English officer travelling on a mission from the Duke of Wellington. Wilson and his fellow conspirators were arrested and sentenced to three months' imprisonment, and a General Order from the Duke of York, Commander-in-Chief, expressed the Prince Regent's high displeasure. The *Gentleman's Magazine* had printed an intercepted letter from Wilson to Lord Grey containing a narrative of their adventure.]

IV

[On Saturday, September 13th, 1834, the Salisburys embarked in the *Ferret* packet from Dover for Calais. This, their third foreign holiday, although it took them only to France and Switzerland surpassed in discomfort and enjoyment their two previous experiences. From Langres on the 19th, Fanny sent her children a lively description of Rheims cathedral ("The windows *en rosette* of painted glass are more beautiful than anything I ever saw"), and Joinville ("where there are no beds to be had on account of a fair. At last we got one room with two beds, which Lizzy (her maid) and I occupied, and Papa and Perugini (his Italian servant) slept on tables in one of the two salons of the inn.") From Lausanne they made an expedition to visit relations of the children's Swiss *bonne*, Blondel ("the lake is delicious, its coloring too beautiful"). They left Lizzy behind at Vevey and rode off courageously "Lord S., Perugini and I on mules, with a fourth to carry the baggage". When the road became practicable for wheel carriages they dismissed the mules and took a char-à-banc, "in comparison with which I should think the worst cart without springs in England would be a *lit de repos*". On September 30th at Grindel-wald they opened their eyes upon "all the glory of the higher Alps" and hired horses. "No mules . . . as they are not equally useful to the inhabitants in winter!" Above the foaming torrent of the Aar Lord S.'s horse fell on a *dalle de granit* and squeezed poor Papa's foot severely against a rock. At the Grimsel hospice they met a dog of the St. Bernard breed who had rescued three persons from being buried in last winter's snows.

The valley of the Rhône would have excited their admiration had they not just come from the most sublime scenes in nature which made all others appear insipid. At Brieg they bade adieu to their horses and got an improved char-à-banc to Vevey where they picked up Lizzy. Geneva was charming, but swarming with English, including the Mahons on their honeymoon. Lyons was a disappointment. "The whole population seems to be composed of the lowest order, at least I hardly saw anything that could even be called a respectable *bourgeois*, much less a gentleman, and here, as in all the other towns of France that I have seen, nothing in the shape of a gentleman's carriage of any description. Louis Philippe's government appears very unpopular here; they have not forgotten the affair of last spring, and openly declare they will have their *revanche*." Grenoble was much better, "something resembling the north of Italy and scarcely inferior to it". Fanny made a beautiful pencil sketch for her album, to follow those of the Lake of Thun and Lyons and precede

La Grande Chartreuse where they had to take to horseback again. Their carriages rejoined them at Voreppe and from Valence Lord S. went to the vineyard of St. Péray and bought a good deal of wine. At Avignon they were persecuted by the Mistral, "far colder than the worst March wind in England", but Marseilles was in a thick fog. Fanny approved of Marseilles. The streets were wide and there was an exhilarating bustle and activity. The people, both men and women, were quite remarkable for their beauty: the former had a look of ferocity. Hières was charming – date trees, bamboos and sugar cane in the open ground, hedges of pomegranate and myrtle. They had to return to Marseilles for St. Rémy, where Fanny obtained a fine sketch of the Arch of Marius and Lord S. went out with the master of the inn to see some specimens of French agriculture. This man said that before the Revolution there had been a hundred châteaux in the neighbourhood. Nîmes had far the most beautiful public garden Fanny had yet seen in France. The first of November brought them perfect weather for their sightseeing at Montpellier, Narbonne, Carcassonne, Toulouse and Bordeaux – "a very fine town more gentlemanlike than any I had seen in France". Lord S. went to the theatre, but neither the pieces offered, nor his account of the audience tempted Fanny to visit any French provincial theatre.

They went to the French protestant church on Sunday, and from this point set off at six a.m. on Thursday, November 13th for their long journey home. With good horses and fine roads they travelled with remarkable rapidity. "We passed through some Landes, a little like the neighbourhood of Bagshot." They had not encountered a single rainy day since they landed, and in consequence the highways were in an excellent state. But the cold was now intense.]

Nov. 17th We resolved to push for Calais and travel all night. We got there between ten and eleven; the English packet had sailed five minutes, and excessively disappointed and tired, we resolved to wait for that of the next day, and ordered beds and breakfasts, when Lord S. accidentally opening a letter from Mr. Lushington supposed to contain only an anodyne plaister as a preventive of sea-sickness, read the words "The Whig Government is out!"

We immediately determined on crossing in a French packet which was just going to start, and which I had before rejected. Quillacq confirmed the news, and informed us that several couriers had gone

142

thro' Calais the preceding day, with the news of the Duke of Wellington's accession to office.

V

[The Duke had, in fact, recommended to His Majesty to send for Sir Robert Peel,[1] but there was a difficulty about this. Although Melbourne's ministry had long been considered sick almost to death and indeed he had told the King so, an actual death, that of Lord Spencer, had to take place before it finally and suddenly collapsed. Sir Robert Peel was on holiday in Italy. Until he could be found the Duke was discharging the routine business at the Treasury, Home, Foreign and Colonial offices. Naturally, hopes of employment were running high in the divided Conservative party, and the indignant Whigs were vocally critical. The circumstances of Sir Robert Peel's summons home to his country were romantic. The King's letter was eventually delivered to him at a ball given in Rome in the *palazzo* of the Duchess Torlonia, on November 25th. The Salisburys arrived at Dover on the 18th.]

We had an excellent passage; on landing found Col. Ellison on the quay ready to receive us, who gave us some account of all that had been passing, which it appears was a complete surprise to everybody. The excitement and fatigue I had gone through had quite knocked me up and I went to bed about seven.

November 19th, Wednesday Got up, still very tired. Mrs. Ellison lent me her maid, the *fourgon* not having yet landed. Sir R. Wilson came in — gives a very good account of things; the country very quiet. The French I thought seemed much annoyed at the change — Quillacq was in fear of a war. We left Dover at once, not choosing to wait for the Boulogne packet by which we expect the *fourgon* to arrive, and which was to come in at three. Dined at Sittingbourne and got to town about between ten and eleven.

November 20th, Thursday I never was more tired in my life, in addition to a horrid cold which I caught coming up in the open carriage. A great many people came to see me.

Lord Cowley called and gave us an account of what had happened

[1] Peel's father had died and he had succeeded to the family baronetcy in 1830.

between Lord Melbourne and the King, which he had from the Duke. Lord Melbourne went down to Brighton on Thursday, 14th and having announced Lord Althorp's removal, proposed three persons as leader of the House of Commons — Spring Rice,[1] Abercrombie[2] and Lord John Russell. To the latter the King decidedly objected on account of his declared opinions on the Church. . . . Lord M. acknowledged to the King that there was a serious division in the Cabinet on the subject of the Irish Church, that certain of its members were prepared to bring forward very strong measures on that subject, and that should H.M. be inconveniently pressed upon it, Lords Lansdowne[3] and Spring Rice were prepared to resign.

But on the other hand, if the Radical part of the Cabinet were defeated, they would join Hume and O'Connell.[4] The King then said that if these difficulties were to come upon him in the middle of a session his situation would be one of extreme embarrassment: that both Lord Grey and Lord Melbourne when he entered office told him that the Whig Government could not go on without Lord Althorp, and that under these circumstances he thought it better at once to consider it dissolved. Lord Melbourne took up the letter to the Duke in his pocket, and the story is that he did not communicate what had passed to any of his colleagues but Brougham and Palmerston, who each sent a paragraph to their respective newspapers, by means of which Lord Holland and Lord Lansdowne received the first intimation of their dismissal the next morning at breakfast.

Lady Brownlow[5] came to me and told me that she had never seen the King look so happy: that it had been an object of remark with all the people of the Court, the good spirits he had seemed to enjoy the evening after the interview with Lord Melbourne. The general feeling seems sanguine, but nothing can be done till Sir R. Peel comes. He has been heard of at Venice on the 7th on his way to

[1] Thomas Spring Rice (1790–1866), Irish statesman, Colonial Secretary 1834, Chancellor of the Exchequer 1835, Baron Monteagle 1839.

[2] James Abercromby (1776–1858), Speaker of the House of Commons 1835, Baron Dunfermline 1839.

[3] Henry Petty, 3rd Marquess of Lansdowne (1730–1863), Secretary for Home Department 1827, Lord President of Council 1834.

[4] Daniel O'Connell (1775–1847), Irish politician, devoted to Catholic Emancipation; his notice for repeal of the Union rejected in Commons April 27th, 1834.

[5] Lady Brownlow was Lady of the Bedchamber to Queen Adelaide.

Florence. Lord Ellenborough seems to think there must be a dissolution. I wish it could be avoided: the House of Commons under the Reform Bill is not elected by the property and intelligence of the country, and does not represent their real sentiments which I am confident are with us. Besides I am sure there will be a great many rats.[1]

We dined at the Duke's: he looks perfectly well and as composed and cool and *"l'esprit aussi libre"* as if he had nothing on earth to do, instead of the affairs of these kingdoms on his hands. The Duke told us he had sent a letter of "four lines" to Lord Brougham, stating that he had "H.M.'s commands to request him to deliver up the Seal on Friday next at 2 o'clock", and got an answer of four sides of paper in return, at the end of which he did not know whether he meant to deliver up the Seal or no — very characteristic on both sides. Our dinner was a most agreeable one — everybody in good spirits, very little politics talked. It really was a moment worth living for to see that great man once more where he ought to be, appreciated as he deserved by his King, and at the head of this great country — if it does but last. But one must not embitter such moments by thoughts like these! . . .

November 21st, Friday We got to Hatfield to dinner. Found the children all well.

November 22nd Saturday Lord Verulam and Edward Grimston came here. I spoke to him strongly on the subject of permitting Edward to stand for St. Albans, and I hope with effect.

If there is to be a dissolution we must all make the greatest efforts. Heaven knows that it is to *us* a very serious thing after all the exertions we have made before; but it is a matter of duty and therefore it must be.

25th, Tuesday I went to town alone for a couple of nights.

26th, Wednesday The Duke came to see me between eleven and twelve. I cannot repeat word for word his kind expressions, but they will never be erased from my remembrance. He called me his friend, twice over, with emphasis, as if he would have said "my first and best friend", and expressed a confidence in me which I feel with a gratitude and pleasure I cannot express. "With you," he said, "I think aloud."

[1] In the event Peel gained 200 seats, but was still in a minority in the Commons.

. . . He told me that on the day before the King left town last, he (the K.) sent the Duke of Wellington a letter from himself to Stanley, in Sir H. Taylor's[1] hand, preparing as it were, Stanley to receive a proposition to join Sir R. Peel's Government, on the ground, chiefly, of their mutual support of the Church of England. This letter the Duke, of course, stopped. Sir H. Taylor told the Duke the next morning that he had had nothing to do with it, and that he was anxious to get the King out of town, as he wanted to *go too fast.*

Peel has been heard of the 14th at Rome: he cannot be here before the 4th at soonest. It is an awful time altogether. It is playing our last stake. I dined to-day with the Duke, Lord Cowley, Lord Strangford, Mr. Irving, Mr. Shaw (the Protestant lawyer) and Edward Drummond were of the party. It was said the Duke of Rutland, in the event of the Duke of Gloucester's death, who is very ill, would offer himself for the Chancellorship of Cambridge. Lord Cowley observed that he had no idea that the Duke of Rutland was a learned man. "It is not the least necessary," said the Duke laughing, "to be a learned man in order to be Chancellor of a University. We can do just as well without. We all know that, don't we?" We looked at some of the H.B. caricatures.[2] He seemed particularly diverted with that which represents him carrying off the bone of power in his mouth while the two other dogs, Durham and Brougham, are fighting for it.

He gets up every morning at six, and shaves by candlelight, and does not get to bed till near twelve, I told him I thought he gave himself too little rest. "I am perfectly well," he said, "and whether a man has a little more sleep or a little less, what does it signify?"

27th, Thursday Returned to Hatfield. All going on well in Herts.

Monday, 1st December Lord S. went up to town to see J. Talbot about Ingestre's standing and Lord Mahon. All right: they will both stand, I hope without opposition. Canvassing is going on with the utmost ardour on both sides all over the country. News came of the death of the poor Duke of Gloucester. He is, after all, much to be re-

[1] Lieut. Gen. Sir Herbert Taylor (1775–1839) aide-de-camp and private secretary to the Duke of York, George III, Queen Charlotte and William IV; Military secretary to Wellington when Commander-in-Chief, 1827; deputy-secretary to Palmerston when Secretary at War.

[2] Henry Bunbury (1750–1811) caricaturist.

gretted. He did a great deal of good in his neighbourhood and his folly was in his words not his actions.

3rd Went over to Gorhambury to settle with Lord Verulam about the second candidate for St. Albans, as Lord S. does not like to be seen riding over there so often.

7th, Sunday Lord Ellenborough, Lord S. and I amused ourselves in the evening settling the new Cabinet. I fancy he wants India. It was rather amusing, each endeavouring to discover the other's expectations and degree of information. Lord E. I have no doubt will be a useful member of the Government; he is talented and active, but I think his views are too *liberal*; in fact expediency is everything with him rather than principle. He talks of concessions to the Dissenters, which is hopeless and absurd. He does not give a very brilliant account of the state of the elections, though at the same time he talks of our acquiring an addition of 200 in the House of Commons. He proposes that the Lord Mayor should give Peel a dinner in order to afford him an opportunity of declaring the principles on which his Government is to be conducted, before the elections. I think it is a good plan.

9th Peel arrived this morning in town. Now that the interregnum is over business will begin. Stanley is sent for.

10th, Wednesday No news. A letter from Lord Ellenborough to say Parliament will be dissolved between the 20th and 24th.

12th Stanley has declined to accept office but returned a friendly answer. The Duke of Buckingham is seen hovering about in London and Lord Londonderry has professed himself willing to accept any of three places which he has named.

14th A messenger arrived from Peel offering Lord S. the place of Master of the Horse. A very kind note came at the same time to me from the Duke to *congratulate* me upon it.

15th, Monday I am getting very anxious to hear from the Duke again. I am so afraid he will take it ill.

All this day I was very *fidgetty*. The post at last brought the dreaded letter – very kind, and not at all offended, at least I think not, in tone.[1] It is evident that the Duke would have offered Lord S. a place of business if he *could*, and he expresses a regret that he did not speak

[1] All the correspondence about Lord S. refusing the offer is in the Wellington Letters under date.

to me on the subject when he saw me in town. I wish he had, tho' probably the result would have been the same.

16th Lord S. went up to town, saw Peel and the Duke. The former received him coldly at first, but on Lord S. renewing his assurances of zealous support, his manner became more cordial, and in the course of conversation the Duke asked him if he would have preferred a place of business, to which of course Lord S. replied in the affirmative. I hear Peel behaved with extreme bad taste at a dinner given by the Duke, when he made a speech in returning thanks for his health in which no allusion whatever was made to the Duke or to what he had done for him. Our party look depressed in consequence. But they need not fear. The Duke is too high-minded to take notice of such petty jealousy: one only regrets to see such a man as Peel capable of it.

18th I am glad Peel took an opportunity of complimenting the Duke in his speech at the Lord Mayor's dinner.

Christmas Day The Duke was to have come down, but was detained by business in town. Lady Cowper attempted to begin a correspondence last night with Lord S. on the subject of the Hertford election . . . I answered her letter.

30th Parliament at last dissolved. Cowper is bribing at Hertford. No other means gives him a chance of success, as the feelings of the people are thoroughly with us.

31st, Wednesday Sat up to see the New Year in. It is an awful moment. No year in my recollection was ever ushered in with such tremendous chances depending upon its course. I dare hardly repeat the question, "What will it produce?" Yet the last has produced more good and less evil than we could have hoped or looked for. We can only look to His mercy and protection amid the dark events that await us, Who has already in more than one instance caused circumstances to work together so wonderfully for our good.

PART V
1835

[The year 1835, looked forward to with so much anxiety, proved one of almost unrelieved disappointment, and towards its close Hatfield almost became the scene of a major tragedy.

The Election opened so badly that for the first twelve days of January Fanny made no entries in her diary. "The defeat at Hertford has taken away my spirits completely." Lord Ingestre had failed at Hertford. At St. Albans Grimston, Abel Smith and Rowland Alston of Pishiobury were duly elected, and a little satisfaction was wrung from the defeat of Palmerston in Hampshire. Several foreign diplomats who had abhorred his sway arrived to enliven the English scene. Pozzo di Borgo and Sébastiani, two newcomers began to make frequent appearances in the journal. Count Carlo Pozzo di Borgo (1764–1842), who had succeeded Prince Lieven, was a Corsican by birth and had been "General Paoli's right hand man" until he quarrelled with his compatriot. He had been educated at Pisa and was a good linguist, speaking English in a penetrating voice. In Corsica he had been mistrusted by Sir John Moore and on the ejection of Lord Minto from the Viceroyalty had become something of an Old Man of the Sea to that capable Whig diplomat whom he had accompanied to the British Embassy in Vienna. His future was solved by his entering the Russian service. Comte François Sébastiani, French Marshal and diplomat born in Corsica 1772, was Ambassador to Great Britain 1835–41. Madame Sébastiani's appearance startled Fanny. "The most made-up looking person I ever saw — like a wooden doll." The Duke, somewhat against his inclination, had accepted the post of Foreign Minister. This meant that he was unusually busy and more than once, when expected at Hatfield, he was "again prevented by business". He wrote wearily, "We have now given the Reform Bill a fair first trial, but I own I am not very confident of success."

He admitted to having been unwell with a violent cold and was said to look ill. His eye was not bright, but Fanny was indignant when Lady Frances Egerton and her brother went about saying he was out of spirits, "nothing does so much harm". At first she began to hope that Peel would grow in stature. He was reported to be "in excellent spirits and extremely sanguine".

On February 2nd she entered dutifully: "Another anniversary has passed of our wedding day. I may indeed regard it as one of the most fortunate of my life. This, and the other succeeding days we spent alone at Hatfield. I am never sorry for these little intervals of quiet. Lord S. was occupied in settling his accounts etc. . . ." These were not cheerful reading. He eventually found he had lost £3,000 on the election. "I lived chiefly alone. From the weather I could not derive much enjoyment; it was cold and miserable."

On February 14th they "went to town for the year". The result of the Speaker's election was now eagerly and even confidently awaited. "Alas! all our hopes are vanished." A dinner given at Grafton Street to celebrate the return of Manners-Sutton was a sad affair. "Terrible long faces." James Abercromby, later Baron Dunfermline, Liberal M.P. for Edinburgh, defeated Charles Manners-Sutton, afterwards Viscount Canterbury by ten votes. Manners-Sutton had occupied the Chair for seventeen years with impartiality but had recently been considered to have identified himself too closely with the Tory party. The Peels unavoidably failed; he had gone to see His Majesty. Notwithstanding all the efforts of the hostess, gloom and despondency reigned. The Duke feared that the effect abroad would be very bad. A week later they dined with the Peels.]

February 20th I was anxious to see how he took it. I sat next him at dinner and never saw him more agreeable and amusing. He told me the King was perfectly calm and collected, and had behaved admirably at the reception of the news. "And really," Sir R. added, "asked me several very sensible questions about it." He then went on telling *me*, to my infinite entertainment, of the successful flattery he had employed in the various transactions and negotiations about offices. "I used to scribble off these letters at once. I had not time to consider . . . But I never yet found the amount of flattery too large for any man to swallow. To Lord Londonderry I made the offer of the Mastership of the Buckhounds *or* of the Embassy to Russia. I laugh when I think of my impudence in proposing both to the same man, but I told him that few people possessed that extent of acquirement and variety of talent which could have justified me in offering him at once two situations so different. Lord Wilton, when offered the Buckhounds, refused on the ground of wishing to decline *any* office in the Household, but I was not discouraged, and when I proposed the Lord Stewardship I heard no more of the objection. To Lord Chesterfield I wrapped up the offer of the Buckhounds by terming it 'High office in connection with the personal service of the King'. (The very words Peel had used in his letter to Lord S. all of which he appeared to have forgotten.) 'And I added that I was induced to make the offer to him as those high offices ought to be filled by persons whose *weight, character* and influence could adorn them.' (These being precisely the qualities wanting in Lord Chesterfield.) There never was such a blessing as the refusal of Lord Roden to be Steward. I never was so glad of an answer in my life. But the next day he changed his mind and wrote a recantation. However, I took care to inform him that the office was already offered to another, to my infinite regret . . ."

He told me also that when he first heard the news at Rome, he thought it an injudicious measure of the King, but he supposed the King must be secure of the assistance of Stanley and Graham. [The Tories under Peel had returned stronger, but not in sufficient numbers to have a majority over the combined votes of the Whigs, Radicals and Irish.]

Tuesday February 24th Opening of Parliament.

[The Houses of Parliament had been burnt down while the Salisburys were in France. The King had suggested that the new palace begun nine years before by George IV on the site of the old Buckingham House might be used, as he had no wish to live in something so magnificent and still incomplete. But it was decided that the old House of Lords could be sufficiently restored to provide a temporary home for Parliament during rebuilding.]

There was a report that the Radicals were to get up a mob to hiss the King. Lord S. went to the Police, and also employed himself to collect as many people together as he could to applaud. They could not, however, amount to any considerable number. The King was generally very well received; an immense crowd, very quiet and civil . . . The Opposition had thoughts at one time of trying to beat us in the Lords tonight by a surprise, many of the Peers on our side being out of town not dreaming their presence could be required. However, Govt. got notice of it in time and collected a majority of about 2 to 1, so that they did not think it wise to push it to a division. Brougham made an insane speech and was completely set

153

down by the Chancellor. The H. of C. adjourned after a splendid speech from Peel . . .

Thursday, 26th Dined today at the Duke's – a dinner for the Foreign Ministers . . .

The Duke looked well, better than I have seen him since I came to town. He was in tolerable spirits. He told me he still was of opinion the Radicals would get up an attack upon him – that Peel had been with him this morning, and that they had had "quite a tender scene", Peel declaring "He would stand or fall with him". "And he is quite right," said the Duke. I asked him if Peel was firm. He answered in the affirmative but in a doubtful tone . . .

Friday, 27th Another disappointment! A majority of seven against us. [Lord Morpeth's amendment on the Address, regretting the dissolution.] Sir J. Graham spoke on our side, and a far more satisfactory speech than Stanley's, which was trimming, mean and egotistical . . . The Duke dined here: we had the F. Egertons, Clanwilliams and De Ros's to meet him. He did not seem as much dispirited as I feared he would. "With good temper and firmness I think we shall get through," he said. "But I can't agree with some people that a minority is a pleasant thing . . ." When the ladies had gone away he talked of his campaigns in Portugal with his usual inimitable simplicity and bonhomie. "I found Craddock doing nothing when I came, so I went to Oporto immediately and set things in a train, and in a week the French were out of Portugal."

I am very angry with Lady F. Egerton and her brother Henry Greville for spreading about that the Duke is out of spirits. Nothing does so much harm.

[Harriet Greville, daughter of Charles Greville, grandson of the 5th Earl of Warwick, who married in 1822 Lord Francis Egerton, poet-statesman, afterwards 1st Earl of Ellesmere, was an authoress of many original works and translations, some privately printed, and sister of Fulke Greville and Henry Greville, political diarists. The Francis Egertons lived in Bridgewater House, St. James, to which he had succeeded in 1803 as heir of his grand-uncle the last Duke of Bridgewater. Barry re-built it for them in 1847.]

Saturday, February 28th The address of the H. of C. was taken up to the King today, never was there such a rabble as the members who presented it, dressed in colored neckcloths, and boots, and looking as if they had not changed their clothes since the debate began. They rushed in a most tumultuous manner with a sort of howl, as if they really personated the mob triumphant over the King and forcing their way into his palace. The King answer very dignified and firm and well delivered . . .

Monday, March 2nd Went to see the picture Wilkie is doing for us of the Duke of Wellington. It is finely colored but I have seen likenesses of him that have pleased me better. However, I was fully rewarded for my trouble by seeing the "Columbus" just finished. I have no pretensions to be a judge of painting, but I scarcely ever saw a picture that gratified me more. The head of Columbus is the finest conception possible: the calmness, the serenity, the self-confidence expressed in it are of the noblest character. You could not look at it for an instant even if unacquainted with the subject without saying "That is the countenance of a really great man." There is another sketch of a "Serenade" and a larger one of the interview between Napoleon and the Pope at Fontainebleau. I think he has made Napoleon too corpulent (as he was in his latter days). But Wilkie is very likely not aware at what period of his life this interview took place: his ignorance of the commonest historical facts even if connected with his pictures is quite surprising.

I met the Lockharts at his (Wilkie's) house. Mrs. Lockhart mentioned a curious anecdote of the Duke which (she) had from Dr. Hume. After the Battle of Waterloo, the Duke desired Dr. Hume to obtain a list of the killed and wounded and bring it him in the morning. Hume accordingly went next morning about five into the Duke's room and found him asleep. He deposited the paper on the bed and on returning some hours afterwards found the Duke awake, having perused the list. His countenance was not apparently changed except that under his eyes were two whitish streaks. He had retired the night before without washing his face which was covered with the mud of the field, and the two white streaks were the traces left of tears which had descended. Willkie talks of doing a picture of Nelson sealing the letter with wax at the siege of Copenhagen, as a pendant to Colombus . . .

Sunday, March 8th Dined at Ld. Westmorland's. He is grown terribly old and gets drunk after dinner. Pozzo, the Jerseys and Burghersh dined there, and the Duke. Lady G. Fane never ceased pouring her eloquence into the ear of the latter, but it won't do. Lady Jersey quite altered, a positive old woman.

The Duke looking well. I am to take my children to him to see his services of plate, china etc. on Tuesday. He is so fond of children and good-natured to them. He is to go with us some night to see *King Arthur* but regrets he was not able to go on the same night with the children to see their delight in it. "That is what I should have liked."

He takes a strong view about the national system of education in Ireland. i.e. the excluding the Bible from the schools, and told Lord S. it was positively contrary to the Scripture.

Lord Londonderry told me he had asked Ld. Russell the other day what were his views if he succeeded in turning out Ministers. "We must come to American institutions, that will be the end of it," he replied. The Duke of Bedford is said to have declared that the choice was now between despotism and anarchy in his opinion – and that he preferred anarchy. On hearing this, the Duke said, "I can tell Johnny Bedford, if we have anarchy, I'll have Woburn" . . .

Wednesday, 11th Contrary to expectation the Malt Tax was decided at one sitting last night – 158 majority for Ministers. Almost all the Whigs voted with them . . . However, Friday will be the trial, upon voting the supplies . . . Mrs. Baring's at night. Met the Lockharts who asked me to dine there to meet Wordsworth.

Friday, 13th Hume backed out of the intended motion for refusing the supplies, in the most shabby manner. Peel made an example of him . . .

Saturday, 14th A sad mess in the H. of C. last night about Lord Londonderry's appointment.

Sunday, 15th Dined with the Lockharts. Their house is very comfortable and pretty, though small. The chief ornaments are portraits of Sir Walter Scott, pictures of his study etc. The Bishop of Exeter, Wordsworth and his wife and Mr. Morier (the author of *Hajii Baba*) dined there. The Bishop was extremely agreeable and full of anecdote. Mr. Wordsworth spoke little, but both he and his wife look like patterns of patriarchal old age, with their simple dress and manners, no pretension to what they are not, no attempt to disguise their age, or to *make effect*, which is quite refreshing in the middle of London Society. Mr. Lockhart has a beautiful boy very like a portrait of his

Grandfather in his childhood but handsomer, and fit to be the infant hero of such a romance as his grandfather would write.

[The Lockhart's home was in Sussex Place, Regent's Park. This was their younger son, Walter Scott (1826–53), "Wa-Wa" to his grandfather. He joined the army and became estranged from his father, but there was a reconciliation before his premature death. The elder son, Little John, had died aged ten in 1831.]

Monday, 18th Lord Londonderry has resigned in a very handsome manner . . .

[The attack in the Commons was by an Irish, seconded by a Scottish member. Lord Londonderry had been appointed to St. Petersburg. Unfortunately, Lord Dudley had stated in the Lords that Londonderry had already received emoluments of about £160,000, cand Londonderry had made a disparaging comment on the Poles, alling them "rebellious subjects" of the Russian Emperor. His application for a pension of £2,000 as retiring Ambassador to Vienna had been refused by Lord Liverpool in 1823, but he had brought home with him the Embassy service and plate. His resignation saved Peel, but according to Greville left the impression abroad that His Majesty had made an appointment which the House of Commons had cancelled. Londonderry and his wife, undeterred, proceeded to Russia as tourists.]

Lord Ellenborough told me Peel was sadly out of spirits the day after the attack on Lord Londonderry.

Thursday, 19th Dined with the F. Egertons. Met the Duke. Lord Canterbury dined there. He told us some amusing anecdotes of the Duke of Cumberland — among others that the D. of C. mentioning the other day that he had a letter from the Duchess, "I'll tell you what she says, 'G-- d--- you', says she . . ."

Saturday, March 21st The Duke asked me what I heard of things in general. I replied I thought our party were in greater spirits since the Dissenters' Marriage Bill was brought in, and that everybody thought Peel was doing admirably well. "Then they think I did right in putting him there?" he said. I told him I thought many of our party had a great hankering after Stanley (implying of course that they had no disinclination to remove *him* to make way for Stanley). "*I* should wish to bring in Stanley too," he said, "if I thought it would do any good, but I do not think it could. Our people in places wish to keep their places and they have a hankering after Stanley because they fancy he would enable them to do so."

He would not allow in direct terms that our prospects are bettered, he is *determined* to see things *en noir*. But his language as to the prospects of the Ministry is certainly changed . . .

He thinks the present Emperor of Austria will do well till difficulties arise, and then the want of the late Emperor will be felt,[1] which Metternich cannot supply. He does not believe the Archduke Charles to be too Liberal. The present Emperor is very deficient in intellect; when the Duke was presented to him at the Congress of Vienna a person stood behind him to prompt him what he should say.

The Duke went with us to Lady Peel's in the evening – an immense crowd, all the Conservatives in London and about half a dozen Whigs. Lord John Russell's marriage[2] is declared.

Peel rises in reputation every day; he is so immeasurably superior to all his opponents that they shrink into nothing before him, and own themselves that he is the only man who can now govern the country with any prospect of success. I regard him as a *Dieu donné*, as raised up by a special Providence for the salvation of the country from civil dissensions, as the Duke was from foreign conquest . . .

Wednesday, 25th Lady Jersey's child's ball. The Duke came late. I asked him if there was any fear of Peel's resigning Monday (on the Irish Church Bill) as is very much reported. He said Peel was very much disposed to do so – that he had a dreadful scene with him yesterday and that he (the Duke) had written to him the strongest letter possible on the subject to-day. I said, "But surely, does he not see that his own reputation must be sacrificed if he gives way without absolute necessity?" The Duke said, "I don't know. He has very bad judgment upon those points – and some people are so wonderfully sensitive. But I think he'll stay."

"I see no occasion for resigning".

We could talk no more as there were people near us, but he promised to call and tell me how things stood on Sunday. Peel was there, and I remarked how much his manner was changed – all that

---

[1] Francis I, father of Marie-Louise, was succeeded on March 2nd, 1835 by Ferdinand I, an amiable epileptic, subject to fits of insanity, who abdicated 1848.

[2] Lord John Russell married, April 11th, Adelaide, daughter of Thomas Lister and widow of Thomas, 2nd Lord Ribblesdale. She died 1838.

buoyancy which struck me so much when I first came to town, is gone, and there is an air of thoughtfulness and care instead. Lord S. had a long conversation with Sir Henry Hardinge who rather seemed to defend the necessity of Peel's retirement on Monday — said that he was harassed to death, that he was not supported by the young aristocracy and could not endure standing there night after night to be defeated — that he could not be expected to hold office longer than was consistent with the honor of a public man etc. Lord S. came home in a terrible state about it. I never saw him so annoyed; he talked of going to Peel and making him a remonstrance on the subject etc. I went to bed more dispirited than I have been since they came into office. Ellenborough and Lyndhurst at least are very stout.

26th I was unwell all day and remained on my sofa. I am not sorry for there is nothing pleasant to hear in the world. Lady R. Grosvenor dined here.

27th, *Friday* Mlle. Este tells me the King is firm *at present*. She regrets Lord Frederick Fitzclarence is so much about him; but there are others to counteract him. "Who?" I said. "Oh! there *are* others — the Queen." "But I thought he never allowed the Queen to speak to him upon politics?" "Oh! I beg your pardon! She *has* influence" . . . People *croak* so dreadfully, I am beyond measure low. They say we shall go out on Monday — and Peel's going out in my opinion is the end of the monarchy. Rogers called on me this morning and told me Lord Grey, whom he has just seen, was as much annoyed at the idea of Ministers going out as we were, and that his friends would not advise him to undertake forming a Ministry at present as the H. of C. was so much too radical for him that he would have no more chance of governing it than Peel. But Lord Howick is ready to go any lengths. Many of the Whigs are frightened at the prospect of the country, even that sovereign idiot the Duke of Devonshire.

Sunday, March 29th The Duke called upon me as he promised. I will endeavour to set down our conversation as faithfully as I can.

"It is very bad — very bad," he said, as soon as he came into the room. He then told me that he had a terrible scene with Peel on Tuesday at Peel's house. Peel was in a dreadful state of agitation, his countenance and all his features working and twitching in a thousand ways. "You never saw a man in such a state of agitation. There I sat, all the time, as cool as possible. The fact is that he wants to resign and he wanted me to tell him he was right. That I would not do. I said to him, 'Nobody has a right to desire you to remain longer than you think fit; but I implore you for the sake of the country, and for the sake of your own credit, do not resign without you have so clear a case for it that your party and country may be satisfied it is *impossible* for you to do otherwise.' He was very much out of temper all that day from what I said to him and next morning, Wednesday, he wrote me a letter of eight sides of paper, which I answered by a very short one . . . Friday, there was a meeting of those members of the Cabinet who are in the House of Commons, and there we had the same scene over again from Peel. Then they told me that they thought they should not be able to carry through the Army Estimates that evening. 'Very well,' I said, 'then there is your case for resigning, if you cannot get the supplies, there is a case which must be plain to everybody.' Yesterday, after the majorities, Peel was in better spirits: today again he is rather low. I am just come from a Cabinet: nothing has been decided as to our line. After the decision on the Irish Tithe Bill we shall hold another Cabinet and be guided by circumstances, if the debate goes against us or the resolution is carried against us by a large majority, I do not see how we can well remain . . ."

I said that I deeply regretted to find that this was his feeling, and I asked him, "Supposing you were certain of carrying the Mutiny Bill and the Supplies, and that *you* were in Peel's place, would you resign?"

"I declare to God that unless I could carry the Irish Tithe Bill or a similar measure, nothing would induce me to remain in office. A Tithe Bill must be carried this year. The Irish clergy are starving and after this year there will not be one chance of recovering a shilling."

Me "But you will carry the Tithe Bill even if this resolution passes?"

Duke "But the resolution is of great consequence. I thought it of less importance at first, but when you come to look at it, it is of great consequence — it attacks the foundation of all property."

Me "The worst is that the people of this country have no strong feeling about this question, and will not understand that there is any

160

necessity for your resigning — nor will they take it up when you have resigned."

Duke "But do they not see that the Union with Ireland depends upon the Protestant Church? Have they not read of the times of Charles I? Don't they read history?"

Me "Who does, to profit by it? But supposing you have resigned — *et puis?* Have you any idea what is to happen, any view or theory of any sort?"

Duke "None upon earth — none whatever — anything is upon the cards."

I urged upon him in the strongest manner that I could, every reason I could suggest against their resigning.

The Duke (in a very emphatic manner) " — Lady Salisbury, it is all very true — what you say is quite true. But — what can we do? . . . The only thing that I can see a chance for the country is that the King should try and compose a Ministry out of the different parties — Lord Grey, Stanley and Peel and so on. And yet that is a dream — a mere vision . . ."

The Duke left me wretchedly out of spirits . . .

Pozzo di Borgo told Lord S. the other day, speaking of Talleyrand, that he was a traitor to Napoleon from the time of Erfurth. He always pretended he had dissuaded Napoleon from the Spanish War whereas Napoleon averred that they had only differed as to the means, not the end. Napoleon's fault, Pozzo said, was leaving Talleyrand in office after the violent quarrel he had with him on his return from Russia: — "*Après qu'on s'est servi de semblables expressions on doit faire arrêter le ministre au bas de l'escalier.*"

Wednesday, April 1st Debate adjourned again . . . In a note I wrote to the Duke, I said that I heard the King would not accept the resignation of Ministers, should it even be tendered, if he had any ground for hoping they might be induced to remain. 'This is true, I was told so by Mlle. D'Este.' In the answer, the Duke merely said that "they were in a very critical situation, and that it was impossible to say what would be done". Lord S. wished me (in consequence of what the Duke said to him yesterday "that if he were the King he would not accept the resignation") to tell Mlle D'Este that I was convinced Ministers would retain office if the King persisted in refusing to accept their resignation — that she might convey this assurance to the Queen. I did so, this day, at three o'clock when I saw Mlle. d'Este.

Without quoting any authority, I stated that it was my firm conviction that Ministers would be prevailed upon eventually to remain if the King persisted in refusing their resignations and desired her to tell the Queen so, as a statement she had heard from me, but not as a message from me. When I saw her in the evening at Devonshire House she told me she had made this statement both to the Queen and to the Duchess of Gloucester — to the latter because she was to see the King this evening, which the Queen possibly might not do. Mlle. d'Este went beyond her commission, however, in telling the Queen that she (Mlle. d'Este) was persuaded that I had heard it from the Duke of Wellington, tho' I had named no authority to her.

She knows nothing on the subject, as I never told her that I had *any* ground for thinking so beyond my own impression — nor did I ever name the Duke of Wellington. I am sorry she made this speech to the Queen. When she told me of it I said nothing except, "Remember that I never gave you any ground for that conjecture, nor ever told you I had any authority for the opinion." I am sorry too that she told the Duchess of Gloucester who is notoriously indiscreet. I am horribly afraid I shall get in some mess by it. However, I have asserted nothing that is not true, and I think I have done right — and then what signifies? I requested Mlle. d'Este to tell the Queen Lord John Russell's speech to Lord Londonderry, and the opinion expressed by Lord Glanville that if the King was not prepared to assent to the demands of the Whig Radicals he might abdicate. I understand the Ministers, in their dispatches, had already hinted something to him of the latter.

When I got home I saw Lord Douro, who made me a declaration, and I dismissed him. I think I have done a good morning's work altogether. It is a pity it is the First of April.

[According to Creevey, Douro in 1830 became engaged to the daughter of his father's medical adviser, Dr. Hume. The Duke remarked, "Ah! rather young, are you not, Douro, to be married? Suppose you stay till the year is out, and then if you are in the same mind, it's all very well." In April 1836, Douro asked Lady Westmeath, should Lady de Rothesay and her daughter go to Naples, to tell him what she thinks, not of the beauty, that is clear, but of the sense and sensibility of the young lady. He doubts if she has enough heart or head, and her mother is a catamaran! Besides Graham, Redesdale and Grimston are all nibblers.[1] Lord Douro married, in April 1839, Lady Elisabeth Hay, daughter of the 8th Marquess of Tweeddale, and died without issue.]

Thursday, April 2nd Dined at the Duke's — a great dinner for the Austrian Ambassador. He seemed in better spirits and told me Peel was so. I said that a letter of John Wortley's from Yorkshire had stated that people there had no idea of Ministers resigning on this question. He said, "Your argument on that subject cannot be answered," and afterwards "We must come to a dissolution at all events". I said, "Yes, but it would make all the difference whether it was our measure or our enemies'." I asked him if he thought the Duchess of Kent's object (as I have heard it conjectured) is to get the King to abdicate in Victoria's favour. "There's no saying — very likely, The worst is, it would create no feeling if he did abdicate — should Parliament be dissolved again, and an equally bad H. of C.s returned. I think he very likely might, provided he got a good pension."

I asked him if he thought Lady Peel had any influence over her husband. "No, she is not a clever woman. Peel did not wish to marry a clever woman . . ."

[On March 30th, Lord John Russell had proposed a motion that the House should resolve itself into a committee to consider the revenues of the Church of Ireland. On April 3rd, it was carried by a majority of thirty-three. Russell then moved a further resolution that surplus revenue should be applied locally to the General Education of Christians, and on this motion the Government were defeated by a majority of twenty-five. On April 7th, Lord John moved that no measure upon the subject of tithes in Ireland could lead to a satisfactory and final adjustment which did not embody the principle of the foregoing resolutions. After a gallant speech, Peel was defeated by a majority of twenty-seven. Next morning he placed his resignation in the hands of the King.]

Lord Lyndhurst offered to send me the earliest information the next morning of the result of the division. "I am quite satisfied," observed the Duke, "to have it when the newspapers come in at 10 o'clock. If I could do any good by having it before, I would; but

[1] Cecil Papers: VII, 265.

as I can't, I had just as soon wait." "You always look at these things coolly," I said, "Now! you never lay awake with anxiety?"

"No, I don't like lying awake — it does no good. I make it a point never to lie awake . . ."

Monday, April 13th I went to the Duchess of Gloucester by appointment, the first time I had seen her since the Duke's death. She looks well in her weeds — in better health, I think, than last year. She mentioned him incidentally, but quite as a person who had been dead for years. She is making her house more comfortable and will be much happier I think altogether.

She told me she saw the King every day and told him everything she heard, and desired me to tell her all I could, that she might repeat it. She said he was very anxious to hear what was the public opinion, that he read the newspapers, and to-day she knew he had read *The Times, Morning Post* and *M. Herald.*

Sunday, 26th I had a conversation with Sir H. Hardinge. He told me that he had a conversation with Peel yesterday on the subject of the Corporation Reform, and of a coalition with Stanley and Graham. Peel expressed an opinion that such a union was desirable but added that he would never join any Administration of which the greatest man of the age, he to whom the Conservative party owed most, was not a component part — the Duke of Wellington.

Tuesday, May 12th The meeting of Parliament. Come to town.

Wednesday, 13th The Duke called upon me. He was looking uncommonly well, much better than when I last saw him, and in far better spirits, quite another creature. He said he was very sorry he had not been able to come to Hatfield, that he had a great deal to do at Walmer and S. Saye. "And then, to tell you the truth, I was out of spirits and annoyed at all that had passed. I think we gave up too soon — but Peel would not stay, there was no use in persuading him. I wrote him the strongest and most affectionate letter I could — it would not do . . ." I replied that tho' it went against my own opinion, that I had expressed so strongly before, I must own that the country had not appeared to disapprove of the resignation, nor had their spirit been damped by it; and that the Irish Church had proved to be an excellent question to resign upon as there was such a strong feeling about it. To this he assented, and added, "Certainly, I have never heard from any quarter such strong language as I heard

THE DUKE OF WELLINGTON

By David Wilkie, painted for the collection at Hatfield House, 1835, and exhibited at the Royal Academy that year

"I walked with the Duke and looked out the numbers in the catalogue for him . . . I am afraid I cannot change the opinion I formed the first moment I saw Wilkie's picture of him that it is a decided failure in likeness: he thought so himself and that it was too large in the body. The colouring, though, is good, and it is far superior at all events to the other two pictures of him — that by Pickersgill is like a drunken undertaker, and that by Morton is made of wood. To these two criticisms Lord Aberdeen adds a third, that Wilkie's is like a Spanish beggarman."

(From the Diary of the 2nd Marchioness, May 19th, 1835)

from you, *sitting there*, upon the subject" (pointing to the place where I was sitting). He told me he had been half inclined not to go to the City dinner. "In the first place it was a sort of triumph, and we are not in a situation that calls for an expression of triumph; and then I dislike that sort of thing, and political speeches after dinner (tho' that may be an aristocratic feeling, I daresay it is, that I have no right to indulge). However, I thought I had better go, and that it would be attributed to some petty jealousy if I did not." Speaking of Peel, I remarked how few personal followers he had, considering his great eminence. "No, there is something unconciliating about him," said the Duke. "He has no devoted friends, for he has no confidence in anybody; he never does what I am now doing with you, for example – thinking aloud. Nothing would induce him . . ."

Sunday, 17th We had a great alarm, one of Lady Salisbury's dogs having gone mad. A footman was bit, and had the piece cut out. The Swiss maid had also had her hand licked on a part where the skin was off, and in consequence went through an operation. Lady S. appeared perfectly unmoved, refused for a long time to part with this, or the other dog, which had been bitten, and seemed to have no thought in the whole transaction but her own privation in losing her dogs. I am most thankful for the providential escape of my children, who were in the room with the dog after it had begun to be ailing and were not bitten.

18th May Met the Duke as I was walking in the Park with Mlle. d'Este. He got off his horse and walked with us, saying he was now the idlest man about town – nothing to do. He is in great spirits. I must say it is far the pleasantest to belong to a party in Opposition – no cares or anxieties, everybody at leisure and everybody good-humoured . . .

May 19th Went to the Exhibition with the Duke, Mlle. d'Este and Lord Ellenborough. I walked with the Duke and looked out the numbers in the catalogue for him. He took my little Blanche in the other hand and went with great interest over the whole, although he had already seen it once at the private view. The people all recognized him immediately and made way for him in the most respectful manner. It was extremely crowded. I am afraid I cannot change the opinion I formed the first moment I saw Wilkie's picture of him, that it is a decided failure in likeness. He thought so himself, and that it was too large about the body. The colouring, though, is good, and it is far superior to the two other portraits of him – that by Pickersgill is like a drunken undertaker, and that by Morton made of wood. To these two criticisms Lord Aberdeen adds a third, that Wilkie's is like a Spanish beggarman . . . We went afterwards to see a beautiful collection of Rubens' drawings which had belonged to Sir Thomas Lawrence, and ended by a panorama of the burning of the House of Lord and Commons, and the learned fleas. The last is excessively laughable and really astonishing.''

May 21st Fortunately Lady S's dog is dead, and has so put the madness beyond all doubt in anybody's mind but hers. The other is tied up in the House . . .

We went in the evening to Lady Farquhar's to see the new American beauty, Mrs Wansworth.

May 27th O'Connell was actually at Lansdowne House in the evening, the first time I have heard of him in a gentleman's house.

May 28th The Duke wrote to me in the morning to say that it appeared to be the Duke of Cumberland's wish that all the chief people of the party should take the same course about Lady Lansdowne's assembly in honour of the King's birthday this evening . . . I have not, however, been in Lady Lansdowne's house since Lord Grey's threat of making Peers to carry the Reform Bill, and I was not inclined to go. So I told the Duke I had already sent my excuses . . .

Saturday 30th Rode with the Duke, Lady G. Fane and some men to the Surrey Zoological. The Duke was in high spirits and took much interest in the animals. We saw the wild beasts fed, and among other things a young ourang-outang, just arrived, wrapped up in flannel – in all its way very like a child and nearly the same size in proportion to its age – very disgusting. The man at the head of the establishment followed the Duke putting many questions to him on the habits and nature of different animals which he had seen in India which the Duke answered with the greatest good nature and seemed particularly amused by the entertainment afforded by the animals to two little boys of Lord Burghersh's who were with us, and who ran after the different creatures, mounted on the elephants' backs etc.

June 4th Lady Salisbury has let her dog loose again, it really is too bad. I forbid my children to go near the house.

166

Saturday, June 6th Went to Hatfield for the Whitsun holidays. I took three of the children with me.

I am provoked at hearing that Lady Aylesbury[1] has set about a report that she refused the Duke before she took her present juvenile spouse. It really is too absurd; the Duke scarcely ever spoke to her.

Lord Verulam and Lord Grimston came over to settle about the races.

[The diary does not mention another annual event (which often took place in Hatfield Park — and still does), the meeting of the Hertfordshire Archers. This year it produced a poem "The Umpire Cupid's Survey".

> "First *Salisbury* passed and fixed his wondering view,
> Her perfect shape ten thousand praises drew
> Tall, beauteous and majestic to the sight
> She led the train and sparkled fair as light"

The small silver arrow which was given to the winner was kept in the silver-mounted tortoiseshell cabinet in King James's room. "The whole county joined in this healthful and rational sport."[2]]

Thursday, June 10th Came up early to London on account of the heat. The Duke called upon me. He told me he had seen Peel yesterday — " 'As dry as dust,' as Scott says, could get nothing out of him. He has not made up his mind on the Corporation question — just shows you what the man is — can decide nothing. He told me he had no communication with Stanley upon it, and Hardinge told me the same thing. But Aberdeen told me this morning that Stanley and Peel intended to try and get Ministers to put off the question for another twelve months. I think if they had managed it cleverly they might have turned them upon it — we had a very good case."

The Duke observed also that he had asked Peel what he intended to do about the Foreign Enlistment Bill. Peel gave him no explicit answer but Hardinge told him Peel meant to do nothing about it.

I said, "Those are Peel's odd ways, acquired from not having been used to good society from his birth. But he is a thoroughly honest man and devoted to you." *Duke* "In the first position you are quite

[1] Maria, daughter of Hon. C. Tollemache, m. 1833, Charles Brudenell-Bruce, 1st Marquess of Aylesbury, b. 1773.
[2] Cecil Papers: IX, Nov. 1835, and XII, 175.

right. He *is* thoroughly honest. I never saw a man who adhered more invariably to the truth on all occasions" (a very rare praise for the Duke to give). "As to the second, I have my doubts of that."

I said that the very honesty of his character was a proof of it, as he would never have gone out of his way to make professions that were insincere, as he had done both in public and private, and that I was convinced from all I had observed that he was really attached to the Duke as a Statesman.

The Duke is in great spirits. He took Lord S. to-day to the Merchant Taylors' dinner. He told me there was a lady who sent him tracts — particularly the account of her attempting with a female friend to convert Cook the murderer, and that he thought it so curious, he had read it attentively through . . .

[The Duke had during the past year called upon Miss J. three times, but was alarmed by her evident intention to marry him, which she relinquished only on his death seventeen years later.]

Sunday, June 14th Dined at Pozzo di Borgo's. Sat next the Duke. The Duke amused me with an anecdote of the Duke of St. Albans.[1]

Dining there one day, the Duchess showed him a *plâteau* which, she said in a sentimental tone, was a *cadeau* of the Duke's on the anniversary of their marriage. After the ladies were gone, the Duke of Wellington observed to the Duke of St. Albans, how handsome it was. "Yes," he said, "some of old Coutts's, I believe, furbished up" . . .

Monday, June 15th Dined at the Buccleuchs. Lord Hertford's in the evening. It is amazing what a pause there seems to be in politics. The Whigs do nothing; and seem to be expected to do nothing, their only object is to keep their places. The Conservatives bide their time, the Radicals theirs, and all sides appear glad to have a rest; without any diminution, however, of hatred *de part et d'autre*. Balls and breakfasts are the subject of conversation instead of politics.

Thursday, June 18th (Waterloo) Went with my children at the Duke's invitation, to see the table laid out for his dinner. The room was crowded and remained so, I heard, for several hours. It was *very* gratifying to see that great man, in his advanced age, his white hair and strongly lined features marking indeed his time of life, but his

[1] The Duke of St. Albans was "Burford", Fanny's rejected suitor, now married to the widowed Mrs. Coutts.

eagle eye and commanding aspect still showing all the vigour of youth, enjoying the recompense of his imperishable achievements, as far, at least, as worldly homage can recompense them, in his magnificent palace, his table loaded with the tributes of grateful sovereigns, surrounded by crowds of his fellow countrymen who thronged after a lapse of twenty years to testify their sense of his benefits, and their admiration of his character . . .

Friday, June 19th The breakfast at Sion. A beautiful day and a magnificent fête. The King, being over-fatigued, could not come; the Queen was there . . . The Duke took me in to dinner and sat between the Queen and me. I have never enjoyed myself more than at that delightful breakfast at Sion. I had a long walk with the Duke after dinner — from about eight till past eleven, when we came away with him. His kindness, his expressions of friendship, of real and *friendly* attachment, I can never forget. I sometimes think how can I be worthy of the friendship of such a man, what have *I* done to deserve the highest honour a woman can attain to be *his* friend?

Monday, June 22nd Dined at the Duke's . . . altogether two and thirty at dinner. I sat between Pozzo and Esterhazy, the former was, I believe, very entertaining, telling me anecdotes of Waterloo, but his mouth was so full of venison, and the Styrian singers, who were stationed at the end of the apartment, so loud, that I could not catch one word in ten. The ball afterwards was immensely crowded. The first person who came in the evening when only the dinner party were assembled, was Sir Francis Burdett.[1] He actually seemed to know nobody in the room, and the Duke and the Duke of Cumberland were the only people who went up to him and did the honours of his reception.

Thursday, June 23rd I had not more than time to refresh myself between the Duke's ball and Lord Hertford's breakfast. A very pretty fête — the day not quite so warm as at Sion. The King was prevented coming here also, by his asthma, the Queen and the other Royals came. There was a separate room for the Queen's table, to which people were specially invited . . . I happened to turn round at dinner and perceived a small side table at which sat H.M.'s Privy

[1] Sir Francis Burdett (1770–1844) politician, reformer and champion of liberty of speech, m. Sophia, daughter of Thomas Coutts; father of Angela, Baroness Burdett-Coutts.

Seal and H.M.'s Prime Minister, with three or four other people . . . I pointed them out to the Duke and he to the Queen, who turned round several times to look at them and smiled. However, Lord Melbourne *s'en consola* in the evening with Mrs. Norton.[1]

Sunday, June 28th We made a party to the Zoological Gardens in the Regent's Park — the Duke, the Pozzo di Borgos (the niece and nephew), M. and Mme. Ferrari, Lady Sandwich and one or two men. Our progress was rather impeded by the number of people who came round to see the Duke (the gardens were very crowded), the people hustling, running and whispering to each other, that nobody might lose the sight; children especially dragged along by their parents and hoisted upon the most elevated places, that they might be able to say hereafter "that they had seen *him*" . . .

Tuesday, July 7th A letter from the Duke giving me an account of his entry into Cambridge drawn by the Yeomanry, of whom a large body assembled to meet him.

Thursday, 9th I hear most brilliant accounts of Cambridge and of the enthusiasm displayed for the Duke. Still it cannot be like Oxford! . . .

Friday, July 10th A review in Hyde Park. I went on foot with my children, and Edward Drummond to take care of us, but the crowd and the press were tremendous. We followed the Duke on his way home, and had the satisfaction of hearing him well cheered. There was not much notice taken of the King. The King on arriving on the ground, shook hands with the Duke and said, "You are the only subject I shake hands with." The Duke kissed his hand. It was a pretty sight before the whole field . . .

Sunday, July 12th The Duke was exceedingly amusing in his description of a breakfast at the Duchess of St. Albans the day before. He sat, as he said, in excellent company — Lady Aldborough and the Duchess of Camizaro, the Duchess of St. Albans and Lady Stepney: in short all the demi-reps in town: Queen Mab among others, who succeeded in getting hold of his arm for a certain time, but he would not let her sit next him at dinner. After dinner a cow was produced to be milked, with a crown of gold upon her horns, but

[1] Caroline, daughter of Thomas Sheridan (1808–77), authoress, musician, artist and beauty, m. 1827 Hon. George Norton who attempted unsuccessfully to divorce her in June 1836 naming Lord Melbourne as co-respondent.

the cow did not like her coiffure and the crown was obliged to serve the more ignoble use of a milking stool. "I asked," said the Duke to me, "what the milk was to be done with. 'The milk is for heroes,' was the reply. So then I thought it was high time for me to be off."

Wednesday, July 15th Dined at Lord Aylesbury's to meet the Duke of Cumberland. Speaking of some person, I observed they had at least one good quality, they were zealous Tories. "Ah!" said the Duke of Cumberland, "that covers a multitude of sins. That is the reason you all bear with me. There is not a sin in the calendar that I have not been accused of." True enough.

In the evening, the Duchess of Sutherland's, the first time of their opening their house. I never saw anything so beautiful — the music, the lights, the *locale*, all so perfect. It was more like a splendid vision than a reality.

[Stafford House was built 1825 by Wyatt (on a site once partially occupied by Godolphin House) for the Duke of York, who died before it was completed, on funds advanced by the Marquis of Stafford, afterwards 1st Duke of Sutherland. The Grand Staircase was added by Sir Charles Barry. The House was presented to the Nation in 1912 by Viscount Leverhulme, re-named Lancaster House.]

Saturday, July 18th Went down to Hatfield for a large party . . .

Sunday, July 19th The Duke came down to breakfast — went with us to church. After church I walked with him between three and four hours — a beautiful day, rather hot; it was delightful in the shades of the Park . . . He told me there had been an attempt on Louise Philippe's life[1] by an infernal machine, but it was hushed up. He left us in the evening.

Monday, 20th Returned to London, Found Cranborne just arrived. No improvement, alas! in his eyes . . .

Tuesday, July 21st Peel spoke powerfully last night in the Irish Church Bill. The Duke thinks it possible Ministers may go out on this question of the Pension List which comes on tomorrow. I am sure I devoutly pray they may not! I never dreaded their coming in as I dread their going out — personally and politically. The Duke says he hears the registration is generally going on well, except in the North and in Staffordshire.

[1] Louis Philippe escaped assassination in October 1832, July 1835, June and December 1836 and July 1846.

It is supposed Victoria does not go with her mother in politics. The other day, at their concert, the Duke went up to Princess Sophia[1] on her blind side (she has but one eye) and she, of course, did not perceive him. On which Victoria left her place in the circle and came up and pulled her by the sleeve that she might turn to the Duke. She is so narrowly watched that all these trifles become important indications. The Duchess of Northumberland was enchanted.

Went in the evening with the Duke and a party to the Coliseum.

Thursday, July 23rd The breakfast at Ken Wood. The road was crowded with people all the way anxious to see the King. A triumphal arch was erected on Hampstead Heath, and in most of the houses by the side of the road there were preparations for illuminations. I heard the King was extremely well received by the crowd, and the Duke still more so. We did not arrive till some time after them. It was a beautiful day. The grounds are excessively pretty, and if there had been enough to eat, it would have been perfect . . . The King and Queen and all the Royalties seemed extremely well pleased: the King in particular trotted about with Lord M. in the most active manner, and made innumerable speeches!

[William IV's speeches were becoming a source of anxiety to his well-wishers. The most famous occasion was on his seventy-first birthday banquet for a hundred at Windsor in 1836 when he publicly insulted the Duchess of Kent, Guest of Honour. Princess Victoria burst into tears, and the Duchess ordered her carriage, but was persuaded by Queen Adelaide not to leave precipitately.]

Sunday, July 26th Had service in the Chapel at nine in the morning for the servants for the first time. Intensely hot.

Monday, July 27th Returned to town in the cool of the evening.

Tuesday, July 28th Emily Grimston's marriage to Lord Craven announced at last. I am glad to hear it.

London is a dusty desert, the Parks burnt up, nothing green to be seen. However, I have no right to complain. In the first place I have such reasons for happiness it would be the height of ingratitude in me ever to be dissatisfied. Besides, *vu les circonstances,* I had ten thousand times rather be in London if it was like the sands of Arabia than anywhere else.

[1] Augusta Sophia, sixth child of George III, lived in Kensington Palace: an ally of Conroy.

Saturday, August 8th Went to Hatfield. The Duke, the Wharn-cliffes, Eliots, Stuarts, Lord Clare, Lord Talbot, Lord Douro, Capt. Percy, Lord Fitzgerald, John Talbot, here. The Duke was in great force and exceedingly agreeable after dinner, relating various anecdotes — the history of Thistlewood's conspiracy, which I had already heard him tell at Walmer, and of the attempt to assassinate him at Paris . . . The conversation began by an observation on the extraordinary fact that the attempt the other day on the life of Louis Philippe was known in all parts of France before it could possibly have been communicated by ordinary means. The Duke said the same thing had happened when his life was attempted. The assassin, who had been a military man, stationed himself at the entrance of the *porte-cochère* of the Duke's house one night when the Duke was expected home from a dinner at Mme. Craufurd's, well knowing that the sentinel keeping guard under the arch could not rush out at the moment the carriage was driving in. The shot missed, and the coachman, whipping his horses furiously, drove the carriage into the archway, and the Duke so little thought of assassination at the moment that his idea was on hearing the report, that the coach-man had knocked down the sentry, whose piece had gone off, and he exclaimed "A pretty fellow you are for knocking down the sentry!" The plot was hatched at Brussels; the assassin was not secured till some time after, when he was tried and acquitted, there not being sufficient proof. It appears that, the day after, he came back to the spot to see what had happened, and actually saw the Duke show-ing the place where he had been stationed to Lord Fitzroy Somerset.

This led to a conversation on the best mode of resisting a mob in the streets of a city, and upon the expected riots in the autumn of the year '30 in London. The Duke said he had no doubt an exten-sive plot existed for getting up a serious tumult at that time (i.e. when the Tory Ministers advised the King not to dine in the city). He did not think the mob would ever be able to pursue with success in this country the same plans as at Paris, *viz:* to get into the houses as soon as the troops charged them in the streets, and fire upon the latter from the windows. The different mode of tenanting the houses, each house generally belonging to a single family, would contribute to this.

He also gave us some very amusing accounts of Spain, and of the manners of the Grandees; especially of the fashion still subsisting when he was in the Peninsula, of the whole family, servants and all, dining as in old times, in the same apartment. "I never was asked to dinner but twice, during the whole time I was in Spain (except dining with the King), so much is it out of the Spanish manners. One of these times was in celebration of a marriage, and it was a *vraie noce de Garnache* — all the duennas and escuderos coming to help themselves from the dishes which came on the tables, and then retiring into a corner of the room to eat it, and chattering the whole time. It is a clear proof that *Gil Blas* was not written by a Spaniard, because the author speaks of '*les châteaux*', '*la vie de châteaux*', and there is no such thing. There are no country houses, no country gentry; the *curé* is the man of influence and fills their place. A very happy peasantry!"

Sunday, 9th Had a long walk in Milward's Park with the Duke: very hot, but delicious in the shade. We talked chiefly about different persons in society . . . Of Lady Wilton that she was a very sensible woman as she proved by her conduct, but that he had never discovered the smallest spark of feeling in her.

Tuesday, 19th I am annoyed to find my name was in the newspapers and on placards as a Patroness of the Polish Benefit, nothing could be further from my intention, as I merely went for the sake of a party to Vauxhall. I called upon Mlle. Pozzo today to explain it.

27th Saw the Duke again. He sat a good while with me, talking first of one subject and then another, as it were "thinking aloud" — particularly of the chances public men have of being assassinated, and the best way of guarding against it. "Depend upon it, a thing of that sort is never done upon the impulse of the moment: an assassin always lays a plan and stations himself in some convenient place where he has means of retreat, and where he can reckon upon the person whom he designs to kill passing at a certain hour. If you walk about publicly in frequented places, you are in no danger: no man can attack you without risking his own life, and no man likes to risk his own life." I instanced the cases of madmen. He agreed that proper precautions are not taken about madmen in this country, and that danger might arise from them. He met one one day in St. James's Park, who entered into conversation with him, and the Duke who was quite alone, went on talking with him till he overtook Sir C. Flower who was on horseback, to whom he said, in a low voice, "I have got a madman here — just ride on with me." He did so and they proceeded till they reached, I think, one of the Government Offices, when the Duke entered, saying to the man as he left him, "Good morning, my friend, and I give you one piece of advice: never attempt to talk to me again."

Speaking of his return from the Tower on that memorable anniversary of Waterloo when the mob followed him, and of the two soldiers who walked on each side of his horse, and were, I believe, the means of saving his life (blessed men!), he said that all he desired of them was, whenever he was prevented getting on by the crowd, to place themselves each with his back to one of the stirrups so that the mob might not be able to drag him off his horse.

September 1st Poor Katty Barham has a dead child.

Thursday, 3rd The Radicals were so good as to give notices of motions last night for taking away the legislative power of the H. of Lds. and reducing it to a suspensive one etc. etc. Are they afraid it should be suspected to be their want of will instead of want of power that allows us still to exist? . . .

Saturday, 5th Went to Emily Grimston's marriage at Gorhambury on my way to Hatfield. They were married in the house by the Dean of Carlisle, about thirty people present and a breakfast to the county afterwards. I was heartily glad when it was over — nothing is so melancholy as a wedding when one considers the many chances for its turning out ill; and how often both parties may wish in vain those awful and irrevocable words then said, *unsaid*. I saw poor Katty, inconsolable for the loss of her child, and crying night and day in the midst of the festivities round her. Perhaps in another year her sorrow may be turned into joy and Emily's . . .

Sunday, 6th The Duke came to breakfast. After the Church a long walk with him in Milward's Park. The Duke was inclined to-day to take a gloomy view of the state of affairs . . . "We are on the eve of a great change of society. I am one of those who think the change had better be gradual than sudden: if gradual, we all (the aristocracy) may find our places in it. We may not be what we were, but we shall be something." He told me afterwards many amusing anecdotes of George IV's Court.

"That man was the greatest *vagabond* that ever existed. He was

175

always acting a part to himself. He thought fit to fancy himself in love with Lady Conyngham and jealous of Old Ponsonby, and to acknowledge the S. American States in consequence. It was all a fallacy. He did not really *care for her* one farthing, and he knew her thoroughly and used to complain to me of her meanness and covet-ousness etc. etc. But he thought it necessary to have a *lady* and a rival. He made a declaration in his last illness that he would leave her *everything* he had, and desired Sir. W. Knighton to inform her of it. When he had executed the message — 'Well,' said the King, 'how did she receive it?' 'She was very much affected, Sir, and burst into tears.' 'Oh, she did, did she?' That was all he wanted — to produce an effect. From that hour he never mentioned the will again though he lived six weeks afterwards and the Conynghams took care, when-ever they were with him, that pen, ink and paper should be within reach.''

The Duke did all he could to prevent this nuncupative will being put into writing, and told Lady C. herself that it would bring utter destruction upon her character. The King imagined himself jealous of the Duke of Cumberland, and in his last illness he used to send Lord Conyngham to prevent the Duke of Cumberland being alone with Lady C. on pretence that he was "boring My Lady to death".

The King was an admirer too of Mme. de Lieven, and *there* he professed to be jealous of the Duke of Wellington.

On one occasion, Mme. de Lieven remonstrated with him, saying, *"Mais que dira votre dame?"* *"Oh? elle n'en saura rien! Faites moi entrer chez vous par la petite porte à gauche* (this was at Windsor) *et personne ne me verra, à moins que ce ne soit ce maudit jaloux."* (The Duke of Welling-ton, whose windows were the only ones that looked that way.) This speech Mme. de Lieven wrote off to Lady Granville at Paris. Canning intercepted the letter and brought it back to the King, and the Duke now has it among his papers.

In his last illness the Bishop who was with him (I forget which), allowed him some extraordinary privileges as Head of the Church — for instance that of pronouncing the benediction himself at the end of the service which was read every evening in his bedroom, Lady Conyngham etc . . . included among the assistants.

He liked making a scene with his sisters and taking leave of them, but to everyone else he maintained he was in no danger, and repeated this so often, that at last he believed it himself. The last time the Duke saw him, he said he was getting quite well, and should be able to move soon.

Of George III, the Duke said to me "that he was the best *King* England ever had, and understood *Kingcraft* the most thoroughly; a far superior man in real ability to his son, tho' he had not the same quickness and talent. George III, however, had no scruple in throwing over his friends or his instruments whenever it suited his purpose" (in this he resembled Elizabeth) . . .

Tuesday, 8th The Duke dined with us – nobody else. In the course of conversation he was mentioning Clarendon's History. "I have read it several times," he said, "and I was reading it again the other day, and left it with a very unfavourable impression of Charles's military talents, more so than I had at first been led to form.

"The worst of this Corporation Bill is that it will form a little Republic in every town, possessing the power of raising money. In case of anything like a civil war, these would be very formidable instruments in the hands of the democratic party. Charles I was ruined by the money levied by the City of London . . ." We came down at night to Hatfield; got there about one.

Wednesday, 9th The Duke dined and slept here on his way to Wood-ford. He looks a little fagged: no wonder: but he was in very good spirits playing with my little boy, and as good humoured and apparently as entirely without care as if he had nothing on earth to do. This is one of the most wonderful qualities of his mind: the power of throwing aside all care in a moment, and completely turning his attention from the more serious subjects which engage him, to the amusement of the moment. Nothing can exceed his good nature and kindness in going to Woodford at this time, when every moment is precious to him and he has not had a day to bestow upon his own affairs for many months. Besides, nothing can be more irksome to a man of his active mind than a visit to a solitary broken-hearted man like Mr. Arbuthnot who has lost all energy and interest in everything.

Monday, 14th Lord S. went to Lancashire, leaving me here with the children. I have long since formed the resolution of giving up that place, and allowing it to be let. I do not think I have any right to put Lord S. to the expense of keeping it up, when so many other things press heavily upon him. Besides, my enjoyment of it can be but at rare intervals and for a very short time. It is a pang to part with it. It is connected with all my earliest recollections, and a few years ago I should have thought it impossible. But I am sure it is right. Lord S. has felt himself bound in duty in these critical times to go to great expense in elections; it is my business to relieve him as far as it is in my power. However, it would have been too painful for me to go down and see it again, knowing it was for the last time.

[Childwall, now a residential suburb of Liverpool, was let in 1836 for twenty years to John Shaw Leigh, son of Bamber Gascoyne's agent. Since 1913, it has been included within the City boundaries of Liverpool. The House was presented to the Liverpool Corporation by the 5th Marquess of Salisbury in 1947, and was demolished because it was riddled with dry rot. Childwall Hall County College, opened in 1955, was erected on the site. The Local History Department contains a large collection of deeds and other records presented by the Marquess of Salisbury.

I remained quite alone from this time, except –

Wednesday, September 16th Dined at Gorhambury, and returned in the evening, till

Thursday, September 24th Lady Salisbury came. I have passed a great deal of time with my children; the weather very rainy and scarcely allowed me to go out. I regret to see that Cranborne's infirmities increase, and his case appears to me to grow daily more distressing and more hopeless.

Friday, September 25th Lord S. returned.

Sunday, September 27th The Yeomanry assembled here for a week's training. We had very bad weather all the week, almost continual rain.

Friday, October 2nd Our Yeomanry week concluded with a dinner to the whole of the troops in the cloister. Seventeen of the Officers have been living in the house here ever since Sunday. The dinner was laid for 216, but owing to the wet weather not above 150 were present. It went off extremely well; no politics alluded to: the Duke's health drank, and *not* His Majesty's Ministers. They all seemed pleased.

Saturday, October 3rd Went to town to consult Quin[1] for Cran-

[1] Frederic Hervey Foster Quin (1799–1878), England's first homeopathic physician.

borne. He would say nothing positive, but is to see him again. Returned to dinner . . .

Wednesday, October 7th The Fancy Bazaar at St. Albans for the benefit of the repairs of the Abbey. I declined having a stall but was obliged to go and buy. They cleared above £500 which I am glad of.

[Engravings from drawings by Buckler of the south aisle of the nave of St. Albans Abbey as it appeared in 1832 show it with the roof gone, timbers lying about and saplings sprouting. The Lady Chapel was walled off as a Grammar School and a public way led through the Chancel; the west front was a ruin. Major restoration began after a report by Sir G. Scott 1871, failed on his death and was not resumed until Lord Grimthorpe intervened in 1880 and spent, reputedly, £130,000 on his own designs.]

Friday, October 9th Lady Salisbury left us. Her memory fails so dreadfully it is quite painful to be with her. The Queen's visit to Oxford and S. Saye is fixed. We are to meet her at the latter on the 21st. I had much rather have my quiet visit at Walmer *now*.

Saturday, October 10th Cranborne has seen Quin again. He gives but very slender hopes of his recovery. I am prepared for the worst, and even a fatal termination would be a mercy compared with his present miserable state; but whatever be the result I fear it must be lingering. He is going to leave us soon and be placed with a clergyman in Devonshire. I will try to turn my mind from this *one* drawback and how much, how very much, I have to be thankful for.

We remained alone till the 20th — cold damp, autumnal weather. Mildred has hurt her knee jumping from a window and is laid up. I am uneasy about it, but they assure me it is of no consequence.

Tuesday, 20th October Mr. Thomas[1] gives me a satisfactory account of the knee, and I am relieved from the apprehension of its being anything serious. We went to Town, I took a long walk with Lord S. We went and lunched at the Carlton where we found nobody but Lord Strangford, a good deal surprised to see me there. Then we took a hackney coach which landed us in St. Mary Axe, walked to a lamp shop and a jeweller's and came back in another hackney coach — incog.

Wednesday, 21st October To-day we dined with the Queen instead. Got to S. Saye about four; the Duke arrived shortly after, the Queen

---

[1] William Lloyd Thomas, F.R.C.S.

not till near eight, having been delayed by visiting Blenheim and by the cross roads. She seemed extremely well pleased with her whole expedition. There came with her the Duchess of Saxe Weimar[1] who is only one degree less hideous than the Queen, the Prince of Hesse Philipsthal, Prince George of Cambridge, a little Saxe Weimar boy, Lord Howe, Lord Denbigh, Lord and Lady Mayo, W. Ashley and Miss Eden, the heroine.[2] There was nobody else to meet the Queen but the Jerseys, Lord Rosslyn and ourselves. A few neighbours, in addition, filled the dining-room completely. I do not think the Queen's manner is a good one as Queen; whether it is shyness or what, I do not know, but she keeps herself too much apart, and does not find something to say to everybody as the Duchess of Gloucester would. Saxe Weimer has exactly the same German-housekeeper look as the Duchess of Kent, only more ugly; but she seems good natured.

The Queen was very tolerably civil to us — more so than I expected. Lady Jersey never left her for a single moment when she could avoid it and talked incessantly. I wonder if the Queen liked it; they say she is jealous of her.

In the night, the furnace that heats the pipes for warming the house, communicated it to a beam, but the fire was soon put out. Lord S. and I were the only people disturbed, as we slept in that part of the house.

Thursday, October 22nd We were all down to breakfast to receive the Queen by half past nine . . . After breakfast we all walked in the grounds and went to see Copenhagen. Poor Dear! He gets very old; he is blind of one eye and very stiff in his joints, 27 years old. He came up to us and seemed to like being patted and caressed. The Duke stroked him with great affection and said, "Poor fellow, poor old fellow!" They give him mashes and nourishing messes; I heard Lord Denbigh recommending some new receipt of that sort to the groom who was with him. The Queen went away about twelve escorted by the Hampshire Yeomanry. Nobody stayed to-day except the Jerseys and Lord Rosslyn. Lady Jersey talked all dinner time and

[1] Ida, Princess of Saxe-Meiningen, wife of Duke Bernard of Saxe-Weimar, younger sister of Queen Adelaide.

[2] Presumably Emily Eden, the authoress. She often stayed at Panshanger with Lady Cowper, who thought she would make an excellent wife for her brother Lord Melbourne; but he never came to the point.

all the evening, but I was the only permanent listener. The four men took it in turns to go to sleep . . .

Sunday, October 28th Lord S. has settled to go down now to place Cranborne with a Clergyman in Devonshire.

[The Rev. Henry Lyte (1793–1847), Vicar of Berryhead, near Brixham, had originally intended to be a doctor. He was the author of several hymns, including "Abide with me" and "Praise, my soul, the King of Heaven". He was a happy choice as tutor for Cranborne, and afterwards detected signs of future greatness in Robert.]

It poured all day; no soul in London, and altogether it was very dismal. We dined with Lady Salisbury.

Saturday, October 31st Lord S. arrived early in the morning from Devonshire. We left town for Walmer a little before nine, but the roads were so heavy, we did not get there till half past seven . . . Found the Duke quite well and looking well.

Sunday, November 1st Lady F. Egerton told me that when Lord Melbourne was at Oatlands the other day, she asked him if he did not think the Duke of Marlborough was not a person of proper character to have been admitted into the Queen's society at Oxford. He answered, with his usual *nonchalance*, "Why, you know, after one has had O'Connell, one may have anybody!" The Duchess of Sutherland told him how much she was shocked at Lord Mulgrave asking O'Connell to dinner, and Lord Melbourne said, with great *bonhomie*, "Well, if *you* think that, what must other people think?" . . .

Wednesday, 4th Had a walk with the Duke. A blowing day — we went over the Downs, about four or five miles . . . I asked him about the life of Picton, just out. He told me he never had any quarrel with Picton, and did not know from what the report could arise. The only thing like a disagreement that he recollected was that one day the 28th Regiment were running away, "and Picton," said the Duke, "who was a very violent vulgar fellow, was blackguarding and abusing them furiously, and I said, 'Come, there's no use in that — no use in abusing them. They all run away sometimes. They'll stand still by and by and you'll have them all back again. What we have to do is to support them.' And in short I took him up for it — but that was all that passed . . . He was a very brave man and a good soldier. General Miranda first mentioned him to me, and told me he had great abilities, but that it might be dangerous to employ him in the West Indies, as he was beyond measure ambitious and might try to get himself made a King. I was not much afraid of his making himself a King, so that did not signify."

Sunday, November 9th Lady Burghersh and Mr. Arbuthnot were both unwell, so we were only four at dinner, the Duke, Lord Rosslyn and ourselves.

In the evening, the Duke told us some anecdotes of the Peninsular Campaigns; among others of the reason he had to suspect Col. de Burgh, a man recommended by Sir Willoughby Gordon,[1] of giving intelligence to the enemy. In their advance upon Madrid, after the Battle of Salamanca, de Burgh was sent on to see if the enemy had evacuated the town. An escort accompanied him and shortly returned without him. From their accounts the Duke concluded he was made prisoner, but shortly after came down some French Cavalry to attack a body of Portuguese, with whose situation de Burgh was perfectly acquainted. They drove in the Portuguese and carried off six pieces of cannon, which were however retaken by a regiment of Germans. Subsequently, on the march, Alava expressed to the Duke his suspicions of de Burgh, who had returned to the camp a few hours after the affair with the Portuguese.

After entering Madrid, the Duke went one day to see *some ladies* of Joseph's party (I think he got into this part of the story before he was aware), where he appeared in the disguise of a *Commissaire de la Quatrième Division*, and there again he found de Burgh. This the Duke considered an additional proof of his correspondence with the enemy. A day or two after, the Duke was riding with his staff in the Prado, and one of these ladies recognized him. *"Ah! Monsieur le Commissaire de la Quatrième Division, vous m'avez joué un mauvais tour!"* The Duke spoke of the extraordinary negligence in the Duke of York's Army when he was with it in Flanders. They had generally an *avant poste* of considerable numbers posted twelve or fifteen miles from the main body which was continually driven in and cut to pieces: no intelligence, no knowledge of the enemy's movements, no anything. One day when the Duke was dining at headquarters there was a good deal of firing heard in the direction of the *avant poste*; nobody stirred,

[1] Sir Willoughby Gordon, Bart. (1773–1851), Military Secretary of the Duke of York when C.-in-C. Quarter-Master-General Peninsula 1811-12, Quarter-Master-General, Horse Guards till his death. Renowned for his tactlessness.

however, or seemed to think it worth enquiring into; and somebody coming in who was going to England, the Duke of York said, "Mind you tell my brother we are always in fire here."

One trait which the Duke related of himself amused me as it shewed even in that early time, how his master mind took the lead in military affairs. There were some entrenchments thrown up upon the bank of a river which the Duke foresaw would be destroyed immediately by the enemy unless they were defended by artillery. He took upon himself to go and make a representation at head-quarters of the necessity of sending some artillery; accordingly, the next day, there arrived one gun. "Well," said the Duke. "And where's the rest? What? Is that all?" "Oh yes," they replied, "the truth is that the others are not ready, but Sir Charles Grey came down and so we contrived to get off this one, and we told him the guns were gone."

Wednesday, November 11th The Duke receives numerous letters every morning from persons unknown to him . . . Nothing can be more quiet and less exciting than his life. He gets up early, breakfasts before ten and then goes into his room to read and answer his letters and seldom reappears till luncheon time, when he never eats more than a jelly or a biscuit — often nothing. After luncheon I always walk or ride with him for an hour or two, and he was often occupied again till dinner time. We dined at 7, and seldom sat beyond half past eleven. Twice a week he goes out at this season with the harriers, and writes his letters when he comes home. He is consulted upon all sorts of affairs, public and private, by all sorts of people, and the letters he receives, all of which he makes a point of answering immediately, are endless.

But with all this he never seems absent or bored for an instant, always gay, always cheerful, entering with interest into everything that passes, even the most absolute trifles, and extracting amusement from them. His mind is equally energetic to whatever its powers may be turned, and he does not appear to know what a heavy hour is, or ever to feel low spirits or *ennui*.

Thursday, November 12th Mr. Arbuthnot was telling me to-day of a dinner at which Sir Walter Scott met the Duke at his house. Mr. A. drew out the latter who talked in the most amusing and interesting manner of his military exploits. The next day Arbuthnot met Scott in the street. "I was coming to you," said the latter, "to thank you for the great delight you gave me yesterday in hearing Caesar himself talk of his campaigns. . ."

Tuesday, November 17th Returned to Hatfield.

Wednesday, November 18th A beautiful Aurora Borealis was visible this evening, I never saw one before. . .

Wednesday, November 25th Lady Salisbury's affairs seem near a crisis. Her income is so much reduced that it is impossible for her to go on and some measures must be taken about it.

[*Extract from* The Times, *November 30th, 1835.*

Fire at Hatfield House
It is with feelings of the deepest regret that we announce to our readers the fact that a portion of this venerable pile, so long the ornament and pride of our country, has been destroyed by fire, and that the Dowager Marchioness of Salisbury, who presided for so many years over its princely hospitalities, with a grace, a courtesy and a kindness which has endeared her memory to all who were brought into contact with her, has perished in the flames.]

Friday, November 27th I have not written in my journal since this frightful day (I am writing now on the 18th December) but I will try and recollect what I can and set it down.

I was sitting in my dressing room about half past five [p.m.], Lord S. in his dressing gown had just laid down to sleep on my sofa, when I heard an impatient knock at the door. It was the house-keeper, who exclaimed, quite breathless: — "There is fire, a great smoke, from the Dowager Lady's room!" We both instantly rushed to the Chapel, and a great smoke came out. He said, "Keep this door shut!" and passed through and closed it.

Lady S.'s maid was in the Chapel crying violently and much agitated. I remained a moment to soothe her, and told her to stay there and tranquilise herself. I then went through the Gallery, down the Adam and Eve Staircase, and up the staircase beyond the Chapel, with the hope of getting to Lady S.'s room, but the smoke at the top was so intense, I could not proceed. I then got one or two of the men to try and force the door of the Green Room, leading to the Tower staircase, but this also was impossible. Coming back through the Chapel, I met William Talbot and suggested to him to get ladders, to try and enter at her windows.

[The Hon. William Talbot (1814–1888), sixth son of the 2nd Earl Talbot, was one of the two guests staying in the house. The courage and address shown by him so much impressed Lord Salisbury that he offered him the reversion of the living at Hatfield, when it became vacant. Talbot had been in the Navy, but took orders and remained Rector of Bishop's Hatfield till his death. Charlotte Sneyd was the other house-guest. She had arrived on the 23rd.]

After this, I scarcely know what happened, Miss Sneyd joined me and we wandered about, not knowing what to do — crowds of people sweeping through the house, asking for directions, and suggesting measures to be taken — the clang of that awful alarm bell going on all the time till the whole neighbourhood was assembled. We went out into the crowd, and someone said, "They want water, has an express been sent for more engines?" Upon that I walked down to the Inn and ascertained that the expresses were gone. As we returned, for the first time I faced the fire. It was now bursting out of the windows of the west wing on all sides in tremendous grandeur, the showers of flame falling far and wide. The rest of the great pile stood in profound darkness, but in all human probability, a few hours more and not a vestige would be left. From the first moment I had felt hopeless of Lady S.'s fate, but now to see that magnificent palace burning before my eyes was a trial. I felt it would be a hard sacrifice, but I felt at the same time that it was the Will of God, no fault of ours had occasioned it, and, above all, that there *might* be far more worse trials and much more difficult to bear.

Suddenly, I recollected that I had never seen Lord S. since the first moment of the fire. It was a shocking thought. I begged Miss Sneyd to go and enquire in the crowd and try to learn some news of him, which she did, but as I afterwards heard, without success. However, she framed an answer to satisfy me and I remained convinced that he was safe.

[Lord S. had been in great danger. Perugini, the resident confectioner, who had attended him as valet on his continental tours, and Nicolas Hellwin, head cook, had to grapple with him to restrain him from attempting to force the door of the Dowager's room.]

I employed myself afterwards in helping to carry books and manuscripts from the library, which the flames were now rapidly approaching. I got a message from Lord S. while I was still thus employed (tho' my strength was beginning to fail me) to desire me to go to Mardall's the steward's where the children were already gone. As I passed the Gallery, I gave it one parting look, thought of its beauty and its grandeur and the many hours I had passed there, and resigned myself to behold it no more. We proceeded to Mardall's, having to pass under a shower of sparks and flame. Mr. Peele[1] joined us in the way, and spoke a few words of consolation. I thought how far worse it might have been if my husband or my children had been lost. I found the children at Mardall's. We were all sitting sadly together when Faithfull[2] came in and said they had a hope of stopping the fire before it even reached the Chapel. I scarcely believed it at first, but afterwards we went out and went towards the House, and saw the flames indeed rapidly declining.

It was a most providential deliverance. The wind suddenly changed, and drove back the flames, the west wing of the House alone being destroyed. The activity and daring of all our tenants and neighbours was beyond all praise; and all the neighbouring gentry showed every kindness and rendered us every assistance possible.

Without Lord S.'s own exertions and presence of mind, it could not have been saved.

Miss Sneyd and I slept that night at the Inn, or rather *lay* there. Every moment I fancied I heard a rush of people summoned by another outbreak of the fire, and the alarm bell was always sounding in my ears.

Saturday, November 28th Spent this melancholy day chiefly about the house, seeing what was saved. Lord S. was terribly exhausted. I think too, he feels his mother's death very much.

If it had happened in the common course of nature, I could not pretend to grieve, her conduct had not been such as to inspire me with respect or affection, tho' personally, to me, she had always been kind and obliging. Her memory was rapidly failing, in a short time she must have become quite childish, and her pecuniary embarrassments alone would not only have been the greatest annoyance to us, but would have made her miserable. She was 85, and I trust, and try to persuade myself, that she died by suffocation. It is too shocking to think of a person you have lived with, and saw a few hours before, should have died in torture too horrible for the worst of criminals.

[1] The Chaplain of Hatfield House.　　　[2] The Rector of Bishop's Hatfield.

Oh no! I *will* not believe it. For the rest God is judge. She had far more excuses and more temptations, probably, in the course of her long life than many of us have, and I trust stands acquitted in His sight.

[Charlotte Sneyd wrote a letter to her brother Ralph on December 5th, describing the events of the night of November 27th. Her sister Harriet had written on December 1st to say that Charlotte had arrived safely at Cheverells but "quite fagged and knocked up".[1] The short account in *The Times* of Monday, November 30th was produced by Charlotte at the request of the Salisburys. Her bedroom had been next to Lady Salisbury's and William Talbot's just above. Lord Salisbury had been much distressed as he had been mistakenly told that the housemaid who had first perceived smoke issuing from the Dowager's *suite* had run away, leaving a door open. He feared that his mother might have tottered to this door, opened it herself and called in vain for assistance. But it was certain that when the door was opened, all was over already, or the dog who was in the room with his mistress would have run out. "As for the behaviour of Lord and Lady Salisbury throughout the whole time, I can hardly trust myself to speak of it. I feel such admiration for them, I scarcely thought so much deep feeling could have been compatible with so much cool presence of mind and activity — perfectly fearless of danger for themselves and so alive to it for everybody else!" Harriet heard from her sister that the Dowager's affairs had been "in such a state that Lord S. was on the eve of going to town to take steps for selling the house in Arlington Street. She had taken all her jewels to Hatfield." Charlotte mourned the Garter and the pearl necklace. Press accounts said that the Dowager had just dismissed her maid, who had dressed her for dinner, and had asked the maid to add a bedside candle to the two on the narrow kidney-table: — she was going to write invitations to a *conversazione*. The maid departed to tea in the housekeeper's room and it was surmised that the old lady might have set light to a lofty head-dress, bending to write. One of her footmen who attempted to enter her *suite* was overcome on the threshold and had to be dragged out. Fire engines from St. Albans, Barnet and Hertford were finally assisted by one from London. The Yeomanry, under the command of Lord Verulam's heir and one of his brothers, performed

[1] Sneyd MSS., University of Keele, S9 RS/HS 52.

good service, guarding furniture and treasures from the house, covering them with rick-cloths and tarpaulins, controlling the crowd, and assisting the firemen. Lord Verulam himself rode over to offer hospitality to the whole family, but Lord Salisbury would not quit his home where a fresh outburst from charred beams had broken out again at two a.m.]

Sunday, November 29th Returned to the House.

Monday and the following days Remained at Hatfield. I began to feel the depression consequent on such painful excitement more now than at the time. I was so weak I could scarcely go out of the house.

Some of the ruins fell in almost every day, but it has hitherto been impossible to make any successful search for her remains. W. Talbot stayed with us till the Saturday, very useful and kind.

On this Monday, I had two letters from the Duke, one forwarded to London the other here, offering to take us in, children and all, at S. Saye for as long a time as he remains there. This I declined, as Lord S. could not leave Hatfield, but I proposed to go to him for a week. We fixed Tuesday in the next week . . . The children were left behind.

We shall not be losers to any amount in property, the insurance being equal to the damage done.

Tuesday, December 9th Went to Strathfield Saye. The Duke was all kindness — when was he not? Nobody there the first day but Lord Charles — and afterwards Lord Rosslyn and Lord Strangford, and on the Sunday, Edward Drummond. The Duke went out hunting twice while we were there. He rides very hard, like a young man, and does not appear in the least tired or sleepy in the evening.

I was idle about writing this journal and did not set down things as I heard them, as I ought to have done. A story I remember Arbuthnot's telling us at Walmer which would be after the Whigs' hearts as illustrating the old Tory rule. Lord Westmorland, years ago, applied to Lord Liverpool for a Bishopric for a protégé, but met with no success. The application was renewed and at last Arbuthnot was commissioned to tell him that the person in question did not possess *merit* to entitle him to a bishopric. "*Merit*, indeed!" said Lord Westmorland. "We are come to a pretty pass if they talk of *merit* for a bishopric." I happened to observe that I knew Lord Ellenborough *curled* his hair. The Duke was holding an *allumette* at

188

the moment, just going to light the candle at his desk. I thought he would have dropped it. "God bless my soul!" he said, in the most unfeigned astonishment at the notion of a Cabinet Minister and his colleague curling his hair.

Tuesday, December 15th. Returned to town. Dined with the Cowleys.

[Lady Cowley had written to her sister Lady Westmeath, (estranged from her family after her divorce), that their mother had been growing daily weaker in body and mind and she had never seen their brother so overcome. He had risked his own life. Lord S. took the chance to hold out an olive branch, "Fanny sends her love." The Dowager, who had been inimical to her divorced daughter, was now removed.

At the inquest, William Lloyd Thomas, medical assistant to the family, bore witness that he had examined particularly bones of a head, face and spine discovered in a heap of ashes, and remains of trinkets and a large ring often worn by the deceased. He had no doubt from his examination of the dentistry on the lower jaw, that it was that of the late Dowager Lady Salisbury.

Amongst the annoying details in the Press had been statements in *John Bull* that the young Marchioness had succumbed to a fainting fit during the fire, and the Dowager should never have been left alone as she had already nearly burned down her own house in Arlington Street. "She had many miraculous escapes from the effects of fire, and particularly on the occasion of the last Drawing-Room when her ladyship on her return home set on fire the whole of her headdress, which her maid (providentially present) extinguished after it had burnt the hair from her head."

The pathetic bills for her lavish expenditure over a long life came to rest in Hatfield archives — French perfumes, *Oeillet, Quatre-fleurs, Sultane, Prés-fleuri* — a gauze bonnet with white flowers, the blue habit of the Hatfield Hunt, a Gibraltar muslin robe, a court train of rich yellow satin and silver *lamé* — apple blossom lace for her head and for the satin gown to match.

Lord Salisbury received a multitude of letters of condolence. Madame de Lieven surpassed all in appreciation of the late Marchioness, emotionally describing her in a letter to Lord Grey as "Good as she was great". A great grand-daughter, Lady Gwendolen Cecil, wrote in 1923 "The impression which as 'The Dowager' she left on popular imagination in the neighbourhood was a witness to the force of her personality. Fifty or sixty years after her death, old men and women among the villagers of Hatfield would describe with scrupulous detail the appearance of her carriage, the dress of her servants, the splendours of her Sunday entertainments — would repeat the most commonplace remarks as children they had been privileged to hear from her, and recount with pride the most trivial circumstance which had brought them into momentary contact with her. It had been the custom on fine Sundays during the years of her sway, that the Hatfield butler should announce sonorously to the congregation after matins in Hatfield Parish Church, 'Her Ladyship's band will play on the terrace of Hatfield House this afternoon.' A neighbour, Mr. Fordham of Melbourn Bury, used to say that he had seen cards ankle-deep in the Long Gallery at Hatfield, when the evening had grown old and many packs had been thrown from the card tables."

She left also to Hatfield House as permanent record of Irish elegance, her portrait by Sir Joshua Reynolds and a collection of beautiful eighteenth-century furniture, both of which escaped the fire.[1]]

Some remains of poor Lady S. have been discovered which I am very glad of, as it will put an end to the innumerable discussions and suggestions on the subject from all those people who have no other occupation but meddling in affairs that do not concern them.

Wednesday, December 16th The Coroner's inquest was held at Hatfield. "Accidental death." We got down to Hatfield in the evening. The house is still in the most uncomfortable state, cold, dreary and desolate . . .

Sunday, December 20th The funeral took place this morning, quite private — nobody but Lord S., Lord Cowley, Marcus Hill and John Talbot attending, and about 40 of the servants. It was all over by half past nine, I never saw such a melancholy day for the ceremony — dark and cloudy, with the bitterest north east wind and driving sleet and snow. We came up to town immediately after, and the look of a snowy Sunday in London is enough to make one low-spirited at any time, were there nothing else.

Thursday, December 24th Went down to Hatfield. The Duke came down to us. Nobody else there but William Talbot. I never saw

[1] Cecil Papers: VIII, 259–65, and XII, 350–409.

the Duke in greater spirits, full of anecdote and conversation – as usual, very fond of the children, taking Bobby on his knee and putting questions to him upon the different things he learnt.

Xmas Day After church walked with the Duke. He told me Peel was much out of humour with Lord Lyndhurst. Talked a good deal of Mme. de Lieven. "She is not a clever woman. I am a tolerably good judge and I tell you she is not a clever woman. She is an *intriguante*. She is now writing to people of all parties here in England except to me, for I would not answer her letters. Her house at Paris is a *foyer d'intrigues* and Pozzo is very much annoyed at her intriguing here, and the end will be that she will be recalled to Russia. She is under the greatest obligation to me that a woman can be to a man, I mean an obligation of society, as a *preux chaevalier*, and I once said to her, 'Well, at least your conduct proves that you think me the most honourable man in Europe.'"

She professed at one time the greatest aversion to Canning, and always held that language to the Duke, but one morning he found Canning in her room, and from that moment he resolved that he would never call on her again unless by her special request.

For a long time she was in the habit of showing the Duke all the letters she received from Lord Grey. They were in a sort of school-boy style, full of set expressions and fine phrases.

Lady Conyngham was determined on filling the place of favourite as many years back as the Peace of Amiens. The quarrel of the old Lady Jersey with George IV arose from a dispute about putting her horses in his stables at Carlton House. The dispute about Miss Seymour brought him acquainted with Lady Hertford, and ended in Mrs. Fitzherbert having Miss Seymour and Lady Hertford having the Prince. Lady Hertford wrote to him in his last illness but he did not answer her. "He was very brutal to those women whom he left. He was not at all a gentleman about that." He talked of all Lady Conyngham's faults to the Duke (of whom, however, he occasionally thought it right to be jealous), and ended by saying, "But with my age and infirmities it is not worth while looking out for another." "He wanted to make me his confidant," said the Duke, "when he left Lady Hertford and took to Lady Conyngham; but I never would understand him. No woman was ever really attached to him – Mrs. F. perhaps the most. He was too selfish."

[There was no New Year's visit to Belvoir this year. The Duke of Rutland had been summoned from Gorhambury on Sunday, November 15th to attend the death-bed of his son Lord Robert Manners.]

HATFIELD HOUSE

Sketch by J. Hammond; from a volume in the Library at Hatfield House,
Genealogies and other Illustrations of the Cecil Family

PART VI
1836

[At Hatfield 1836 was bound to be uncomfortable. The house proved to have been insured (rather to the surprise of Lord S.) but inadequately in view of the large expense of having to demolish the ruins before re-building the whole of the west wing. This Lord S. directed himself, according to his own designs. The female staff and some of the male had lost all their clothes and personal belongings (and in one case of an intending bridegroom, his life savings). Lady Grey recounted a touching anecdote of the little Ladies Gascoyne-Cecil bringing to their papa, to help him, all the treasure from their money boxes.[1] The Dowager's fabulous jewellery had been one of her principal assets: Lord Exeter and Blondel identified a bit of a ring, and the chain of her quizzing-glass from which the old lady had lately been inseparable.

Lord S. had decided not to sell 20 Arlington Street ("one of the finest houses in London" wrote Fanny) but here also extensive re-building would be needed to bring it up to modern standards. It was not possible to entertain in the accustomed style at Hatfield, nor to be long absent, once the noisy repairs had begun.]

January 1st I ought rather to have begun with December 31st. We had not a large party for New Year's Eve; recent events made that impossible. Miss Sneyd and William Talbot only were in the house. Still, I did not feel melancholy or distrustful. I have much to be thankful for the past year — many dangers escaped, many happy hours enjoyed, and new sources of happiness opened. It is always fearful to look forwards, especially when all changes must be for the worse, but we are all in the hands of Providence: for ourselves and others dearer than ourselves, that is our only trust.

Politically, we surely stand better in everything essential than we have done for a long while past. The spirit of the country is returning, and we are in a more hopeful position than we could have expected to be a twelve month ago.

Saturday, January 9th Went to Burghley . . .

Sunday, January 10th Went in the morning to Church at Stamford with Lord Exeter, the Duke, Lady Lonsdale, Lady W. P. and Captain

[1] *A Family Chronicle derived from notes and letters selected by Barbarina, the Hon. Lady Grey*, ed. G. Lyster, 1908, 110.

Percy. The Duke admired the sermon preached by Mr. Porter, and said it was the best he ever heard in a country church. It was upon the necessity of religious principle in all classes to the welfare of a nation, but strictly religious in its tendency and not political. The Duke wished it might be printed. "That man understands what he is about; that is a sensible man." After church we went over the house and to the stables — weather tremendously cold. In the afternoon we all attended prayers in the Chapel. The Duke in great spirits, taking great interest in all he saw in the house, a portrait of a Countess of Desmond who lived to be 108 particularly attracted his attention.

Wednesday, January 20th Went for one night to the Hoo. Mr. Young, the actor, read some comic Irish stories in the evening, with great effect. I like him, he is a sensible and gentlemanlike man.

[The Hoo, near Welwyn, was the seat of Thomas Brand, 20th Baron Dacre (1777–1851). He had ridden over during the fire to offer assistance and hospitality. Charles Mayne Young (1777–1856) was educated at Eton, but his father deserted his mother and family, and Young became a clerk in the City before taking the plunge after success in some amateur performances. He was a friend of Sir Walter Scott, played many of Garrick's most famous parts, and supported Kemble at Covent Garden. He was supreme until the arrival on the stage of Kean and Macready.]

Monday, January 25th The Duke tells me in a letter that his visit to Drayton has gone off very well, and that he found Peel more reasonable than usual.

[This was a success for Fanny who had been trying for months to get the Duke to accept an invitation to visit Peel in his own home.]

Wednesday, February 3rd Peel has a great meeting tomorrow of members of the House of Commons, the Duke suggested it.

Thursday, February 4th The meeting went off very well. Peel very affable and open and the young members very well satisfied; quite a new *régime*.

An amendment was agreed upon, after all, by Peel and the Duke after hearing the King's speech. Ministers gave way in the House of Lords. The Duke spoke well I hear, and moderately.

He joined us after the House, at Drury Lane, where we took the children to see the pantomime . . .

Saturday, February 6th Called upon Lady Peel, saw Croker[1] there as usual viewing everything *en noir*.

Tuesday, February 9th Several people in the evening. Hardinge came — told me that they were very anxious i.e., Peel and his friends, to have the Duke come up to town before the second reading of the Irish Corporation Bill, that Peel might consult him before he entered into any definite arrangement with Stanley, and thus avoid the awkwardness of last year . . .

Peel . . . had said to Hardinge, "I wish the Duke could get rid civilly of the Duke of Cumberland."

Wednesday, February 10th Went to dear S. Saye. We found the Duke quite alone. I took the first opportunity in the evening to tell him (the Duke) all that had passed between me and Hardinge, and he entirely concurred with me as to the impossibility of breaking with the Duke of Cumberland . . . He observed that many of the Conservative Peers, though not holding Ultra politics or inclined to support the Duke of Cumberland, were yet of the old Tory, Church and King Party and would be highly disgusted at a quarrel with the Duke of Cumberland, especially if brought on without any provocation on his part. "Besides I have no motive for quarrelling with the Duke of Cumberland, the chief harm he does is to annoy me. *I* am the sufferer, who have to keep him in order. I never allow him to interfere with my measures, and if he does any outrageous thing then it will be time enough to quarrel with him . . ."

Friday, February 12th This morning we heard of the death of Copenhagen. Lord S. suggested to the Duke to have him stuffed, and I proposed erecting a monument to him, but the Duke would not listen to either. The Duke was extremely agreeable at and after dinner, telling us many anecdotes of his campaigns. He spoke of Sir Willoughby Gordon as quite inadequate to the office he filled. He was the object of ridicule to all the young officers from his want of personal activity. "We had him on horseback one day for a good many hours. We got back at 6 o'clock, there was to be a ball. And *we* all went to the ball, but this fellow, just arrived from England, full of beef and porter, was obliged to go to bed immediately, and lay there for twelve hours."

[1] John William Croker (1780–1857), politician, essayist, Secretary to the Admiralty, 1809–30, vigorous opponent of the Reform Bill.

Saturday February 13th The Duke was apprised this morning of the intended appointment of Dr. Hampden[1] as Professor of Divinity at Oxford. I copied for him his answer on the subject, and also his letter to Sir H. Taylor, to put the King on his guard with respect to confirming this appointment, and enclosing the Oxford Address for the King's perusal.

We rode afterwards, a delightful day. Pozzo, Lord Burghersh, Lord Lyndhurst[2] and Lord Rosslyn came to dinner. Pozzo extremely amusing in the evening and full of anecdote. Lord Lyndhurst said something at dinner, before all the servants, strongly reflecting on the King. I forget the words, but there was a silence and the Duke turned the conversation. I was amazingly struck with the contrast between Lord Lyndhurst and the others, who were all such perfect gentlemen; and he with his acuteness and ability constantly reminded one of his origin . . .

Sunday, February 14th After Church rode to see some beautiful pictures at Farley Hill. The Duke told me he had a conversation with Lord Lyndhurst and had assured him he would not throw over the Duke of Cumberland. Lord Lyndhurst described the latter as being very much altered and in low spirits.

A Mrs. Dickison, a strange vulgar woman, dined here and took poor old Pozzo for Count d'Orsay. . .

Tuesday, February 16th The Duke went out hunting. Pozzo was very entertaining at breakfast, telling us anecdotes of his early life. He left Paris after the 10th of August (the attack on the Tuileries, 1792) and retired with Paoli to Corsica. Lucien Bonaparte procured that they should be *decretali* and Pozzo had never met him after this till they both dined at Lord Burghersh's this year. Three Commissaries were sent after them, Salicetti and two others and Pozzo advised Paoli by all means to receive them at their landing and never lose sight of them for an instant, by which means they would have no opportunity of doing harm. But Paoli would not take this

---

[1] Renn Dickson Hampden (1793–1868), Principal of St. Mary's Hall. His Bampton lectures were objected to as unorthodox by High Tories. He persevered in retaining the Regius Professorship of Divinity, but was excluded from the board to select preachers for the University. Bishop of Hereford 1847.

[2] John Singleton Copley, 1st Baron Lyndhurst, son of John Singleton Copley, American portrait painter, and Mary Fernum Clarke of Boston Mass., Lord Chancellor 1826.

advice and persisted in remaining in the mountains till they received intelligence that they were *decretali*. Upon this Pozzo again represented the necessity of more decisive measures. "*Si nous restons ici, mon Général, on finera par vous couper la tête à vous, et pour la mienne, elle tombera comme un oignon. Et comme je ne veut pas cela du tout, si vous vous obstiner à rester, moi je m'en vais; je suis jeune et je pourrai servir quelque part.*" At last Paoli allowed him to take what steps he pleased and Pozzo summoned the nearest commandant, and telling him they were in hourly expectation of an arrest, ordered him by the authority he and Paoli still possessed to escort them safely to Bastia. The man wanted to go and consult the other officers, "*Vous ne sortez pas de là,*" said Pozzo; and finally he escorted them to Bastia and they got possession of the fortresses.

Paoli had issued an order for the arrest of young Napoleon, but he was warned in time, by a friend who made a sign from a window as he was walking in the street at Ajaccio, to make his escape, and he got on board a French vessel on the coast.

After the Peace of Tilsit Alexander wanted to send Pozzo into Turkey to negotiate a peace with the Turks. But Pozzo told him plainly that he could be of no use to him under the circumstances, and while he was acting in the same policy as Bonaparte — that he would be required to give him up: that he (Pozzo) could only be an obstacle to a good understanding between the Emperor and his new ally. "*Enfin, V.M.I. feroit bien me donner un congé illimité de voyager — peut-être dans quelque temps vous me demanderez encore.*" They had quite a scene. "*L'Empereur me serra dans ses bras, et moi je fus presqu' attendri.*" And at last the Emperor agreed. But when Pozzo was at Vienna, Napoleon demanded he should be arrested. It was refused on account of his being in the Emperor of Russia's service. Alexander gave him up and said he no longer belonged to him, *and* Metternich warned Pozzo of his danger, who was obliged to make his escape through Hungary, exposed to all sorts of privations and dangers, to Turkey. He came afterwards on board an English ship to Malta and to England.

The war between France and Russia broke out: Lord Castlereagh wanted Pozzo to write to the Emperor. He only consented on condition of stating it was at Lord C.'s suggestion. The Emperor's answer to this letter was very cold. The fact was he still hoped to make it up with Napoleon and thought Pozzo would be an obstacle. Then came the burning of Moscow, and a most eager letter from the Emperor. *"Benez à moi mon cher, tout de suite etc. etc."* Pozzo went in an English ship to Stockholm, crossed the Gulf of Bothnia on the ice, found the Emperor had already left Petersburg and rejoined him at Kalisch.

Wednesday, February 17th. To my great sorrow we left S. Saye for town. Mr. Lyte dined with us — a good account of poor Cranborne in all but the essential point.

[Mr. Lyte had reported in November that he thought Cranborne the most cheerful person in his house. He was learning to row. He had pathetically inherited his father's longing for a military life. He was frank and had good abilities and an excellent memory. It was very difficult to proceed with his reading and writing as most of the books published were for people who had never seen, and he was partially sighted. In May he needed a new ear-trumpet.[1]]

Thursday, February 18th A *soirée* at the Duchess of Gloucester's — about 30 people. The Duchess of Kent and Victoria, contrary to their custom of late, very civil to us. The Duke of Cumberland seemed very much out of humour . . .

Sunday, February 21st The Duke called here — told me all about Lady Westmeath's letters. A reconciliation is evidently out of the question. She is determined to persevere in her quarrel. However, we have put ourselves in the right, so it don't signify . . .

Saturday, February 27th Dined at the Duchess of Kent's. I had an opportunity of conversing a little with the Princess after dinner and was very much pleased with her. She appears as far as I could judge to have a good deal of intelligence and acuteness. She is too short; her features rather good, like those of the Royal Family. Her countenance is rendered rather heavy when she does not speak, by a falling of the under jaw; but when she speaks it brightens up. Her manner remarkably good. Very ill dressed. It was a mixed party, chiefly foreigners. I cannot help thinking there is a change in the politics of that house . . .

Thursday, March 17th Dined at the Duchess of Gloucester's — very pleasant. An amazing improvement in the *régime* since the Duke of G.'s death. A *soirée* afterwards. I hear that the Peels and Stanley

[1] Cecil Papers: XII, 333–8, 427.

met at a dinner at Lord Grey's yesterday, which went off extremely well . . . In the meantime, nothing can go worse than political affairs.

Saturday, March 19th Saw Lady Cowley, very cross and uncertain about going to S. Saye at Easter. The Duke had asked her as my chaperon in Lord S.'s absence. Impossible to depend upon her. Wrote a note to the Duke when I came home to say so, and to suggest Lady Georgiana de Ros.

Sunday, March 20th The Duke, Lord Lyndhurst, Lord Aberdeen, the F. Egertons and William and B. G. De Ros dined here. We have not dinners on a Sunday in general, but the De Ros's could come no other day to meet the Duke. He very kindly asked them to S. Saye, which they will do, and I hope stay, as I cannot remain there without some woman. He has also asked their two children, to ensure their remaining. With my *three*, it will be a perfect nursery . . .

Wednesday, March 23rd Duchess of Kent's concert. Victoria does the honours remarkably well.

Thursday, March 24th Went to the Drawing Room. Dined with the R. Grosvenors. Lord S. set out for Lancashire and Scotland . . .

Wednesday, March 31st Went to S. Saye taking the three children with me. The De Ros's and their two children arrived the same day and Lord Bathurst.

April 1st, Good Friday Went to Church. It snowed all day and we could not stir out afterwards.

Saturday, April 2nd The Duke went out hunting. Lord Rosslyn came.

Easter Sunday, April 3rd Another wretched day; impossible to go out after church. The Cowleys are coming after all, on Tuesday.

Monday, April 4th The hounds meet near S. Saye. We all went out to see them, the De Ros's and children in the pony phaetons, and I rode . . .

Sunday, April 10th Speaking of Dr. Keatr, the Master of Eton, having subdued a rebellion of the boys there, he treated it with great contempt. "You might as well talk of an insurrection in a fishpond. The fish might just as well talk of an insurrection. People do not know what it is to possess *authority*, and the power *authority* gives them, and which they *ought* to use when requisite. You bully your horse and you get the better of him. Why not bully the human animal too, over whom you have authority, *when it is for his good.*" I do not think that this time he was in such a good humour to *raconter* as I have seen him. Whether he was not feeling quite well, or whether he was overtired or had some secret subject of annoyance, I do not know. I had scarcely any opportunity of being alone with him. He took as usual great delight in the children, and the utmost interest in anything that pleased or amused them . . .

Speaking of bravery in the field, the Duke said, "Every man is brave, there is nothing so common. That is what I used to say when the French talked of '*l'honneur*'. One expects a man to be brave as a matter of course. If he is not, when he goes home, his sister won't speak to him."

Monday, 11th April We all came to town . . .

Wednesday, 13th April Went to the great Conservative dinner in Covent Garden theatre. It was a very fine sight – the pit boarded over so as to be on a level with the stage. I should think there must have been above 1200 at dinner, all respectable and substantial looking persons: great enthusiasm, and every time the Church or the Lords were alluded to bursts of applause were called forth. The boxes were filled entirely with women. I was disappointed, however, in the speaking, which was very indifferent. Neither the Duke nor Peel were there.

Thursday, April 14th Lord S. returned . . .

Thursday, May 5th Went to sit with poor Lady K. Barham after this shocking calamity. [Mr. Barham had become deranged.] Her self-possession and strength of mind are wonderful. He is in confinement and it is hoped may not live.

Monday, May 20th The Duke called here. The Duchess of Kent's ball. That young Prince of Saxe Coburg is very handsome. I hope they will not succeed in getting Victoria to take him, which is the object of the Coburg faction. We dined this day at Sir R. Peel's to meet the Prince of Orange.

[Princess Victoria, born May 1819, was now seventeen and her first cousin, Prince Albert, born August, was not quite seventeen. She liked him extremely and seemed quite ready to fall in with the wishes of her mother and uncles. On ascending the throne a year later she panicked and said she could not be rushed into anything. The arrival of the two Saxe-Coburg Princes at Kensington Palace had aroused the fury of William IV who promptly invited his candidates, the Princes of Orange.]

Tuesday, May 31st Went with the Duke and the children to see the Giraffes, beautiful creatures, particularly *gentlemanlike* looking, and their shape by no means such a caricature on a quadruped as their prints had led me to believe. There are four of them, and they all seem in perfect health. Their African attendants were in an adjacent enclosure, and kept from view by a curtain, but the noise they made was incessant — chattering and playing on a sort of national hurdy-gurdy . . .

[This was not the first giraffe to arrive in England. Agasse painted for George IV a picture, still in the Royal Collection, of the Nubian giraffe, presented to him by Mehemet Ali, Pasha of Egypt, in August 1827. It survived only two seasons, at Windsor.]

Saturday, June 4th Strong reports of Lord Melbourne's resigning on account of the Norton Affair, which is certainly to come on; I don't believe he will . . .

Sunday, June 5th The Duke called and stayed with me a long time . . . Speaking of Lady Jersey, he said: "She is a foolish, vain, selfish woman, she has but one merit, and that in my eyes is a very great one — attachment to her children. I never go to see her unless she sends for me. I am always good friends with her in public: I always have some joke with which I attack her, and never give her an opportunity to begin her grievances."

I said, "It is a standing accusation of the Whigs against you that you used to tell her everything, and show her state papers." "I never told her anything."

Wednesday, June 8th Dined at Lord Aylesbury's to meet the Prince of Orange. *He* is agreeable, but the two sons, the eldest especially, appear very stiff and stupid. They always look as if they were mounting guard. They have been brought up entirely for the Army and think of nothing else.

Sunday, June 12th We dined at Apsley House . . . Douro, just arrived from abroad, after an absence of nine months, during which he has never written to his father, and his return was at last announced by the servant, who when the Duke told him who was expected to dinner, added, "and Lord Douro, your Grace, his servant is just come." The Duke is very much afraid he has formed some connection abroad which may prevent his marrying, for which the Duke is very anxious . . .

Saturday, June 18th Went on foot to the Park to see the review. Nothing could be more gratifying than the reception of the Duke. The crowd followed him home cheering enthusiastically. Mrs. Drummond and I with the children endeavoured to follow but we were almost squeezed to death by the crowd. At last we took refuge in Apsley House where the Duke let us out by the garden gate . . . Dined at Sir R. Peel's . . . Peel was talking of the different period of history at which one should have liked best to have lived. He said, "I should have liked best to have seen the court of Louis XVI just before the French Revolution, as an example of the perfection of luxury and refinement, Louis XIV's too was a very interesting time." Speaking of the strange mixture of profligacy and religion at the latter court, he said, "Our court towards the end of George IV's reign was tending very much to the same sort of thing. Lady Conyngham seemed to think that by the forms of religion she could atone for everything else. I wish," he said, "I could recall Sir R. Walpole from the dead, and spend a few hours with him. I should like to see him at Houghton at his ease among his friends . . ."

Sunday, June 26th Dined at Apsley House — a large party to meet the Prince of Orange . . . I never saw such a brute as Prince Galitzin — a mixture of coxcomb and barbarian that is quite insupportable. He asked me when Apsley House had been completed. *"Après les triomphes du Duc,"* I said. *"Et les fenêtres qu'on lui cassées avec des pierres —vous appelez cela aussi un de ses triomphes, n'est ce pas?"*

Thursday, June 30th Dined at Sir G. Ouseley's to meet the Persian Princes. They appear remarkably intelligent and have adopted all our manners, attitudes, etc. with extraordinary quickness. I conversed a good deal during dinner with one of them by means of Sir Gore's interpreter. He abounded in compliments in a high flown oriental style upon everything in this country, and the ladies in particular (the hair and skins of the English Women are what he professes particular [sic] to admire). However, he spoke with great affection of Shiraz and an evident desire to return. He would not drink wine, as it was their Sabbath eve, but confessed that though the priest would not approve, he had no scruple in drinking it on other days. Upon the whole, if I may take these as a fair sample of the Persians, they appear to me fully to merit the appellation that is given them of "The Frenchmen of the East". Gay, talkative, full of *tact finesse* in conversation, and I should think extremely insincere.

[They had already been to a party at Grafton Street on June 16th. "Their dress is not magnificent, as they were obliged to make their escape from Persia in a hurried manner after a defeat, one of them, however, has a splendid scymiter set with the largest diamonds I ever saw."]

Friday, July 1st I was shocked beyond measure on hearing the Duke had a fall from his horse. Thank God! he is not seriously hurt. A water-cart ran against the horse. It *might* have gone over him while he was on the ground! But he has only bruised his knee, which will however, lay him up for some days . . .

Thursday, July 6th Took the children to a little party in Mrs. Damer's Garden. Then returned and went with Lord S. to see the Duke. He is in great spirits but not yet allowed to put his foot on the ground. Katty Barham dined with us. No change in Mr. Barham . . .

["Minney", Mary Georgiana (1798–1856), d. of Admiral Lord Hugh Seymour and Lady Anne Waldegrave, m. Hon. George Dawson who took the name of Damer on succeeding to the property of his aunt, Lady Caroline Damer. "Minney" was the adopted daughter of Mrs Fitzherbert.]

Friday, July 7th Lord De Ros's breakfast. Left it at half-past eight and went with Lord S. to sit with the Duke for the rest of the evening. He showed us his portrait copied in miniature from Mr. Arbuthnot's picture, and which he is going to send to the Duchess of Cambridge. He has endless visitors all day who appear to amuse him, he does not seem the least bored or fidgetted by being confined to his chair, but takes it with perfect good humour and good spirits, and says it amuses him to look out of his window in the Park and see what is passing. He suffers no pain. He talked of Gurwood's forthcoming volume; there are several letters he has been obliged to suppress, among others one in which he speaks of three general officers they were about to send him out. "The first," he says, "is a madman, the second an idiot, and of the third I know nothing."

He told us that he had more than once been obliged to take notice of the continual *croaking* of the officers in the lines at Torres Vedras. "There was not a single officer but myself who was not anxious to

205

embark at any moment. But I did not care a farthing what they thought — only when a general officer is disposed to find fault with the measures of the Commander in Chief, let him go away. They were all at first for following their own plans instead of obeying me, and that continued a long while, even after the siege of Burgos, when we retreated. (We made a *magnificent* retreat.)" He then went on to say that he had ordered the [blank] to move along a particular road before daylight on the next morning — his own headquarters were a few miles further in advance — He waited till after daylight — nothing happened. At last, riding back, he found that after he had left them the night before they had held a Council of War and five Lieutenant Generals had decided upon moving along a different road — Picton one of them. The Duke rode after them, and was in time to prevent their getting entangled in a swamp, and to turn them back again before the French came up. He told us Lord Ellenborough had been with him, very full of some alterations he wanted to insert in the Irish Church Bill which he was persuaded would bring over some members in the House of Commons to us. "That man," said the Duke, "is the most slippery fellow in the world, when any legislative enactment is in question there is no end to his crotchets — it is his whole delight. Just as another man runs wild about a party of pleasure, or a gaming table, or a woman, Ellenborough runs wild about a clause in an Act of Parliament . . ."

Sunday, July 10th Spent the evening with the Duke . . . Lord S. asked how the Ministers at that time came to send over Brougham to negotiate with Queen Caroline. "Because they were the greatest of fools," he said. "I had nothing to do with it. The person I wished to send was Sir Frederick Lamb.[1] He would have gone to Italy, have made himself agreeable to Mrs. Bergami, and Miss Bergami, and all the Bergami's, and have made them understand that it was their interest to keep her abroad. Lord Liverpool could not understand why I wished to send him, in particular. I was the only one of the Ministers who knew the world at all. I went about the world, and I knew that Brougham was holding very different language at Holland

---

[1] Sir Frederick Lamb (1782–1853), afterwards Baron Beauvale and 3rd Viscount Melbourne, third son of the first Viscount and younger brother of William 2nd Viscount, the Prime Minister, whom he survived by five years; ambassador to Lisbon and Vienna; a diplomatist of ability.

House, and Lady Jersey's, and all those places from what he told to them. I knew that Lord Sefton had said to him, 'Now don't keep her abroad and deprive us of such an amusement for the summer.' But the Ministers would not believe a word I said. Lord Londonderry and I had several conferences with Brougham and Denman, and Brougham assured us, when he returned from Calais, that nothing could be conducted with more decorum than her court there, Bergami and all, and nothing could exceed the respect with which they all approached her.

"She was the most impudent devil that ever lived, never handsome, in my remembrance, and doing everything with an effrontery that supplied the place of cleverness. The Dowager Lady Jersey made the marriage, — simply because she wished to put Mrs. Fitzherbert on the same footing as herself, and deprive her of the claim to the title of lawful wife to the Prince."

Pointing to two boxes under the table, one of considerable size, and one smaller one, under the table, the Duke said, "There! those are filled with the love letters of George IV. I had Sir W. Knighton[1] here the other day, and we destroyed as many more."

Monday, July 11th The Duchess of Buccleuch's breakfast. The fire-works were beautiful, and a great number of people assembled in boats on the river to see them. After they were over, someone in the crowd called out for three cheers for the Tories which were immediately given — three cheers for the Whigs — a dead silence . . .

Friday, July 15th I was surprised and delighted to have a visit from the Duke. He came upstairs, instead of sending for me down to him, which gave me great concern as I feared he might suffer from it . . .

Sunday, July 17th Dined at the Duke's. The Duke was extremely amusing after dinner talking with Gurwood over many circumstances in his campaigns . . . The Duke said Masséna ought to have retired upon the Douro after Bussaco. "He would have found himself eventually in the same position, but with this difference, that he would have preserved his army."

He mentioned the infamous conduct of the Commander of Badajoz and the curious circumstance of his stipulating in the capitulation to march out thro' the breach, which breach was obliged to be made

[1] Sir William Knighton (1776–1836), keeper of the Privy Purse to George IV.

on purpose. Several letters were mentioned as being suppressed, particularly one about Berkeley calling him the foolish Admiral.

The Duke had possession during the War of an Army List of the French which he used constantly to study, and acquired from it such an accurate knowledge of the French Army that whenever he could obtain the name of any officer engaged in operations (for which purpose every scrap of paper accidentally found was ordered to be preserved and every means taken) he could judge pretty accurately what regiments were in the neighbourhood and how posted.

He spoke with commendation of the Portuguese peasantry as the best tempered, gayest people possible, ready to submit cheerfully to every privation, and keep up their spirits under any trial. "They will render you any assistance, provided it involves no personal trouble to themselves. If you go into a village and inquire your way, the whole population will turn out, men, women and children, all eager to explain, and bawling after you at the top of their voices if they see you take a wrong turn. But if you propose that one of them should go with you, off they scamper, as hard as they can, and not a soul is to be seen again."

Before the battle of Bussaco, on going to reconnoitre the posts at daylight he found the commanding officer on one of the most important points drunk. Of course he was instantly sent away, but the cause was not made public. I expressed my surprise at such a thing being possible at such a moment. "Oh! he was nervous. A man gets nervous, thinking of his own responsibility; and then he takes to brandy — want of confidence in himself, there's the evil."

Saturday, July 23rd The Duke was here — settling about my taking a house at Walmer. He talked a great deal of his sons and complained of their want of attention . . .

Friday, July 29th Dined at the Verulams. Sir Henry Hardinge, speaking the other day of the Duke's dispatches, said that it was his habit to sit down for an instant where he could (while giving orders to his troops perhaps to advance upon the enemy), and scribble them off as fast as possible, then take up his glass, give another order, and resume his pen for a few minutes more.

Saturday, August 13th Lord S. set off for Scotland, having paired off with Lord Tavistock . . .

Monday, August 15th and succeeding days. Remained in town alone with my two girls, having sent off the boys to Walmer. Scarcely anybody left here. I dined at home and alone every day, intending to remain till the Prorogation.

Monday, August 22nd Went to Walmer, the two girls with me. Got to my own house about seven; found it very convenient and comfortable. A great delight to be once more at the sea.

Tuesday, August 23rd The Duke arrived last night with Arbuthnot at the Castle. Walked up there this morning with the children. Dined there and met the Hardinges who have got a house there, and Lord Ellenborough. A very agreeable dinner. Hardinge talked a good deal about Picton whom he calls the Radical of the army of that day. The Duke said he was the most foul-mouthed fellow that ever lived. Hardinge mentioned several instances of his over-bearing and violent manner. He told us also some particulars of the death of Sir John Moore, whom he saw after he had received his mortal wound.

[Sir Thomas Picton (1758–1815), Wellington's right hand in the Peninsula, fell at Waterloo. A law unto himself, he went into action in Spain wearing a top hat and carrying an umbrella. He was accused of brutality in the West Indies. Hardinge was actually speaking to Moore when the General was hit on the battlefield of Corunna.]

Sunday, August 28th The papers had just announced the change of the French Ministry. Someone observed that Europe was in a state of great confusion. "Depend upon it," said the Duke, "that the state of confusion will never end in the world until it is *governed*. God Almighty intended the world should be *governed*, and it never will go on well until it is." He said that when he was at Cadiz, Arguëlles[1] had consulted him about the constitution and had said that as they had not the practical experience of France and England, it was requisite for them to have a constitution perfect in theory as their best chance of success. "Think of a country governed by theory, and of Spain governed by public opinion. Why, there is no such thing there."

Monday, August 29th The Duke walked up here to see Cranborne, I walked back with him. Dined at the Castle. The Duke told us a curious anecdote about Romana's evasion from the Island of Zeeland. Canning wanted to find some person whom he could trust to communicate with at the time of the breaking out of the Spanish

[1] Agostin Arguëlles (1776–1844), Spanish statesman, Liberal leader in the Cortes.

patriots. The Duke recommended him a man whom he had employed when Secretary in Ireland, a Scotch priest of the name of Robinson.[1] The only credentials this man had was a stanza of a copy of verses composed by Romana and which he had given to Frere. Robinson, disguised as a sort of pedlar, landed in the Island, and found his mission at first difficult to execute. The French were on the alert and Romana himself turned him away several times, saying *"Qu'est-ce-que vous venez faire ici avec votre chocolat?"* At last Robinson found a moment when nobody was by to say, "I have a message for you from the person to whom you gave these lines," and repeated his stanzas. And upon this communication alone, Romana and his 10,000 men effected their escape to the English Squadron.

Tuesday, August 30th Dined at the Hardinges.

Thursday, 1st September The Duke was talking this morning at breakfast of his former colleagues in Lord Liverpool's Cabinet. He said Lord Westmorland was a man of strong good sense who always perceived immediately the strong point of a case, and explained it in the plainest and sometimes coarsest terms which made him often extremely disagreeable to Lord Liverpool, who, though "a very superior man, was like a sensitive plant" . . . Canning's empire over Lord Liverpool was more that of fear than love. Once, when the Duke and L. had had an interview on business with Canning, and were returning together from Gloucester Lodge, the Duke observed to his companion that what Canning proposed would never do. "No," said Lord L. "I know that. I wish *you* would tell him so." The Duke told us that Ashley Cooper[2] had assured him that it was a letter from Canning which occasioned Lord L.'s paralytic seizure. He had received it, read it, and was found immediately insensible, with it in his hand. When Lord Londonderry died, the King wrote to Lord Liverpool respecting the new arrangements in the Cabinet, but adding a postscript "Let nothing change the journey to India."[3]

[1] *See Narrative of a Secret Mission to the Danish Islands in 1808.* James Robertson, Benedictine monk (d. 1820) gave his MS. to a nephew who published it 1863. He was again employed by Wellington 1813. He founded the first blind asylum in Bavaria at the Scottish Monastery at Ratisbon where he retired and died.

[2] Sir Ashley Cooper (1768–1841), celebrated surgeon, lecturer in Anatomy and Comparative Anatomy to the College of Surgeons.

[3] Canning had accepted the Governor-Generalship of India, but resigned it on hearing of Londonderry's suicide and became Foreign Minister.

Lord Liverpool communicated the letter to his colleagues, but witheld the postscript. Had the Duke been aware of the postcript, he would never have consented to Canning's being admitted into the Cabinet. As it was, he was the only Minister who declared that if the King persevered in his repugnance to Canning, he should not be forced upon him. Peel was written to in the meanwhile, and in his answer expressed his readiness either to undertake the lead of the H. of C.'s or to serve under Canning – or in short to do anything that was required. Arbuthnot met Peel one day coming out of Fife House in considerable perturbation, saying that Lord Londonderry had misrepresented his answer to the King, and that he must go to Carlton House and set it right. Arbuthnot went in, upon this, to Lord Liverpool's and found him in tears, wringing his hands and exclaiming, "Peel will ruin it all."

Thursday, September 8th The Mahons and Hardinge dined here. Lord Mahon entered into a very interesting conversation with the Duke on the subject of Southey's *Peninsular War*. The Duke spoke in very strong terms of reprehension of it, saying that he had a bad opinion of Southey for having written a work so much at variance with facts. That he had, it was true, refused him his papers but that he might have had access to the dispatches in the possession of the Government and at all events might have consulted the published Gazettes . . .

The way I pass my time now is this: we breakfast at ten, after which I go down to my own house to teach the children – return for luncheon at two, when some of them accompany me to dine at our luncheon. Afterwards we go out, and dine at seven.

Friday, September 9th Rode with the Duke and Lord Rosslyn as far as Waldershare. He went his usual rapid pace and did not seem at all the worse for it . . . Nobody was asked to dinner this day or the next, in consideration of Mr. Arbuthnot's feelings, the 10th being the anniversary of Mrs. A.'s birthday, which always used to be kept by the family. Mr. A. speaks of her occasionally with perfect composure, but I am convinced that his feelings for her remain the same. Lady Burghersh told me that he had said to her that if ever a woman went to heaven, Mrs. A. would be that person, as she left the world without a thing to reproach herself with. He told her on another occasion, that he considered every day of his life what there was that

211

he could do which she would have wished him to do if she were alive, and that he did it.

Arbuthnot told me some curious anecdotes of Lord Liverpool's irritation of temper. He would break a chair to pieces by dashing it against the ground, when annoyed at something that had happened, and on one occasion, when the Ministers were assembled at Lord Castlereagh's house, upon it being announced that one of them, Lord G. Cavendish, would not vote for them on some particular question, Lord Liverpool began beating himself with his arms, in the most violent manner, and exclaiming in a sort of scream, "D – – n the Cavendishes! D – – n the Cavendishes!" till at last he burst out of the room, continuing these gestures and exclamations through the hall, to his carriage, to the great astonishment of the servants . . .

Tuesday, September 13th Rode with the Duke and Lord Rosslyn under the cliff to St. Margaret's Bay: dreadful weather. Cranborne left us for Devonshire.

Thursday, September 15th The Duke considers Charles X a more able man than Louis XVIII, but misled by bigotry. He told us it was a fact that Napoleon left a legacy to the man who had attempted to assassinate him (the Duke) at Paris!!!

Friday, 16th Speaking of crime, the Duke said he would have capital punishment inflicted whenever the crime was to a certain extent mischievous to society and could be prevented in no other way – *not* for highway robbery, for that might be prevented by other means, but certainly for burglary and particularly for robbing unoccupied houses, as that fell particularly hard on the industrious poor, who were obliged to leave their houses open to go to work. He spoke strongly against the system of canting going on among the visitors of prisons, and the erecting of every malefactor to a saint. "If you tell them in the newspaper that every fellow that is hung was sure of going to heaven, how will they mind if you preach to them of the danger of going to hell?" He condemned the modern maxim that the object of punishment was rather to reform the criminal than to give an example to society.

Sunday, September 18th After dinner, the Duke spoke of Waterloo. The Prussians were decidedly beat at Ligny and he could distinctly see their field of battle from the Quatre Bras, which was about eight miles off. Napoleon committed a big mistake in not moving his forces by the great road from Mons to Brussels. "It was my business to be prepared for all events, and I had thrown up fortifications at Mons — they could not have delayed him long, still, he would have been obliged to break ground there. But Napoleon committed mistakes, just like other people. The great thing in military affairs is never to make a false step, or to go farther than you ought, especially when you are moving in parallel lines with such a man as Napoleon."

Bourmont[1] the writer, came over to the Prussians before Quatre Bras, and there was another man, Navaillac, who came over to the Duke at the same time, and told him Napoleon's army was a splendid one, full of enthusiasm, and cries of *"Vive l'empereur"* from morning till night. "Which indeed," said the Duke, "I could hear from their camp." "But," says Navaillac, "I hear your men can fight, and they may have some chance, the Prussians have none."

Lord Anglesey committed a great fault in not bringing up his cavalry at Quatre Bras. The Duke had ordered them to march in an extended column, but Lord Anglesey, instead of keeping with the head of his column, remained with the tail, four or five miles behind, so when the Aide-de-camp arrived where Lord Anglesey ought to have been, he found them all gone to bed and nobody to whom he could communicate his orders. The Duke went on to speak of the advantages of moving troops in a lengthened column, so that in the case of any check, there should be plenty of room to fall back without confusion. In this way his retreats through Portugal were conducted, and if Sir John Moore had adopted the same plan, his retreat would have been conducted in perfect order, and he would have been able to have made his option of directing his march upon Vigo or Corunna, as he chose. But his column of march was too close, and his troops *entassés* upon each other.

Tuesday, September 20th The Duke dined this day at Dover to meet King Leopold who had slept there in his way abroad.

Friday, September 23rd Walked with the Duke round the wood for a long while, as it was too stormy to ride. The conversation was most agreeable; it afforded me nothing to set down but much to reflect upon and rejoice in.

[1] Louis de Chaisnes, Comte de Bourmont (1773–1846) declared for the Bourbons in 1814, rejoined Napoleon on his return from Elba, but again deserted after Ligny.

Sunday, September 25th Walked home from Church, and afterwards had a long walk with the Duke, in the wood and to the beach, to see the children land, who had been out in a boat. W. De Ros went off this morning to Stuttgart about this sad affair of Lord De Ros, which I hope may prove without foundation, or at least be hushed up . . .

[Henry Fitzgerald, 22nd Baron De Ros, had been accused of cheating at cards. He was called "The Sarpent" by Emily Eden. His brother William had married Lady Georgiana Gordon-Lennox. Olivia, Lady Cowley, the artist, was one of his sisters.]

Thursday, September 29th Walked for some time with the Duke round the wood. We had a very interesting conversation. I asked him what were his sensations when he felt that the day was won at Waterloo. *Me* "I suppose you must have felt secure of the victory when the Guards withstood the famous charge that was made upon them, and what was your feeling at that moment? Did not it surpass all that one can imagine?" *Duke* "It is very singular, but I have no recollection of any feeling of satisfaction. At the time you mention, I was by no means secure of the victory, nor till long afterwards. But I have no recollection of any sensation of delight, such as you describe, throughout the day. *You* can probably recollect all the moments of great happiness which have occurred to you in your life — Well, I can recollect nothing of the sort on that day — if I experienced it. My thoughts were so entirely occupied with what was to be done to improve the victory, to replace the officers that were lost, to put everything in proper order, that I had not leisure for another idea. I remember our supper that night very well — and then I went to bed, and was called about three o'clock in the morning by Hume to go and see poor Gordon,[1] but he was dead before I got there. Then I came back and had a cup of tea and some toast, wrote my dispatch — and then I rode into Brussels and got there about six in the morning."

Me "But now! while you were riding there! Did it never occur to you that you had placed yourself on such a pinnacle of glory?"

Duke "No. I was entirely occupied with what was necessary to be done.

"At the door of my own hotel I met Creevey; they had no certain accounts yet at Brussels, and he called out to me to ask 'What news?'

[1] Sir Alexander Gordon (1786–1815), A.D.C. to the Duke of Wellington, mortally wounded rallying the Brunswickers at La Haye Sainte.

I said, 'Why, I think we've done for 'em this time.' I saw he looked incredulous, and I said, 'Come up here, and I'll tell you all about it' — and so I did. I stayed all that day in Brussels, making different arrangements.

"Among other things, there was a mutiny among the prisoners — 3,000 we had in the gaol, and only 600 troops to guard them. So I sent orders to the Commanding Officer that if they attempted to break open a single bar, to fire in among them, and I sent them word that I had done so, and after that we heard no more of them. Then the Mayor came in great alarm. They had seen some troops they took for the French and fancied they were coming down upon them. I told them there was no fear, Napoleon's Army were scattered to the devil and half way to Paris by that time. I left Brussels the next morning at four o'clock; the second night I slept at Malplaquet; the third I took Péronne; the fifth day I joined the Prussians at Paris. But it was not till after that, till ten or twelve days after the battle, that I began to reflect on what I had done and to feel it."

Me "But the feeling of satisfaction must have come at last, and I cannot conceive how it was that it did not take possession of your mind immediately — that you did not think how infinitely you had raised your name above every other."

D. "That is a feeling of vanity. One's first thought is for the public service."

M. "But there *must* be a satisfaction, and a lasting one, in that feeling of superiority that you *always* enjoy. It is not in human nature it should be otherwise."

D. "That is true. But still I come constantly into contact with other persons on equal or inferior terms. Perhaps there is no man now existing who would like to meet me on a field of battle — in that line I am superior — But when the war is over, and the troops disbanded, what is this great General more than anybody else?"

M. "But that does not apply to you, you are equally great in the Cabinet and in the field."

D. "But I very often fail to convince those with whom I am acting. I cannot always carry them with me. I may be in the right, but when I have done my utmost to bring them over to my opinion, I often do not succeed."

M. "That may be their fault, not yours. If an angel were to descend

215

he could not always be sure of convincing the wrong-headedness and stupidity of men."

D. "At all events, tho' I feel that I am capable of doing or acquiring anything I choose, still, I am necessarily inferior to every man in *his own* line, tho I may excel him in others. I cannot saw or plane as well as a carpenter, or make shoes like a shoemaker, or understand cultivation like a farmer. Each of these on *his own ground* meets me on terms of superiority. I feel I am but a man."

I asked him what his feelings were after Assaye. He said he had a vivid recollection of the mud encampment in which he slept after the battle, and of waking repeatedly, tormented by the idea of the number of officers who had fallen; and a confused notion that they were *all* killed, which precluded every other sentiment . . .

Saturday, October 1st A hurricane of wind and rain all day. Impossible to stir out. Lord S. arrived to dinner. The letter I got yesterday was from him, inclosing a most infamous anonymous one which he had received abusing him for leaving me at Walmer. However, he treats it with the contempt it deserves. I had told the Duke of it yesterday.

Sunday, October 2nd Went to Church and walked home as usual. Had my last walk with the Duke after luncheon. He talked a great deal of Mrs. Arbuthnot — said there was nothing brilliant about her, but that she was a woman of strong sense, with a mind that turned to matters of fact, and very inquisitive about them, and repeated to me his own well known observation when he was first acquainted with her. "She will be a very well informed woman when she had got answers to all her questions." He said she was everything to Arbuthnot, who tho' a clever man, had an anxious restless mind, always worrying himself when he ought to be acting, and depending upon her for advice, for consolation, for everything.

Wednesday, October 5th Went to Hatfield. Found it in a wretchedly uncomfortable state, no room to live in but the summer dining-room. The new wing, however, is getting on rapidly and will soon be roofed in. The chimneys in the rest of the house have been pulled to pieces to search for any beams that might have been in them, and several have been found. The Kitchen chimney is not yet finished and our dinner is dressed in an oven.

[A letter from Charlotte to Sneyd says that her head is not good

216

enough for her to walk on single planks or climb ladders to inspect the re-building, but the old wall has been preserved where possible and new bricks added to old are skilfully dove-tailed. An immense quantity of the most beautiful old oak is coming from a Church in Ghent. William Talbot had walked from Hemel Hempstead to Hatfield this morning and is to dine at Cheverells (the Sneyd's house near Flamstead and Beechwood, on the Sebright estate) on Tuesday.[1]]

Thursday, October 6th and following days. We remained quite alone at Hatfield occupied in getting the house into some sort of order, re-arranging the pictures, etc.

Monday, October 10th Bobby sent to school for the first time at Mr. Faithfull's.

[The carefully-considered plan for sending Robert, aged six, to a local school attended by many of his young friends, including the Verulam sons, kept by the Rector of Hatfield, a man of utmost probity, was a ghastly failure. He was hideously bullied by other boys, "an existence among devils".]

Tuesday, November 1st Mr. and Mrs. Hale, Mr. and Mrs. Delmé Radcliffe and some other country people come here — on account of the hounds meeting here tomorrow.

Wednesday, 2nd November I had an admirable letter from the Duke in reply to my last. He also sent me his correspondence with Charles Greville on the Lord De Ros affair. The Duke, as he always does, has taken the really friendly, high-minded and disinterested line. He will support De Ros if possible — at all events, he will not give up a friend until the charges are proved against him. But I am afraid De Ros is guilty. The Duke's letter to Charles Greville is most excellent. What a pity that all his letters, even upon the most trivial subjects, are not published. They would teach the world how to act according to sound sense and high principle in every occurence of life.

Mr. Arbuthnot left us.

Thursday, November 3rd Alone.

Friday, November 4th We went to Town for the day and returned to dinner. I had a very painful interview with Lady R. Grosvenor. She reproached me with all my conduct to her since her marriage — I think without foundation. Sure I am that I have been the sufferer and that she deserted me before my sentiments suffered any change.

[1] Keele MSS. S/RS/CAS/19, dated November 8th, 1836.

She made me miserable by her altered conduct – but that is over, and feelings that have once been destroyed cannot be revived. She parted from me in anger, and I conclude we are parted for life. I shall ever regard her with the same esteem and admiration, but affection she herself has thrown away . . .

[The difference had been merely political. Lady Robert's grief on the death of her beloved friend three years later was recognized by Lord S. by the gift of a bracelet, once the property of his "poor Fanny".]

Monday, November 7th The Duke has had four artists at Walmer, a sculptor, and three painters employed by Lord Carrington, the Duke of Buccleuch etc. . . . to take his likeness. They occupy him during the whole of the daylight with the exception of half an hour for breakfast, and the intervals during which their apparatus is changed and which he employs in walking up and down the beach for exercise.

He has sent me an annonymous letter he has received about Miss Jervis that I may compare it with the one that I got at Walmer. I have no doubt it is in the same hand, and I suspect they must both be from some habitué of the house.

Tuesday, November 8th I heard with the most sincere concern of the death of one of my oldest friends, Alicia Blackburne. I was much shocked as I did not in the least expect it. We were friends from childhood, and tho' I have scarcely seen her for years, it recalled many painful feelings of past times to my mind . . .

Sunday, November 13th I was much annoyed to-day on finding that Robert had imbibed ideas at Mr. Faithfull's of overstrained strictness with respect to the Sunday, which must end in producing a conviction that all he sees practised at home is wicked and thereby confusing his ideas of right and wrong. It is very difficult to know what to do. Mr. Faithfull's disposition to Methodistical tenets, discouraging every innocent amusement etc., is producing great mischief in the Parish and neighbourhood.

[There is a voluminous correspondence between Lord S. and Mr. Faithfull[1] "On Sabbath day observance". Robert on his Sunday at home had refused to play at "Lamb", apparently a form of leap-frog, with his sisters because Mr. Faithfull said it was wicked. Miss Faithfull had said he could employ himself better on Sundays "running about cheerfully" and reading good books. Lord S., unfortun-

[1] Cecil Papers: XII, 433 *et seq.*

ately, entirely lost his sense of humour. Eventually, Mr. Faithfull said he had used the word "wrong" not "wicked", and that when Robert had explained that his mother let his sisters play "Lamb" Mrs. Faithfull refrained from further comment.]

Wednesday, November 16th My maid announced her intention of leaving me, as she is going to marry. It is quite an event in my life. She has been with me 25 years!

Lord S. has had a conversation with Faithfull who has promised that there shall be nothing of the sort we object to instilled into Bobby's mind . . .

Sunday, November 27th Bobby fell ill of the measles at school and Mildred at the same time, at home. It is a very favourable sort and does not cause me the least uneasiness. Lord Mahon has given me the memorandum of the duel between the Duke and Lord Winchelsea, written by Dr. Hume who was present on the occasion. It is in the highest degree interesting.

Thursday, December 1st Went to Drayton. Got there to dinner. 100 miles. A very comfortable house, very handsomely fitted up; the pictures beautiful.[1]

Friday December 2nd Bad weather. We could scarcely get out. I had however a view of the outside of the house which I think in bad taste. The country flat and ugly. Sir R. and Lady Peel and their daughter live entirely in their private apartments on one side of the house, when they are alone; no servants inhabit that side. Lady Peel teaches her daughter herself; she seems a clever intelligent girl. In Sir Robert's room hangs the famous *Chapeau de paille* picture of Lady Peel.

[Peel began to be interested in collecting pictures when he was in Paris in 1815 and heard from Lord Whitworth that valuable collections were in the market. He had two galleries, one at 4 Whitehall Gardens and the other at Drayton. He employed Lawrence to paint a kit-cat of his wife to form a companion for the famous Rubens of Susanne Fourment, "Chapeau de Poil" (generally mistakenly called "Chapeau de Paille") for which he was believed to have given over £3,000, in 1823. For Rubens's "Triumph of Silenus", once the property of Cardinal Richelieu, later of the Regent Orleans, he gave £1,000. The bulk of his collection including these, and the popular

[1] Drayton, Peel's house, near Tamworth, rebuilt 1797 by his father and re-decorated by Peel.

Hobbemas "Château de Brederode" and "Avenue, Middleharnis" were sold to the National Gallery, by the fourth Peel baronet. The portrait of Lady Peel is in the Frick collection, New York.]

He sees I fancy little of his relations. Two of his brothers were established near him, but we saw nothing of them, and Lady Alice had not been there for six years. The Jerseys arrived to-day. She was ill and never stirred out of her room while we staid.

[Fanny wrote also on Friday, December 2nd to her younger daughter Blanche, now aged eleven. "I am very much obliged to you for your letter, my dear Blanche, which is a very good one and very tolerably written. I am glad to hear Mildred is so well.

"We got here yesterday about six o'clock. There is a large party in the house . . . None of the boys are at home, only Miss Peel, and her sister, a troublesome disagreeable child of four years old. The house is not very large, but very comfortable. There is a fine library, a dining-room, and a small drawing-room which open into a picture gallery of rather more than half the length of the gallery at Hatfield, lighted by skylight and filled with beautiful pictures. The other three rooms do not communicate with each other but only with the gallery.

"As the house is just finished they are all newly fitted up with a good deal of gilding, and altogether very handsome.

"I have not been out yet, as it pours with rain, but the country looks very ugly and flat.

"Tell Mildred that Lord de Grey means to come to Hatfield to see Bianca. He says he is passionately fond of cats, and that before his daughter Lady Fordwich, married, she always used to have two cats in the stable, a black one which always laid on the back of a grey horse, and a white on the back of a dark brown horse. I think that the white cat in the stables should be taught to lie upon Blacky's back. I saw some cats that did the same in Lord Exeter's stables.

"Pray thank Mrs. Faithfull when you see her, for her account of Bobby. My love to him. Yours affectly.

"I quite agree that the expression 'cuts a figure' is a very vulgar one'."[1]]

Saturday, December 3rd Went to see Tamworth Castle with Lord Ellenborough and Miss Peel — a curious old fortress.

[1] "Miss Peel", Julia, who was now sixteen, married the eldest son of Lord and Lady Jersey.

Peel does not think Stanley cordial with us; in Graham he expresses perfect confidence. He was inquisitive about the Duke. I regret the latter should have declined coming. I think Peel is sore about it. Lord Lyndhurst was asked but is still at Paris. Peel thinks there will be a collision between the Houses the first night of the session — that Ministers will bring it on by the King's speech.

He talks with much pleasure of his expedition into France this year. Louis Philippe received him most graciously, and Peel says he is highly Conservative. He showed me a letter and memorandum he received from Lord Londonderry, with an account of his visit to the Emperor of Russia. Peel is evidently flattered by the attention Londonderry is paying him, and observed that whatever faults he had, he certainly possessed some good qualities, particularly *gratitude!* "He has always been so grateful to me," said Peel, "ever since I declared my resolution to stand by him on the affair of the Embassy." He observed that no man's talent in speaking and in writing could present a greater contrast than Lord Londonderry's . . .

Sunday, December 4th Went to church and walked afterwards. In the evening Peel read a sermon and a few prayers afterwards taken from the comn. service, to the company staying in the house and the servants — very impressive and well read. The sermon an excellent practical one, no cant or methodism.

Monday, December 6th Left Drayton soon after six a.m. Got to S. Saye about half past seven (p.m.) in time for dinner — 107 miles. Found nobody with the Duke but Col. and Lady G. De Ros, and Gerald, his nephew, who is living in the house until the Rectory is fit to receive him.[1]

Tuesday, December 6th Rode with the Duke. We talked chiefly of this unlucky affair of De Ros and of Miss Bagot's marriage. The Duke has never given advice to De Ros, except to come back to England, which was certainly the best advice that could be given him on the supposition of his innocence, and on that supposition only could the Duke advise at all. I told the Duke frankly that I thought him guilty, he made no answer, but I doubt not he is of the same opinion tho' he considers it but just to behave to him as an innocent man till he is proved otherwise.

[1] Hon. and Rev. Gerald Wellesley (1809–82), third son of 1st Baron Cowley, afterwards Dean of Windsor.

We spoke of Peel; he made his usual complaints against him. I told him that I hoped he would go to Drayton, it would please Peel so much. He said he would. "But," he added, "I really wanted to come here. I had things to do; and I can't be sent for at any moment to Drayton", or words to that effect. I said that I knew Peel had complained of not being asked to S. Saye. The Duke seemed struck with that and said, "I have often asked him. I would have asked him to meet the party here, next week, but I was not certain of the day etc. etc. . . ."

I told him all that Peel had said that bore at all upon politics – for they have no communication of the kind.

Wednesday, December 7th Rode again with the Duke. He told me there were great divisions at Oxford and seemed to regret the intolerant spirit displayed by the new Vice-Chancellor, with respect to the lectures of the Regius Professor. He mentioned also a sect, quite new to me, which was springing up among the Divines of the University, who consider that the Reformation went too far . . .

Some of the neighbours dined here. Talking of Pozzo, the Duke told me he was on much better terms with our Ministers than he chose to appear and intimated that he had been a sort of spy at S. Saye . . .

Thursday, December 8th I told the Duke all that had passed between me and Lady Robert. He said that hers was the same turn of mind that existed in others of her family, particularly Lord Cowley and her brother Gerald – an unfortunate disposition to suspect her best friends and think herself neglected by them. And speaking with much feeling, he said, "One can only pity those who are subject to such unfortunate feelings, and do all one can to show them how groundless they are. Have you written to her since?" I said, "No." He looked surprised – "What! you have done nothing? Write to her by all means, immediately, the kindest letter you can." I did.

Saturday, December 10th Speaking of the Duchess de Berri with great contempt, he said that she had been guilty of one of the most wicked actions a person could commit, that of encouraging a people to insurrection . . .

Of George IV and Charles X, the Duke said there was no comparison as to the two in the drawing-room. Charles X was so infinitely superior as a gentleman But on horse-back, at the head of his troops, he was a mere *péquin*.

I received a letter from Lady Robt. written with the same intention as mine, and which had crossed it. Nothing is so foolish and disagreeable as a quarrel, and therefore I am glad this is made up, and I hope we shall always be on good terms for the future. Besides, the Duke wished me to make it up, and that is enough.

Tuesday, December 13th I had a long walk with the Duke. He talked to me confidentially, as he often does, about his sons, whose neglect of him is certainly unpardonable. He showed me a letter he had addressed to Douro this year, pointing out to him the obligations he lay under to marry and continue his family, and a similar one to Charles, in which he made him the very handsome offer of enabling him to marry whom he chose. I think this subject dwells very much upon his mind.

He spoke too on a subject I never heard him approach before — the Duchess. He said she was one of the most foolish women that ever existed — a sort of wise and meditated folly, an obliquity in all her views of things, which it was impossible to remove.

"She was very vain. She thought herself the *prettiest* woman in the world (she had been pretty in her youth), and the cleverest. She used to buy a great many books, and write her name in the title page, but never read them. She always professed a wish to do everything to please me, but if I desired anything might be done, the wish was complied with at the moment and then it was always neglected afterwards.

"In her observations upon other women (and she was very censorious), there never was anything that showed observation or discrimination of character. The remarks she made upon *one* would have done equally for half a dozen others. She spoilt my sons by making everything give way to them, and teaching them to have too high ideas of their own consequence."

He told me she got into debt when she had the management of the house at S. Saye, £10,000, that he implored her to tell him if that was all, and she solemnly asserted that it was — but when she died he discovered debts to the amount of £10,000 or more. These debts preyed upon her mind, and she was constantly wretched about them. He cannot imagine how the money went, but supposes she gave a great deal to a sister of hers who married a Mr. Stewart, who was connected with a banking house that broke.

He laughs extremely at the notion of his being in love with Miss Jervis. "What is the good of being 67 if one cannot speak to a young lady?" He says she is mad, but has talent and intelligence, though with less powers of conversation than any educated person he ever saw . . .

Thursday, December 18th Left S. Saye at 6 in the morning – passed the day in town and got to Hatfield to dinner. Found Mildred quite well. Blanche and Eustace recovering from the measles.

Tuesday, December 20th The ball at Gorhambury.

Wednesday, December 21st Bobby at home for the holidays.

Thursday, December 22nd Everybody else left us, except Mlle. D'Este.

Sunday, Xmas Day A good deal of snow falling.

Monday, December 26th A hurricane of wind and snow. Impossible to go out. Almost all the roads stopped up.

Tuesday, December 27th The snow ceased to fall, but the drifting has completely stopped all communications. Mr. Percy who was to have gone yesterday is unable to move; and of course nobody can come. The Mail from London did not come in this evening, and the Glasgow due this morning at three is not yet arrived.

Wednesday, December 28th To our great surprise Mr. and Miss Sneyd came, having gone round by Barnet from St. Albans. Miss Sneyd set out on Monday from Cheverells, 15 miles off, and was stopped half way, at the inn at St. Albans, by the snow. The mail came in to-night from London, the want of horses had stopped it yesterday. The Glasgow arrived at 12 to-day.

[Miss Sneyd had been fortunate. Christmas 1836 made history in Hertfordshire. A mail coach went off the road in a blizzard north of St. Albans, and south of the town a chariot, containing two ladies, was discovered accidentally, almost buried in a drift.]

Thursday, December 29th Mr. Percy left us for town on the report of the road being clear. The coaches come in, however, very slowly from the north, and the frost continues.

Saturday, December 31st More snow has fallen, but in no great quantities. The roads still bad towards the North, but pretty well cleared about us. Edward Drummond came. We had a gay New

Year's Eve. The children acted charades, danced, etc., and brought the New Year in joyfully. May it answer to its commencement, and may I feel the thankfulness I ought for the many, many blessings of which it finds me in possession, and for the causes of happiness, so far beyond my hopes, or deserts, of which the last has been productive.

PART VII

1837: January–September

"A RAINY MORNING IN THE COUNTRY"

Sketch by Olivia Wellesley, née De Ros; from an Album of the 2nd Marchioness of Salisbury

"The Duke of Wellington was talking of the life in country houses in the winter, and observed upon the immense waste of time in the manner of passing the day and the inconvenience of it to a man like him who when he was either out or receiving company at home could scarcely find time to answer his letters. 'I, who have been engaged in business, commanding armies *or something of that sort* all my life, can scarcely conceive how people contrive to pass their time so totally without occupation.' "

A Rainy morning in the ...

I

Monday, January 2nd The weather begins to look like a thaw; the roads are improving. The neglect in not clearing them more rapidly is generally complained of. Lord Aberdeen called here on his way to Belvoir.

Tuesday, January 3rd Set off at five in the morning for Belvoir. We started so early in order to be prepared for any accidents or stoppages we might meet with on the road. We took four horses and accomplished the journey much sooner than we expected, as we got in soon after four — 100 miles. The Duke overtook us on the road near Stamford. He was snowed up the other day at the inn in Marlborough in his way to Badminton.

Wednesday, January 4th The Duke of Rutland's birthday began as usual, by the firing of cannon, announcing that he had attained the age of 59 years. The weather so bad I allowed myself a rest to-day . . . A ball as usual in the evening at which all the servants and tenants danced. I began it with the Duke of Rutland. The Duke could not dance on account of his lameness.

Thursday, January 5th Never stirred all day. The Duke occupied almost all day in writing — never appeared in the living rooms between breakfast and dinner the whole time of his stay. In the evening John Wortley was speaking of an anecdote in the new edition to Lady Mary Wortley Montagu's Letters of the irruption of ladies into the House of Lords commanded by the Duchess of Queensberry. The question was who could be put at the head of a similar manoeuvre to-day at the present day. "Tell me exactly what they would be required to do," said the Duke "and I will name you a commander." After a moment's reflection he said, "The Duchess of Northumberland."

Friday, January 6th I thought he was tired in the evening. He went to bed early. We danced the Coquette till one o'clock, with the servants to make out. Drew the Queen to Comte Zichy's[1] King, it being Twelfth Night.

[1] Count Eugène Zichy, described by Queen Victoria as "renowned for his magnificent turquoises and famous valsing—a good natured *élégant*".

Saturday, January 7th Drove out by way of seeing the hounds throw off in a snowdrift, for the snow was by no means gone, saw nothing of course — except Bottesford Church, where there are really some very curious monuments of the Rutland family. Went in the afternoon to Belton . . .

Sunday, January 8th Went to church in the morning, and in the afternoon attended the Chapel in the House. An admirable organist, the large golden candlesticks on the altar, and the massive silver crucifix at one end of the gallery, besides a *soupçon* of incense, reminded one more of the Catholic service than I should have expected in the house of such an ultra-Protestant. *I* always regret that our service has not more of these accompaniments and I am fully of opinion that with respect to these outward appeals to the senses, our Reformation went too far.

Monday, January 9th Started for Hatfield at seven. The Duke and Lord Aberdeen at the same time, and we all arrived nearly at the same moment — at six o'clock. The Duke was in great force and did not seem at all tired.

Talking in the evening of the siege of Badajos, Lord S. asked him if there had not been some mistake committed there in the attack. He said no — that when he had carried the castle he knew the place was taken, and called the men off from the breach in the wall. The next morning, at daylight, he went in, and as he crossed the great square he was saluted by a *feu de joie* with ball cartridge, by some of his own troops, who were completely drunk and had stationed themselves all round the square for that purpose. Speaking of plunder, he said, "It is impossible to prevent it entirely, but after a certain time you must stop it for your own sake. The troops begin plundering each other and eventually their officers, and everything is in confusion."

He said that his letter to Whitbread[1] in the 7th volume originated in an attack made by him upon the Duke in the house of Commons, after the passage of the Douro. The Duke wrote to him, in consequence, a letter which does not appear. And after the retreat of Masséna, Whitbread wrote again, acknowledging his error, which produced the published reply from the Duke . . .

Saturday, January 14th and following days. I had a little touch of the influenza and kept the house . . .

[1] Samuel Whitbread (1758–1815), Whig politician, social and financial reformer.

Sunday, January 21st Received the account of Lord Rosslyn's death. I have scarcely ever been more grieved. Notwithstanding his great age, his health and activity might have led me to hope his days would be yet much prolonged. I have spent so many happy hours in his society, the remembrance of him is so associated with all I have enjoyed and valued most, that I deplore his loss with a bitterness of feeling that it is long since I have experienced. And to many a sad reflection it gives rise! He was universally popular and will be universally regretted. In him the Duke has lost a real and steady friend and a most useful assistant, whose place, politically, it will be difficult to fill.

Monday, January 22nd Nobody left here but Hardinge and Sir Walter [James]. The former very agreeable and full of anecdote, but I think he is an intriguer. He is in correspondence with Sir H. Taylor and told me the King was inclined to try a Ministry of Lord Grey's and was actually corresponding with him, more, however, *complimentarily* than politically. Hardinge complains bitterly of the Duke's not going to Drayton etc. . . . Whether he really wishes him to keep well with Peel, for the present, or is preparing an excuse for Peel to break with him, I don't see yet . . .

Saturday, January 28th Lord Wharncliffe[1] here, and several other people were to have come, but were kept away by various causes and we had him all alone.

He looks forward, I am sure, to being shortly in office. He says that Peel is in high spirits from his reception at Glasgow and Lord Lyndhurst returned *en jeune garçon* from Paris, with innumerable conquests and a new wig, ready to fight the more serious battles of the Constitution. Nobody knows or guesses what line Brougham will take. The announcement of the intentions of the Radicals as contained in the speeches at the Bath dinner, and in Molesworth's[2] articles in the *Westminster Review* are said to have dismayed the Whigs and increased Lord Melbourne's desire to be out of the scrape. Lord Wharncliffe

[1] John Stuart-Wortley-Mackenzie, 1st Baron Wharncliffe (1776–1845). He was elected in 1818 as Member for Yorkshire, the most important County Constituency in Great Britain. A moderate Tory; his daughter married John Chetwynd Talbot, a Hatfield nephew. Lord Privy Seal in Peel's Ministry 1834, President of the Council 1841, but opposed Peel on the Corn Laws.
[2] Sir William Molesworth (1810–55), friend of Jeremy Bentham and John Stuart Mill.

told me that the King thought Lord Melbourne's conduct on the occasion of the Conservatives last coming into office was ungentlemanlike and unwarrantable; for he gave the King in his last conversation with him, previous to going out of office, every reason to suppose that he was perfectly satisfied and even recommended him to send for the Duke. The King always speaks of Lord Grey as a gentleman, and a man who has acted honourably by him. Lord Wharncliffe told me that when the plan of the first Reform bill was presented to the King for his approbation, Lord Grey had an audience of him at Brighton which lasted about two hours, at the end of which time he came out and informed Sir H. Taylor that the King had agreed to the bill in all its details, and even seemed surprised himself at this prompt acquiescence. Taylor was so much astonished at it that he could not forbear saying, when the King made a boast of it afterwards, "I thought Your Majesty would have taken more time for consideration — a fortnight, or something of that sort."

Monday, January 30th We came up to Town for the season. Lord S. dined at the Duke's — the dinner usually given to the leading Peers of the party . . .

Thursday, February 2nd Went to the Olympic theatre with Mlle. D'Este, the Duke, William De Ros and Captain Percy — very good . . .

Sunday, February 5th The Duke called here before he went out of town to ask us and the children to spend the Easter at S. Saye. Lady G. De Ros spent the evening here, full of anxiety about the approaching trial. It is to be hoped that at least Lord De Ros may get a verdict as will enable his friends to support him. Of his *real guilt* I have not a doubt . . .

Thursday, February 9th The Duke called here. He will not allow that there is likely to be a change in the Ministry, which seems to be the universal opinion. But I think it is because he is determined not to allow it. Dined at Mlle. D'Este's.

Friday, February 10th The Duke called and brought me a gold chain as a souvenir. [Of her wedding-day, February 2nd.] I was going to say something about the value I put upon it. I won't. One should only attempt to put down what one can express. The trial is this day. I got a note in the evening from John Talbot to say it was going decidedly against De Ros.

Saturday, February 11th The Verdict *is* against him. Those poor people, how I pity them! — under the greatest of earthly misfortunes — disgrace. Though it can, in no way attach to them personally. But it is dreadful to be ashamed of the name one bears.

Sunday, February 12th We had some discussion what should be done about Lord de Ros. I am clearly of opinion that Lord S. having supported him in the utmost as long as his guilt was doubtful, owed it to himself and to Society to draw back, now it was proved. He has decided to adopt that course.

Monday, February 13th Poor Lady Georgiana came to drink tea here. She is quite overwhelmed. But I am glad to find that she seems prepared for the course her friends must necessarily take on this sad occasion, and does not expect or wish her brother-in-law to be received.

A few of his former set have been to call upon him, but in such a case of clear proof he cannot but be exiled from Society . . .

Sunday, February 19th Dined with the Lockharts to meet the Bishop of Exeter. Mr. Lockhart showed me a curious passage in "Don Juan", certainly alluding to Lord . . .

> "There was the preux Chevalier de la Ruse,
>   Whom France and Fortune lately deign'd to waft here,
> Whose chiefly harmless talent was to amuse;
>   But the clubs found it rather serious laughter,
> Because — such was his magic power to please —
>   The dice seem'd charm'd too, with his repartees."[1]

Whist was De Ros's game. Byron was incorrect in speaking of loaded dice. De Ros was accused by a fellow Clubman Mr. Cummings of marking cards and shuffling so that he obtained high cards. The Duke, never suspecting that De Ros was guilty, had advised him to come to England and face it out, bringing an action for slander in the court of King's Bench. Lyndhurst, Alvanley and others of the Salisburys' circle attended the trial at which clubmen divulged that they often played very deep—winning up to £30,000, and had continued to play with De Ros in spite of their suspicions. He left England for Rotterdam directly after he was declared guilty, but

[1] "Don Juan", Canto XIII, v. LXXXVI: See Annual Register 1837, Chronicle p. 13.

returned to die in seclusion "of a dropsy", in his villa in Grove Road, St. John's Wood, March 29th, 1839. He was buried in Kensal Green Cemetery, and his brother William succeeded to the title.[1]

Wednesday, February 22nd Lady K. Barham and her brothers and Lord Ellenborough dined here. The latter, talking over the possibility of a new Govt., mentioned a proposition he had heard from someone — not a member of the House of Lords — that the Duke should go to Ireland. It is an absurdity. The House of Lords could not go on without him. He has it in his pocket. I am sure the proposition is Hardinge's to get rid of the Duke . . .

Friday, March 3rd Lady Stanhope's. The Ministers brought forward their measures upon Church Rates this evening which it is supposed, on our side, will do them great injury with the country. They seem suddenly to have suspended all their haste, and talk no more of immediate resignation.

[The Cabinet was playing for time. The King was ill and his death would mean a dissolution and General Election.]

Thursday, March 16th I heard from General Gascoyne that the King still hankers after a coalition Ministry — Spring Rice and Lord Lansdowne to be added to the Tories. He remains of opinion that the Reform Bill was a beneficial measure, and that in a few years, perhaps seven or eight, all party divisions will subside and the country will enjoy more prosperity than before — and that he trusted he should live to see it, as he conceived his life to be as good a one as that of any man of his age.

Monday, March 20th Went to S. Saye with the three children. Found only Lord Douro and Gerald with the Duke. After dinner, speaking of Lord de Ros and an intention that had been entertained by Lord Winchelsea to move that he should be expelled from the House of Lords, the conversation reverted to Lord George Germaine, and the circumstances of his expulsion from the Army. The Duke observed that his conduct was probably occasioned by something worse than cowardice — by a factious spirit.

[Lord George Germain (1716–85) M.P., after a distinguished military career (he was wounded at Fontenoy) was dismissed the service after Minden where he had failed to respond promptly to

[1] There are many allusions to the affair in Cecil Papers — Letters of the Duke of Wellington, 235 *et seq.*

repeated orders to advance with the British cavalry, to support Prince Ferdinand of Brunswick, the Allied Commander-in-Chief. He was refused a court-martial in England and officiously warned that if the finding of the court was adverse he would certainly be shot, like Byng. He persevered, and in spite of a spirited defence was found guilty, and dismissed from all his military posts and the privy council, in April 1760. After the accession of George III his name was restored to the privy council and he was received at court. He was created Viscount Sackville 1782; a motion in the Lords that he was an unfit person for the peerage being still under sentence of courtmartial was rejected. He was haughty and bad-tempered in official intercourse.]

Speaking of Evans he said it would not be possible for him to form the projected junction with Espartere on account of the nature of the country, and that he would be forced to retire.

[General Sir George de Lacy Evans (1787–1870), Peninsular veteran and radical reformer, had accepted the command of a British Legion, raised by General Alava, Spanish Ambassador in London, and allowed by Melbourne's Ministry and the King, to serve the Queen-Regent in Spain. In May 1836, Evans raised the siege of San Sebastian, with heavy loss, in October defeated a Carlist attack. The campaign of 1837 opened with his defeat at Hernani, but in May he took Hernani and Fuenterrabia. In June, the remnant of his gallant legion was brought back to England, the two years for which it had been recruited having expired. It had been starved and neglected by the Spanish Government. The Duke had disapproved of the whole concern.]

Tuesday, March 21st When we were at breakfast this morning the accounts came of Evans' repulse and defeat at Hernani; and we were all struck with the correspondence of the event with the Duke's predictions.

The Duke told me that he thought they were in a scrape about the Irish Municipal Bill; however, they should have thought about that last year, before they brought in the measure. "I won't give way."

Colonel and Lady Georgiana De Ros and their children came today. With his usual consideration, the Duke had not asked anyone to meet them for the first day or two. She looks very ill, and he seems depressed, but shook it off a good deal after being here a short time.

235

The Duke expressed a very high opinion, in the course of conversation this evening, of the English Navy, as it was when he knew it. Every officer, he said, on quarter-deck, understood his profession, and was capable of putting his ship in any position required. Some conversation ensued about Rodney and the new line of battle introduced by him, which I cannot now recollect.

Of James II he said that his work was the most able military book he knew. His conception of James's character is that he was a man of great ability and the mistakes of his life were wholly owing to his extreme bigotry. He thought little of William III as a military man.

Of Charles X he repeated what I have heard him so often say, that he was a *péquin*, who did not know how to show himself to the troops: and telling a story of an old serjeant in the 33rd regiment who, whenever a man was deficient in any capacity, always observed, "He! why, what could you expect of him? D – – n him, he *can't form!*"

The Emperors Alexander and Nicholas, the King of Prussia and the Emperor of Austria, though they could not command armies, could at least show themselves to the troops. He told us that when the French Royal Family came over here, after the *trois jours*, Lord Burghersh went to see the Duc d'Angoulême, and in his downright way asked him why *he* did not go out and head the troops in Paris, as his father did not. *"Il ne me l'a pas ordonné"* replied the dutiful son.

He was reading over to me this morning some of his letters, preparatory to their being published in the 8th. volume of the Dispatches, which is coming out. He laughed very much at the postcripts of one or two of the letters, intimating where the hounds were to meet, and at a letter to a Portuguese who complains of the use made of his stables – dated Freinada, 4th February.

We were all looking in the evening over some Spanish Maps of the Duke's and trying to trace the movements of the Carlists and Christinos. The Duke showed us the line of country Evans ought to have occupied, along the valley of the Borunda. His position at St. Sebastian, he said, was a false one, maintained solely to afford the British ships an opportunity for co-operation, and that it was impossible from the nature of the country that he could keep up his communications in that situation.

Wednesday, March 22nd Another horrible day; the snow quite deep.

Somebody said the accounts of Evans' troops plundering were exaggerated. "I should be sorry," the Duke said, "to be a clean shirt on a hedge in their way."

Thursday, March 23rd Lord S. and Ed. Drummond arrived after dinner . . . The Duke showed me today the correspondence with Dr. Hampden — so admirable for temper, good sense and clear argument that I am quite grieved the other is at last sensible of the mischief it would do him to publish it . . .

He was talking of the dreadful state of the country after Masséna's retreat. When the French retired from Santarem, the road by which they were to go was choked up by mud. Such was their wanton love of destruction that they tossed the mud into the houses on each side of the way. And whenever the British occupied a town or a village after them, nothing was so common, upon opening a door of a closet or a store-room, as for a dead body, set upright, to come tumbling down.

The Portuguese have an extraordinary fondness for illuminations and illuminated every village the night he slept there . . . Speaking of the incapacity of the Spaniards, he said, "No Spaniard ever could learn anything."

There were six young Spaniards, of the best families, with the Army, but they never could learn anything, tho' they came for that purpose. The whole of the French Army might have been stopped in their retreat on the Bidassoa had it not been for the impossibility of the Duke's communicating with Sir T. Graham.

Gurwood told us that Louis Philippe had said, "Do you think I would send my troops to assist a nation who were 800 years driving out the Moors? And, after all, to come back, if they ever did come back, imbued with constitutional principles?" . . .

Easter Day Went to Church. The Duke did not go out again. Heard to my great concern of the death of poor Louise Fane.

[*Gentleman's Magazine* March 23rd, "In Lower Berkeley St. in her 15th year, the Hon. Maria Louisa Fane, eldest daughter of Lord Burghersh." Louisa Fane was the only daughter of the Duke's niece Priscilla Wellesley who had married the heir to Lord Westmorland.]

Monday, March 27th Lord S. returned to town. Lord Redesdale and Miss Mitford here. The Duke went out hunting . . .

Tuesday, March 28th I think the Duke feels for poor Lady Burghersh's

237

loss deeply. He hears every day from her friends. He seemed anxious while poor Louisa's fate was in suspense, and when the fatal news arrived he said in a hurried voice, two or three times, "Poor thing! Poor thing!" and then after a few moments' silence he seemed to make an effort and throw it off his mind, and there has been no mention of it since. But with me alone he has recurred to it once or twice. Those who are intimate with him alone know the command he possesses over his feelings, and the impossibility of knowing what is passing in his mind from his countenance or manner in general society.

Thursday, March 30th The Duke went with Gerald to attend a meeting for the building of Churches at Winchester, but returned to dinner. I went in the morning with Miss Mitford and the De Ros's to Bramshill. I had a violent pain in my side on the way there, and felt otherwise unwell.

Friday, April 1st Lord Redesdale and his sister left us. I felt still very unwell and send for the apothecary who says it is an attack of liver.

Saturday, April 2nd No better, but still I can go about, and trust not to be laid up here.

Sunday April 3rd Better; the first fine day. In the evening he gave us some very amusing accounts of Mme. de Stael. He says she was the most agreeable woman he ever saw, "If you kept her light," but apt to get heavy in hand and run into discussions. He has read, or attempted to read, her *Allemagne*. All he observed upon it was, " *Was there* ever such a book! and *not true!* She talks of the State of Germany, which she knew nothing about."

[Germaine, Baronne de Staël (1766–1817), daughter of Jacques Necker, Swiss Statesman and financier, married Baron de Staël Holstein, Swedish Ambassador to France, 1786, and published *D' l' Allemagne* 1809.]

He told us an amusing anecdote about an Indian *vakeel* who came into his camp before the Battle of Assaye. The Duke asked him the number of the enemy which he reported pretty correctly, and afterwards showed him his own forces, their number and dis-

---

[1] See *Madame de Staël et les Anglais*; Sir Gavin De Beer, Geneva 1967; *The unpublished correspondence of Madame de Staël and the Duke of Wellington* 1815–17 ed: Comte Victor de Pange, Paris, 1965.

positions. He then asked him what he thought would be the event. The *vakeel*, with Eastern politeness, made an equivocal answer to the effect that the battle was not always to the strong. However, when the Duke saw him after the victory he confessed that he had considered him a madman.

Tuesday, April 5th Went to Town. I was obliged to go for some days to the Clarendon Hotel, as the House in Arlington St. was not ready to receive us. Dined this day with the Cowleys.

Thursday, April 7th The Duke called here. I felt still so unwell that I sent for Dr. Hume.

Saturday, April 9th Removed to Arlington Street where we remained for some time in a most uncomfortable state — the house full of workmen and hardly a habitable room. I got rather worse than better and shut myself up and seriously set about being cured.

Sunday, April 10th The Duke here; I showed him all that is in a tolerable state in the house.

From this time I continued for the next fortnight very unwell and neglected this journal for a considerable time. I will put down here, however, anything that occurs to me as remarkable in the interval before I resume it.

Tuesday, April 12th Was in the greatest alarm for my poor little Eustace who had an attack of inflammation on the chest. Thank God! he recovered, but we were not quite easy about him for several days.

It was in the end of April, I think or, beginning of May[1] when I heard of the death of Mrs. Lockhart. She was a most excellent person and is an irreparable loss to her husband and family. In the beginning of May, Cranborne came up from Devonshire to receive the benefit of the advice of a Mr. Turnbull who has effected some wonderful cures of blind people. They are accomplished entirely by friction with certain preparations. His progress hitherto (*June 18th*) has been most satisfactory, though slow. It would indeed be a blessing we have long ceased to hope for if he could regain his sight.

[Dr. William Turnbull, junior, published in 1805, with a memoir, the medical treatises of his father (who died in 1796) a Hawick practitioner who had come south as physician to the Eastern Dispensary. Turnbull junior's treatment produced no lasting success in the

[1] Mrs. Lockhart died May 17th, 1837.

case of Cranborne, which continued to be sad. A German attendant stole the blind boy's watch, and borrowed money, the next was tactless and bad mannered. Cranborne continued to move between Devonshire and Hatfield. He was put on a steamer at Dartmouth and arrived at a wharf on the Thames.[1]]

June 8th Dined with the Sébastianis. The Duke brought us home in his carriage. Speaking of the King's illness and of Sir H. Halford's report of it, he said, "That man has so many thousand people pass through his hands that he talks of a death with the utmost coolness. I do believe there is not a more unfeeling race of people upon earth than physicians and surgeons — except poets. Nothing like poets! They *describe* feelings *beautifully*, but I'll be hanged if they ever had the sensation of one of them. Look at Lord Byron — he was the chief of them — and a more hard-hearted unfeeling wretch never existed."

Sunday, June 18th The Duke called here. The King not expected to live through the day. He expressed a wish this morning that he might live to see the sun of Waterloo set. Pozzo said of him the other day, at a dinner in this house. *"Il a vécu pour ruiner son pays, il est mort pour l'embarrasser."*

Nevertheless, it is impossible not to feel the deepest concern and alarm at the termination of his reign, disastrous as it has been, on the principle of "rather to bear with the ills we have, than to fly to others that we know not of".

Never was there a state of such complete uncertainty as to the disposition of the successor, and the prospects of the future reign. Everybody has their own anecdote of rumour to repeat of some saying or doing of the Princess, and all without the slightest authority. Some say that she has a great admiration for the Duke, some that she is entirely in her mother's hands, some that she is frivolous and ill-educated, others that she has a great deal of firmness and *caractère*.

Lord Durham[2] is said to have been sent for by the Duchess of Kent. The Whigs are *said* to regret the King's death, and the Radicals to be triumphant. Others again assert that neither the Duchess nor Conroy are really of the Radical Party. Much is thought of the

---

[1] Cecil Papers: XII, 28, 45.

[2] John Lambton, 1st Earl of Durham (1792–1840), an ardent Reformer, head of the advanced section of the Whig party, was on his way home. He had retired from the Embassy at St. Petersburg.

influence of Leopold – himself governed by Louis Philippe. The Princess, too, is generally thought to hate Conroy. In short, amidst these conflicting reports and influences and motives, the only thing that seems certain is that it is impossible to make any reasonable conjecture whatever.

Lord Fitzgerald, Hardinge, Lord Ellenborough and Lord Mahon were with me today – all of course anxious and eager, but not dispirited. Lord Durham is expected, they say, at the end of the week. Lord Ellenborough thinks he will *go the whole hog* with the Radicals.

I have betted Mr. Cornewall 5 shillings to 10 that the new Queen will send for the Duke, to advise her what course to take. I shall lose.

We dined alone and walked out after dinner. There was something melancholy, and that reminded one of the uncertainty of things, in passing St. James's Palace, and seeing the Park on this beautiful evening, the anniversary of our greatest victory, swarming with people in their holiday dresses, the subjects of him who was lying on his bed of death. Every moment I fancied I heard the distant sound of St. Paul's bell, announcing the event.

Monday, June 19th I have not had an account as usual from Mlle. D'Este. I suppose because he is at the last extremity. Esterhazy has put off his dinner where we were to have been today.

3. o'clock The accounts I hear are as bad as possible. They say he cannot outlive the night.

Seven The Duke's dinner takes place, at the King's express desire.

Tuesday, June 20th The King died this morning at half past two.

II

Victoria

Tuesday, June 20th 11 a.m. Lord S. has been up to the Duke's to get some information about the Privy Council – found the Duke at breakfast and settled to go with him and Lord Cowley. He returned here to put on his uniform and is just gone to join them and proceed to Kensington.

Half past 1 Lord S. is returned. He says the young Queen made her entry into her Council with singular grace and self possession. This is his account of the proceedings.

"The Council met. The President informed the Council that H.M. had died at 20 minutes past 2 this morning, and that Princess Alexandrina Victoria succeeded to the throne.

"The Council agreed to a proclamation, and ordered it to be made by the Heralds etc. By the Mayor and Aldermen at Temple Bar — by the Lord Advocate of Scotland.

"The council sent a deputation to inform Her Majesty of her accession to the throne.

"The Queen came in and took her seat at the head of the table. She read an address which was a perfect matter of form, containing nothing from which any political inference could be drawn. There was an allusion to the virtues of the late Sovereign, and the *immature* age at which she was called upon to succeed him.

"Then she took the oath according to the Bill of Rights, and to support the reformed religion. Both the address and the declaration were read by her in a perfectly steady and composed tone, and her manner altogether was remarkably cool and dignified, 'tho her appearance was quite that of a child."

[The scene described by Lord S. is represented by Wilkie in his well-known conversation piece, "Queen Victoria's First Council". Melbourne holds the pen and has Palmerston and Russell on his left and right. The Duke stands in front of the pillar, with Peel on his left. Lord S. is third from the extreme right of the picture. The Duke of Sussex is the prominent figure seated, wearing a skull cap. In fact the Queen did not wear white. Mourning had been delivered at the Palace some days before. The black dress worn by the Queen is an exhibit of the London Museum, Kensington Palace.]

The Privy Council then took the oaths and kissed the Queen's hand — afterwards signed the proclamation and some witnessed the Queen's declaration.

Most of the Conservative Peers did not receive their summons to attend in time. Whether this was by design or accident I know not. But they were on the alert and mustered very strong. Lord S. did not get his summons till after he came home at half past one.

Reports that Parliament is to be dissolved in a month. It appears as if the Whigs remain in. The Duchess of Gloucester told Lord Cowley that the Duchess of Kent had never taken any notice of her or Princess Augusta, since her (The Duchess's) return from Windsor three weeks ago. Neither has she sent ever to enquire after the King, though the Queen wrote her a letter to inform her of his state of health some time ago.

The shops are, most of them partly closed today, but I see no marks of feeling of any sort otherwise. One would not suppose that anything extraordinary had happened.

Wednesday, June 21st Went at nine in the morning to join a water party on board the Duke of Rutland's yacht. Lady Alice and Colonel Peel and Lord Forester and ourselves proceeded to Woolwich in a steamer, where we found the yacht, with the Duke of Rutland, Lady Adeliza Manners, and the Duke of Portland on board.

We went down the river to Purfleet and then returned to Woolwich, went over the dock yard, dinner on board the yacht and came back to town by steam about ten o'clock. We had a beautiful day and everything as perfect as wind and water could make it, but I was never more bored. Found the Duke had called during my absence — *ennui de plus* . . . Lord Forester told me, and I think him good authority, for all he hears is from Lord Duncannon thro' Mrs. Fox, that the Queen had given the whole appointment of her household to Lord Melbourne, with the sole reservation of Sir John Conroy to whom she decidedly objected. The Queen was proclaimed to-day. I heard that the acclamations were not very great.

Thursday, June 22nd Saw Mlle. D'Este, in great affliction for the King's death. The Queen Dowager seems to be a very unamiable woman, harsh, selfish and without affection; and even in the King's last moments endeavoured to keep some of those he loved best from him, thro' a petty jealousy of his regard for them. She performed her duty to him as a machine, without feelings and consequently without the wear and tear that it occasions. The King seems to have been universally beloved by those about him. His faults were more those of the head than the heart, and I believe him to have been full of kindly feelings and wishing always to do right and to promote the happiness of all who depended upon him.

The Queen Dowager sent Prince Ernest of Hohenlohe[1] to Victoria and the Duchess of Kent on Sunday to inform them of the desperate state of the King. Victoria burst into tears and was anxious to go to him immediately, but was overruled . . . There was to have been a

[1] Prince Ernest was the husband of Queen Victoria's half-sister, Féodore.

243

great dinner at Pozzo's, which was put off on account of the King's death, and as all evening parties are put off for a few days, people are at a loss how to pass the evening.

Friday, June 23rd The Duke, the Lothians, Hardinges, Lord Ellenborough, Lord Bathurst, Lord Aberdeen and Mr. Bankes dined here.

The Queen told Lord Melbourne she wished not to have a private secretary. He replied that it certainly was not a constitutional office but that he thought H.M. would find it difficult to transact business without. "Well," she said, "That may be so, but at all events I'll try."

She is to live at Buckingham House. The Queen Dowager wrote to the Queen immediately on the King's death. The Archbishop of Canterbury and Lord Conyngham were the bearers. The young Queen wrote her answer, unassisted, immediately upon the receipt of it, and directed it to the Queen. They suggested it should be the Queen Dowager. "No," she said, "let it go as it is."

Lord Bathurst mentioned in the course of the evening a small equestrian figure of the Duke at Waterloo which is now making at Garrard's and appealed to him to know whether he wore his cloak on that day, as it would add much to the grace of the figure. "It was a showery day," said the Duke, "though it got finer in the afternoon. But I had my cloak on and off fifty times. I remember very well putting it on often, because I never get wet when I can help it, and then when it grew fine I took it off, and fastened it on my saddle."

Sunday, June 25th Dined with the Verulams.

I hear Conroy's disappointment and vexation are very visible and the Duchess of Kent herself is in very low spirits and does nothing but cry. Victoria, it appears, never took anything upon herself till the moment she became Queen, but now she comes out as a most decided personage.

Wednesday, June 28th A large dinner here — the Duke, the Jerseys etc. In a fit of absence I had unfortunately asked Lady Dunmore[1]

---

[1] Susan, daughter of Archibald, 9th Duke of Hamilton, m. 1803 George Murray, 5th Earl of Dunmore. She was an aunt of Mlle. d'Este. Her sister-in-law had been Lady Augusta Murray whose marriage to the Duke of Sussex was forbidden by George III.

and Lady Jersey to meet — a terrible scene in consequence on the part of the latter. The other behaved like a reasonable well bred woman.

Lady Cadogan's in the evening.

No news, the court appointments go on slowly. The Queen, they say, behaved admirably in her interview with the Queen Dowager on Monday. Lord Hill[1] is charmed with her — her punctuality, her attention to business, her anxiety to do right, the observations she makes etc. etc. He does not believe a word of the report that he is to be turned out. Others say that her papers are much in arrear for want of signature . . .

Sunday, July 2nd The Duke called here. Very anxious about the elections. Much better report of Westminster, and altogether accounts favourable. Lord S. subscribes £2,000 to the elections, in case we escape a contest for the County, of which there seems no prospect. We have finally given up having anything to do with Hertford — such a relief to one's mind and to one's pocket. However, Mahon and Cowper would, I should think be undisturbed. Money terribly wanted in the Conservative Party. I don't know how it is with the others.

Monday, July 3rd The Duke called here. Complained terribly of the incessant persecution of notes and letters on all subjects from everybody. Told me he had written fifty notes or letters that morning — that he had a secretary, an assistant and a librarian, and not one of them did anything.

"I declare that I dread going into my own house, from the heaps of letters that are ready to receive me there." The other morning he had a visit from a man who had made repeated applications to see him on business of importance, a baronet, who has published one or two pamphlets. The interview began with highflown compliments on his side, which the Duke soon put an end to, saying, "We did not meet to make compliments. You stated you had something to say to me." "Yes, my Lord, I have a question to put. I wish to ascertain whether, if your Grace were to return to office you would support principles of moderate Reform."

"That is your question, is it?"

[1] Rowland, 1st Viscount Hill (1772–1842), "Daddy Hill", Peninsular veteran, appointed Commander-in-Chief 1828, while the Duke was Prime Minister, and held office over fourteen years.

"Yes, my Lord."

"Then allow me to put a question in return. What right have you to ask me?"

Thursday, July 6th I got a letter from Lord Douro in answer to one of mine in which I attacked him for having committed himself in his speeches on the subject of the Poor Laws at Norwich; an indiscretion which I knew would annoy the Duke particularly. However, I did not mention the Duke in any way. Douro's answer denies the accusation, and adds, "tho' I do not hold myself responsible to the Carlton Club, I should be glad my father knew etc. etc." I wrote a word of this to the Duke and got a very amiable answer in return, but with a postscript recommending me not to allow myself to be made a channel of communication to him from anyone for things which they did not like to say themselves. The postcript was so abrupt and strong that I was completely overset by it. I wrote instantly to explain that it was not a *message* from Lord Douro, and that I had no previous communication with him on the subject, but that I had transmitted the information as he seemed to wish his father should have it.

Dined at Lord Downshire's — a dinner to Lord Combermere on account of Lord Hillsboro's approaching marriage to Miss Cotton. . .

[A family occasion. Lord Hillsborough, heir to Lord Downshire, a heavy-looking young man of five and twenty, known to his contemporaries as "The Mountain", was marrying a daughter of Stapleton Cotton, Peninsular Cavalry Commander, 1st Viscount Combermere.]

Friday, July 7th Got a note the first thing from the Duke, an explanation of his opinion but *not* a *softening*. He observes that conveying an indirect message is more calculated to put me in a false position than a direct one.

I don't know what to make of it — and it annoys me to death. I had no idea I had done anything to displease him; but he is very sensitive on all subjects relating to Douro. I am only afraid he should suspect me of wishing to make a *tracasserie*.

I wish Douro, Norwich, and the Poor Laws were at the bottom of the sea.

I wrote in return a recapitulation of the whole transaction exactly as it passed, and of my motives — truth is always the best with him —

and added I hoped he was not angry. Another note assured me he was not angry.[1] He evidently is so, however, with Douro — a bitter note about *him*, which I must say his whole conduct to his father amply justifies.

Saturday, July 8th I am relieved from my anxiety by a visit from the Duke. Nothing *could* be more kind, and I am sure he never intended to say a word which could give me pain. He told me I must not be surprised when he pointed out to me what I ought to do, and explained his reasons for desiring I should not put myself in the position of transmitting communications to him which the parties concerned were reluctant to make themselves.

This day was the King's funeral. Lord S. attended it and did not return till two the next morning. [The funeral according to custom took place at night. It began at nine p.m.] A very fine spectacle, by all accounts, especially the procession descending the staircase of the Castle.

Sunday, July 9th The Duke called here. The Queen, it seems, is determined to ride at the review. The Ministers have in vain endeavoured to dissuade her. Some person (the Duke could not remember who) asked him the other day his opinion on the subject, which he gave at length, without any idea of it being transmitted to the Queen. Yesterday, at the funeral, Lord Hill told him that the Queen was made aware of his opinion, but that she nevertheless persisted in her resolution.

He thinks that in the first place, the difficulty of procuring a horse for her that could be entirely depended upon would be very great; that it is very doubtful, even if she is a good horsewoman, that she would go well and gracefully through a review, and that it would be much more dignified for her to appear in her *calèche*, surrounded by her court.

"I would not wish," he said, "a better subject for a caricature, than this young Queen, alone, without any woman to attend her, without that brilliant *cortège* of young men and ladies who ought to appear in a scene of that kind, and surrounded only by such youths as Lord Hill and me, Lord Aberdeen and the Duke of Argyll. And if it rains, and she gets wet, or if any other *contretemps* happens, what

[1] These three letters are in the Cecil Papers: Letters of the Duke of Wellington, July 6th, (2) 7th.

is to be done? All these things sound very little, but they must be considered in a display of that sort. And as to the soldiers, I know *them*; they won't care about it one sixpence. It is a childish fancy, because she has read of Queen Elizabeth at Tilbury Fort. But *there* was a threat of foreign invasion, there was an occasion which called for a display *then*. What occasion is there now?"

[The review was cancelled for Hyde Park in May and took place at Windsor in August. The Queen rode.]

Monday, July 10th Lord Hertford's. London is thinning rapidly; all the men gone to their elections. Accounts continue good, but the other party, I understand, are equally confident and talk of an increase of 30.

Tuesday, July 11th Breakfast at Ken Wood. No men, and few eatables; very dull. The Queen, they say, is far from strong, and so knocked up every evening with the fatigues of the day that she goes to bed at nine o'clock . . .

Wednesday, July 12th Dined with the Londonderry's at Rose Bank.[1] The Ravensworths, Lord Strangford, Lord Eglinton and D'Israeli.[2] I never met him before. He bears the mark of the Jew strongly about him, and at times his way of speaking reminded me so much of Lord Lyndhurst, I could almost have thought him in the room. He is evidently very clever, but superlatively vulgar . . .

Monday, July 17th The Prorogation of Parliament by the Queen. I went with the Cowleys about $\frac{1}{2}$ past twelve. We found, however, no difficulty in getting places, all those of the peeresses who had sent in their names being marked. The only annoyance I had arose from a mistake, by which I had unluckily put on white feathers instead of black, and as not more than two or three other peeresses had done the same, I felt very awkward, and conspicuous in the midst of the black. However, all the orders of this new court on such subjects are so uncertain and confused that I only wonder there are not more blunders. Two days ago the Duchess of Sutherland positively announced that all peeresses were to be in white, and she was obliged to write a note yesterday to Madame Pozzo to contradict it.

The scene was really a very striking one and nothing was wanting

---

[1] Rose Bank was the Londonderrys' Thames-side villa, near Hammersmith Bridge.
[2] Benjamin D'Israeli, afterwards 1st Earl of Beaconsfield (1804–81), at this date a successful novelist but without a seat in Parliament.

to render it perfect but a more imposing *locale*. That temporary House of Lords is a very shabby concern. The House was extremely full – the peers in their robes certainly one of the most beautiful and dignified costumes in the world (it is wonderful how well men *do* look, when they are well dressed), the peeresses with their plumes, and the *Corps Diplomatique*, with the different uniforms and orders of their respective countries, made altogether a very fine *coup d'oeil*.

All rose when the Queen entered, preceded by the Beefeaters and the Officers of the Household. She ascended her throne with perfect ease and dignity, and tho' every sound was hushed and every eye turned upon her, her composure did not seem to fail her for an instant. She looked well, tho' rather heated, and her want of height was not so apparent when she was seated. But it certainly requires all the prestige of royalty to cheat one into the belief of her being pretty – tho' I am sure at that moment, she appeared beautiful in the eyes of half the spectators. Her countenance betrayed no emotion whatever, except that at one moment I thought I saw a lurking inclination to laugh. The Commons read their address – the Queen's assent was given in the usual form to several bills – and then she read her speech. Her voice is clear and harmonious, her delivery *admirable* – and altogether I never saw a thing better done. At the conclusion she rose and retired, with her suite, curtesying to such of the peeresses as were near her when she went out, but speaking to no one.

The Duchess of Kent had a seat close to the throne. The Duke of Sussex remained nearby the front of it. Since the operation on his eyes he wears a black skull cap, which combined with his enormous grisly whiskers, almost amounting to a beard, and his immense figure arrayed in robes of State, gave him the appearance of some old portrait of Holbein's time.

The Duchess of Northumberland sat next me, and was affected to tears during the Queen's speech. She told me that, from a child, she had always been remarkable for reading well, and for another quality, which in her situation was *invaluable*, never leaving any subject until she had made herself mistress of it. It is evident, that the Duchess has a great personal affection and *esteem* for her. This looks well, she must be worthy of it! The Duchess said the Queen would not go out of town yet, "She likes Society."

Wednesday, July 19th A small dinner party here. The Duke was to have dined here but was invited by the Queen — "as Chancellor of Oxford" the more singular as there was nothing connected with Oxford in the dinner . . .

Saturday, July 22nd Two new Peers made. Old Coke of Norfolk[1] one — surely the Queen cannot know what he said of her Grandfather. It is scandalous. I am afraid this but too clearly proves that she is entirely in their hands.

They are using the Government influence openly, and in the most shameful manner, in the elections, and bribing everywhere *à pleines mains*. Where does it all come from? . . .

I sent my girls and Eustace this morning to Hatfield; Cranborne remains with me. I become daily more hopeless of his regaining his sight.

Sunday, July 23rd Dined with Mlle. D'Este. There is an opposition at Hertford, but I hope Mahon is in no danger. The Queen, by all accounts, is a clever, determined little virago, delighted at her sudden emancipation from all constraint. She told somebody that when she woke in the night, she said to herself, "Is it possible that I am my own mistress?" She is very haughty to her household and has once or twice snubbed her ladies, even the "Grand-Duchess", and to two of her Maids of Honour she has never yet spoken — one of whom (Miss Spring Rice) takes it in great dudgeon.

The Queen told Lord Melbourne that Conroy had always thwarted her from a child and that she detested him.

[Conroy had antagonized Baroness Lehzen, "Daisy", whom Victoria regarded as giving her a true mother's love. When the princess was recovering from typhoid, aged sixteen, he tried to get her to sign a document pledging herself, on her accession, to appoint him private secretary. Later she discovered that, with her mother, he had tried to get her coming of age delayed, so that should William IV die before it, the Duchess might become Regent.]

The Whigs themselves say that they expect she will turn them out some fine day from sheer perverseness because they are supported by her Mother and her *entourage*. In that case, they are acting foolishly to surround her so entirely with their own party. Lord Melbourne

---

[1] Thomas Coke, 1st Earl of Leicester (1752–1842), celebrated agriculturalist and protectionist, but favoured the Reform Bill.

told Lord Conyngham that he was determined everything about the Court should be Whig, down to the housemaids. She shews no regard for her mother's opinion, but rather puts herself in opposition to it. In the meantime Conroy has been writing to canvass a naval officer at Portsmouth for the Whigs, which pretty well shews de Duchess of Kent's sentiments.

It is said that there is to be a concert at Court on Friday, but that the Ministers have remonstrated against the expense, as the lighting up of Buckingham Palace, even for one night, will cost £1,000.

Tuesday, July 25th Good accounts from Hertford. A terrible letter in to-day's *Times* from Lord John Russell to Lord Mulgrave conveying the Queen's approbation of his Administration. It is past a doubt now that she is heart and soul with them. She is not the sort of person to have allowed that letter to be sent without fully weighing and concurring in its expressions. It must influence the elections and I expect the worst.

5 o'clock Marylebone gone — which was reckoned certain, and the City decided against us by six!!! Encouraging! Hertford is safe — but Mahon had a squeak for it.

Wednesday, July 26th I am in rather better spirits today. We have won great victories at Liverpool, Bath and Hull, and altogether it appears that we have obtained an increase of five upon the borough elections already decided. We have still the counties, which I hope will go in favour — but then Ireland!

Norwich is safe, notwithstanding the most unexampled bribery. For the last ten votes the Whigs gave £1000. They are mad with fury at the result of Liverpool.

Thursday, July 27th This afternoon I understand the last accounts reduce our majority to *one*.

The Duke called here. He told me that as he went through the Green Park yesterday, he was hooted, and they called out "Waterloo, Ah!" and hissed, as a term of reproach. . .

Saturday, July 29th The Duke called here, told me he understood the Ministers were not in spirits and that Lord Melbourne talked of the possibility of going out of office and being succeeded by the Duke of Richmond.

Wednesday, August 2nd I dined with the Queen. The party were Count Pozzo and Count and Countess Charles Pozzo, M. de

251

Mandelslow, the Württemberg Minister, Mr. and Mrs. Stevenson (the American Minister and his wife,[1]) Count and Countess Ludolf, Lord and Lady Seymour, and Lord and Lady Cowley, and the household.

I went, as appointed, at half past seven. The rest of the company arrived nearly at the same moment, and we were ushered into a large and handsome room where we remained standing nearly half an hour till the Queen and the Duchess of Kent and their *suite* arrived. They had scarcely time to speak a few words to everybody when the dinner was announced in the adjoining room. Nothing could be better mounted than the whole establishment — the dinner excellent and extremely *rapid*. After dinner the Queen's health was drank in silence, and she retired with the ladies a short time afterwards, to a room called the Music Room, adjoining that which we had first occupied, where we all remained standing full half an hour till the men came out.

Nothing could be more amiable in manner than the Queen, to everybody. When the men joined we went into a third drawing-room, and she seated herself on a sofa, desiring me and Mme. Pozzo to sit on each side of her — Pozzo and Lord Cowley each occupying an arm chair at the ends of the sofa — the Duchess of Kent opposite, with Lady Seymour and Mrs. Stevenson on one side, and Countess Ludolf and Lady Charlemont on the other. The rest of the men remained standing. After a little while, the Duchess of Kent made a whist table with Lord and Lady Cowley and Mr. Stevenson, and I had a good deal of conversation with the Queen. As far as I can judge, I think her decidedly clever, quick of observation with a great turn for seizing the ridiculous, perfectly unaffected and natural and, I should suppose, disliking the reverse of these qualities in others. She has no affectation of being older than she is, and does not pretend to conceal that she has the tastes and feelings of a girl, at the same time she preserves most perfectly the dignity of her station.

She told me she was delighted to leave Kensington and come to Buckingham Palace, where the view was so much gayer, and she

[1] Andrew Stevenson (1784–1857) congressman from Virginia, speaker of the House of Representatives. He m. 1st Mary Page White, 2nd (1812) Sarah Coles, 3rd Mary Schaff of Georgetown D.C. "A courtly and talented man; but he was a machine politician, and his career lacks the stamp of a strong personality." (*Dictionary of American Biography*.)

could see from her dressing room the people walking and driving in the park – that she delighted in London and was charmed with the pretence which Parliament meeting in November would afford her, of coming to town. She preferred driving in the streets, she told me, infinitely to driving out of town – the Regent's Park was quite country enough.

She appeared acquainted with the history of everybody in Society, and could talk of them as if she had passed her life in the world on the same footing as others. She had a great deal to do, she said, and always went to bed quite sleepy and tired. She observed in a low voice on the American *tournure* and manners of Mrs. Stevenson, and seemed much diverted with her – and to an observation of mine she replied that she thought the Americans must be a very disagreeable people, and that it was impossible to see any of them without being reminded of the books which had been lately written about them and which she was afraid were all true in the main points. Altogether, I never saw anything more perfect than her manner; if any fault could be found, it might be that she laughs a little too much. To the Duchess of Kent it appeared to me perfectly respectable.

At half past ten the Royalties took leave of us, and we departed as soon as they had quitted the room. Lord Seymour told me at dinner that the Whigs expected to gain two in Scotland and six in Ireland. *"Comment vont les élections?"* said Pozzo to me. *"A merveille!"* I am not sure he was pleased . . .

Monday, August 7th Left town to meet Lord S. at Hatfield. Found him just arrived before me.

Was much amused, tho' not surprised to see announced in this day's paper Lord Lyndhurst's marriage to Miss Goldsmid at Paris . . . I do not find the House at Hatfield much more advanced than when I left it in January. The cloister is unpaved, the West Wing inaccessible and it is impossible to receive above four or five people for the present.

Wednesday, August 9th Went to town to dine at Apsley House. Miss Jervis sang beautifully. Giannora and one or two of the Opera people came to sing with her. I told the Duke his marriage was announced both with Miss Jervis and Lady G. Fane, to his great amusement.

Thursday, August 10th He called upon me before I left town. He seems in good spirits about the election upon the whole — lays the whole blame of our failures in the boroughs upon the alterations Peel forced on the Lords in the English Municipal Bill, said that Ellice kept the Ministers in perpetual alarm by telling them that if the Tories ever got firmly seated in power, they would be impeached . . . The Duke is invited to dine with the Queen on Friday. I think that a good sign.

In the evening we came down to Hatfield. Quite alone there.

Saturday, August 12th We lead a patriarchal life, dining at five, and going out, with all the children, after dinner. The weather lovely.

Monday, August 14th To our great surprise, as we were sitting after dinner, about six o'clock, the Duke walked in. He had written a note to say that he intended to sleep here in his way to Woodford, but it had not been forwarded in time. We ordered him some dinner immediately and he walked up and down the terrace with us and the children till it was ready, and sat up talking in the evening, till near twelve, in great spirits. He told us in the course of conversation that he always made it a rule not to give his name to charitable subscriptions unless he was perfectly well acquainted with the case. "I do not think it right. I had much rather give the money myself. I have a right to do what I like with my own money, but I have no right to give my name as an inducement to others to contribute."

The King of Württemberg called upon the Duke the other day in town, and had a conversation with him of above two hours. He is a clever man, the Duke said, but quite ignorant of English affairs as all foreigners are, and at a loss to understand why the Conservatives should contend for the ascendancy of the Protestant Church in Ireland when the two religions go on so amicably upon equal terms on the Continent.

The Duke told him that such an impression showed that he understood nothing at all of the subject. And subsequently in their conversation the King of Württemberg told somebody that he had never clearly understood the state of affairs in England till the Duke explained it to him. He condemned the conduct of the King of Hanover, and said the Diet would be obliged to interfere. Speaking of this letter, the Duke said, "I treated him with contempt and he has never forgiven me. There is nothing so foolish as to treat anyone with contempt. It is the only thing that is never forgiven."

[Queen Victoria wrote to her uncle Leopold on August 9th to say that the King was coming over in strict incognito, under the name of the Duke of Teck. He was her second cousin, his mother was sister of Queen Caroline (of Brunswick) and daughter of Victoria's grand-aunt, Augusta, Duchess of Brunswick, sister of George III. Ernest, Duke of Cumberland, who had succeeded his brother as King of Hanover had caused a storm by cancelling the Constitution granted by William IV in 1833. Wellington had advised him to leave England instantly on the death of William IV, not to expose himself to be mobbed and hooted in the streets, but he had insisted on remaining to swear allegiance to his niece and take his seat in the House of Lords.]

Speaking of drunkenness as the great vice of the English nation, he expressed an opinion that the use of wine, spirits and strong liquors of every kind was prejudicious to health and longevity in all situations and climates, and that mankind would benefit if the use of them was utterly unknown except as medicines.

With his usual kindness he has asked Lady R. Grosvenor's children to come to stay at Walmer Castle during her absence with Lord Robert abroad. He seldom sees Lord or Lady Robert, who live in a different Society, and with people of violent politics, but meeting Lady Robert in the Park by chance, she told him she was under great difficulties about leaving her children as she was obliged to go abroad on account of Lord Robert's health, and he immediately made her this offer which was accepted with delight.

[The Duke had written on July 10th:
My dear Lady Salisbury,

I have been considering of what you said to me yesterday. I shall be delighted to see you at Walmer with all your children for as long a time as you will stay. But I strongly recommend you not to come without Lord Salisbury. One would suppose that you might hope to go through the world without giving reason for scandal; and that I am beyond the age to afford any ground for it. But it is not so. There was plenty of it last year. There will be more if your visit should be repeated this year without the company of Lord S. and I earnestly recommend that you should refrain from making it.

Believe me ever yours most affectionately, W.[1]]

[1] Cecil Papers: Letters of the Duke of Wellington, 250.

255

Thursday, August 22nd Went by steam to Margate and thence in a fly to Walmer. A beautiful day and calm voyage. Mildred, Blanche and Robert with us. Found the Duke alone except Mr. Arbuthnot.

Wednesday, August 23rd Walked with the Duke on the Beach. Speaking of the composition of political parties at present, he said, "We are in a curious state — the House of Commons is a deliberate assembly — and what is it composed of? Two parties diametrically opposed to each other. There are no half dozen members who have not completely made up their minds on every single point, and all are exasperated to the last degree against the other side. I do not believe in the reaction as it is generally understood. Those who were Radicals remain Radicals, but the difference in the elections arises from the number of Conservatives who have been awakened to a sense of their danger. The Destructive party consist of four classes — first the old Dissenting party, who have always been inimical to the existing order in the Church and the State, the representatives of the Puritans, 2nd the atheist, and republicans in principle, who are prepared to ally themselves with the papists as a means of bringing about a revolution; thirdly, the Catholic party, and finally, the old Whig nobility and gentry, who are induced by party feeling to patronize measures they cannot approve. From this latter class alone, we can hope for converts."

[Lord John Russell has sent to the Queen on August 15th a general statement of the election results, complete except for one or two Irish counties. While the extreme Radicals had been defeated in several cases, the number of O'Connell's followers had decidedly increased. The general balance of parties was not much affected.]

Peel called upon the Duke a few days before King William's death. There was at that time a report that the Duke was in communication with Kensington, and Peel probably wished to ascertain its truth. The Duke told him frankly that he knew nothing of the future Queen's intention, and Peel observed that if she proposed to form a Tory Government, he, for one, could not undertake office. A few days after, he told Lord Aberdeen positively that he would accept office if she sent for him. The Duke was much hurt at his conduct on this occasion, and the duplicity to him.

Thursday, August 24th Rode with the Duke. Nobody to dinner. He (the D.) told us in the evening that soon after King William's accession he consulted him about the time to be fixed for the Coronation. The Duke recommended it should be delayed till the long days in the spring, and added that he strongly advised H.M. not to avoid the ceremony, as there were certain oaths to be taken by the Sovereign on that occasion which it was very desirable should not be omitted. This accounts for the line the Duke afterwards took upon the subject in the House of Lords.

Speaking of the possibility of a civil war in this country, Lord S. rather seemed to consider it as a desirable event. The Duke, as he always does, strongly espoused the opposite side and showed the danger and mischief of it. "But you have no doubt you would be implicitly obeyed by all who commanded troops on your side?" said Lord S. "There is nothing on earth that I am more certain of than that *I should not. I have often turned it over in my mind* and I have seen the difficulties attending it; that among others. Look at that book" (the Dispatches), "and see the impossibility of directing the Spanish armies — of getting them to obey orders — of saving them from being beat! It would be ten times worse — Beside, who is to support and provision your troops?" . . .

Friday, August 25th I rode again with the Duke. He told me that when Office was first proposed to him by Lord Castlereagh, after the Congress of Aix la Chapelle, he had the greatest dislike to accepting it, and the only thing that determined him was the assurance that if he refused to join he should weaken the Ministry and become a rallying point for the disaffected.

Sunday, August 27th Went to Church in the morning — a charity sermon, very plain and sensible. The preacher dwelt upon the necessity of *religious* education. The Duke observed as we came out of the church that it was wonderful the clergy did not enforce this topic more frequently, as the last command of our Saviour was "to go and preach the gospel".

In the evening the Duke talked a great deal of his campaigns. Sir George Murray, he said, was an excellent subordinate officer, but not fit to be entrusted with a great command. His defect was the not being able to form troops *upon the ground.* He could form them very well on paper, but he had not practice enough in the other way. He had served too much upon the staff, and he was conscious of it himself and intended to go into the line and not serve upon the staff any more. Soult had the same defect — he had served also too much upon the staff. Murray was always opposed to the plan of retiring behind the lines of Torres Vedras, and earnestly entreated the Duke not to do it. The Duke replied that he thought it his duty to remain as long as possible in the country, provided he always maintained the communication with the ships. Murray maintained that the lines must be forced, etc. etc . . . Again, before the battle of Vittoria, he had an interview with the Duke and entreated him not to pass the Ebro. The news of the Battles of Lutzen and Bautzen had then just been received, but notwithstanding, Murray implored him to take up a position on the Madrid side of the Ebro. "For," said he, "these victories are nothing. The Allies will soon be beat, and then you will have an imposing position upon the Ebro to meet the course of events." "I think I should have a more imposing one upon the Pyrenees," said the Duke. "In short, I am determined to cross the Ebro, and *I will*."

The Ebro was crossed, Vittoria was fought, and the news of that battle arrived in the camp of the Allies while they were deliberating upon the continuance of an armistice, and Austria was still un-decided. That event determined them, and ruined Napoleon — such were the consequences of rejecting Sir George Murray's advice.

"Nothing so true," said the Duke, "as the proverb 'Better an army of stags commanded by a lion, than an army of lions commanded by a stag'." In proof of this he instanced his own troops, which but a few months before Vimeiro, were surrounded in a church at Buenos Ayres under Whitelocke and forced by the Spanish Bourgeoisie to lay down their arms.

[Lieutenant-General John Whitelocke was cashiered. He pleaded that the expedition had been sent at the wrong season, and under the impression that the inhabitants would be friendly. His son-in-law, Sir Gore Ouseley, a familiar figure at Hatfield, provided for him.]

"But in war, *I* am like a good player at some game. I know exactly what I can do, and what I cannot do with the materials I have in my hands. Nothing could be better than the British Army at the close of the Peninsular War, yet some of their best troops had a signal failure at Bergen-op-Zoom."

General Coote got possession of the ramparts of the town in the night, by surprise. The French officers within heard a cannonading still going on in the outworks, determined to try their fortune, and climbing up by a ramp, gained the rampart and succeeded in dividing General Coote's forces, which were at last obliged to capitulate for a safe retreat. On hearing of this, Sir Andrew Bernard observed upon Lord Lynedoch's negligence in not coming soon enough to their support. "The Duke," said he, "would have been there in an hour." "And," said the Duke to us, "so I should."

[Lynedoch commanded the troops sent to Holland to co-operate with Bülow's Prussians against Antwerp in November 1813. He failed to carry the fortress of Bergen-op-Zoom by assault on the night of March 8th, 1814. Wellington's comment in his dispatch was merely, "Night attacks on good troops are seldom successful."]

Monday, August 28th The Duke went over to Ramsgate to receive the King and Queen of the Belgians who were to land there today. The Duke staid to dinner and returned at night.

Tuesday, August 29th Lord Winchelsea came over from Dover to luncheon. The Duke and I rode back with him part of the way. He told us that the Whigs said the Queen was Tory in her heart. Lord S. asked the Duke how it came that the French did not attack him on the retreat from Burgos. "Because they found out that our bullets were not made of butter."

Wednesday, August 30th Lord Fitzroy Somerset and Sir Herbert Taylor came from Dover at luncheon time and remained with him some time which prevented our ride.

The Hardinges and Mr. and Mrs. Welby dined here. After they were all gone, in the evening, the Duke was exceedingly amusing — talking over Napoleon's first campaign in Italy, the battle of Marengo etc. etc . . . The Austrians never concentrated their troops sufficiently. They would make a long line through a great extent of country which was easily broken through, and the communications never could be re-established. Marengo was lost by the Commander in Chief going to bed (he was very old) in the middle of the day, supposing the battle won. A body of Austrian troops, detached from the rest, were suddenly attacked by the French. Their pieces were not even loaded; there was nobody to give directions or re-establish order, and the rout became general. The French troops got between them and the Po.

[On June 13th, 1800, General Desaix told Napoleon that the

battle was "completely lost" by five p.m. "But there is still time to win the second battle." General Mélas, Austrian Commander-in-Chief (1729–1806), thinking his victory complete, had retired to his headquarters leaving his second-in-command to do the tidying up. General Zach was captured with all his staff.]

The Nassau troops in the French Peninsular Army were remarkably good. "I followed them from the Tagus to the Bidassoa; they always behaved well. It was always an effort to dislodge them – a serious affair. The French put foreign troops in their posts of danger in the front and rear guards. We do not – tho' they always accused me of doing it." These Nassau troops, about 3,000 came over to the Duke after he entered the French frontier, upon his causing a proclamation of the Duke of Nassau's to be circulated among them.

He spoke of the extraordinary propensity to desert in the British Army, especially in a case which frequently occurred – desertion from the besieging army into a besieged place. "Tho' they knew they must be taken, for when we lay our bloody hands upon a place we are sure to take it sooner or later. But they liked being dry and under cover. And then, that extraordinary caprice which always pervades the English Character! And they were ill-treated by the enemy. Those who deserted in France were treated as the lowest of mortals – slaves and scavengers. Nothing but English caprice can account for it – just what makes our noblemen associate with stage-coach drivers, and become stage-coach drivers themselves."

The Army at Waterloo was very bad. The foreign troops all behaved ill, even those Nassau men who had fought so well under the French in the Peninsula, though they were commanded by the same man. They were afraid of the French. The Dutch, the Brunswickers, none of the foreigners, behaved well, except the German Legion at la Haye Sainte. The reason why we were forced to give up la Haye Sainte was that the commanding officer had neglected to break down a part of the garden wall to introduce ammunition. "I ought to have thought of that, but one cannot think of everything."

For four days previous to the 16th (the 12th, 13th, 14th and 15th), he never went further than twenty yards from his own house in Brussels, that they might know where to find him.

Napoleon committed a great mistake in endeavouring to cut in between the Prussians and the English. He ought to have gone by the direct road — by Mons. He committed another error in directing the march of a body of troops towards the English front on the day of the 16th. He afterwards recalled them, so that they were ineffective the whole day.

"I wonder what they would have said to me if I had done such a thing as that. But I have always avoided a false move. I preferred being too late in my movement to the having to alter it."

Arbuthnot told us that Napoleon said to Captain Maitland[1] that the Duke equalled him in everything, and excelled him in one thing — caution.

The Duke described Lord Anglesey's charge, and the mischief it was near occasioning. He had himself gone to his quarters, and was at dinner when they brought him a message from Lord Anglesey to desire him to come immediately, for he was in great difficulties. And Lord Anglesey had the impudence next morning (he was Senior Officer after the Duke) to ask him, in case anything should happen to him, in which case Lord Anglesey might be called upon to take the command, to tell him what his plans were. "Plans! I have no plans. I shall be guided by circumstances . . ."

Thursday, August 31st At breakfast this morning the Duke was talking of Evans — of his General Orders that the troops should have hot breakfasts, and beds 18 inches from the ground, when there were neither beds nor breakfasts to be had etc. He said that he had never seen him in his life, which he ascribed to his being generally in the rear of the army, sketching fields of battle — he is an excellent draughtsman, which was his original recommendation. He went afterwards to America, and Captain Ross being killed, Evans was employed to write the dispatch in which he mentioned himself as "This fine young man". The Duke was on horseback at Waterloo, on Copenhagen, from five in the morning till eleven that night.

There is an unfortunate boy living here at Walmer and confined by a spinal complaint without hopes of recovery. He is the son of some old friends of the Duke's in India, of the name of Gordon, now dead, and the Duke most kindly went yesterday to see him and sit with him.

What the Duke fears is that Leopold, whom he conceives to have

[1] See *Narrative of the Surrender of Bonaparte and of his residence on board H.M.S. Bellerophon*, by Capt. Frederick Maitland, C.B., 1826 p. 222.

great influence over Victoria, should give her liberal ideas upon the Church.

[*Note* There is no trace of the Diary from September 1st, 1837 to January 1st, 1838.]

PART VIII
1838: January–August

I

Monday, January 1st Left Hatfield for Burghley. A large party there — the Duke, the Wiltons, F. Egertons, Lord Burghersh, Lord Alford, Lord Maidstone, the Becketts, Lord Aberdeen, the Duke of Rutland etc.

Wednesday, January 3rd Went to Belvoir. Most of the same people there, the F. Egertons excepted. The Duke and Duchess of Sutherland and the Duke of Newcastle in addition, also Lord Fitzgerald, Lord Rokeby, Sir S. French, Mr. Irving and all the married daughters of the house with their respective husbands. We were about 40 at dinner.

Thursday, January 4th The birthday. The Duke of Rutland made an excellent speech after dinner, complimentary to The Duke. In the evening the ball. I danced with Lord Burghersh, Lord Aberdeen and Lord Fitzgerald.

Saturday, January 6th A good many of our party gone. The Duke has been suffering all day from lumbago. He was in great spirits however, in the evening and told us many anecdotes relative to his campaigns.

Masséna[1] was the best tactician of Napoleon's Generals — Marmont[2] clever but not equal to him. Soult[3] was the best administrator of an army, the best *stratégiste*, but he did not understand managing his troops in the field. "He gave me less trouble than any of the others. We thought great things of Suchet[4] and those others who were employed in the East of Spain."

Soult knew nothing of the Allies having entered Paris when he fought the Battle of Toulouse. It was impossible he should. The English army was between him and Paris. The battle was fought on the 10th, the English occupied Toulouse the 12th and the same

[1] André Masséna, Duc de Rivoli, Prince d'Essling, Marshal of France (1756–1817), named by Napoleon "the favourite child of Fortune".

[2] Auguste-Frederic, Duc de Marmont, Duc de Raguse (1774–1852), Marshal of France. He left Memoirs.

[3] Nicolas Soult, Duc de Dalmatia (1768–1851), Marshal of France. Turned the day at Austerlitz. Minister for War and Foreign Affairs to Louis-Philippe.

[4] Louis-Gabriel Suchet, Duc d'Albufera (1772–1826), Marshal of France.

day received the intelligence brought by Col. Cooke and Col. St. Simon from Paris. The Duke sent them on to Soult, who would not believe the news at first, was furious, and ordered St. Simon into arrest. Soult was more sulky and ill-conditioned than the other French Generals. All that were within reach came to the Duke's camp, after the Peace was announced, but he did not.

The claim of the French to the victory of Toulouse was ridiculous. The day after the battle the only ground they possessed beyond the town was a strip about half a mile broad between the Garonne and the Canal of Languedoc — and the Duke was preparing to attack them there when Soult retreated, and the Duke was at the theatre at Toulouse on the night of the 12th. Some time afterwards Suchet wanted to have a plan drawn of this battle. He sent it to the Duke; but it was so far from the truth he would not sanction it.

"They wished to have a plan to show the manoeuvres for three days before the battle — and it was very *curious* manoeuvring — Soult on one side and I on the other." After the battle the Duke made up his mind to attack Soult, as the latter took no steps in consequence of the capitulation of Paris. He made every preparation to that effect when Garnier came to him from Soult. The Duke represented to him how much it was to be lamented that unnecessary bloodshed should take place, and gave him a message to Soult, deprecating his conduct and the continuance of the war. "At the same time," he said, "be so kind as to tell him that my troops march tomorrow morning." "Oh yes," says Garnier, "I saw them all as I came along — *voilà bien la légère et telle et telle division. Je les connois toutes.*" However, the message had its effect.

"If Soult had succeeded in joining Suchet, I should still have been a match for them both. I could have done anything with that army. It was in such perfect order."

After the Battle of La Nivelle there was a certain battalion shut up in a redoubt on a hill which was carried by the English. The Commandant was brought to the Duke who had some intelligence of the Battle of Leipsic and wanted to get the truth out of this man. But he was sulky and would not know anything. "Try him after dinner," said the Duke. Accordingly he dined at headquarters and *everybody* asked him to drink a glass of Madeira. By and by the Duke turned suddenly on him and said. "*Où est le quartier général de*

266

l'Empereur?" "*Monseigneur il n'y a pas de quartier général. Il n'y a ni armée ni quartier général.*" And it was true, such was the *déroute* that the Allies might have penetrated to Paris at that time with the most perfect ease.

Lord Burghersh, who was with the Allied Sovereigns, told us that he was present when a deserter from Soult's army was brought in. Some question was made about the possibility of getting to Paris, upon which this man said, "*Si le prince Anglais qui est là-bas étoit auprès de vous, vous y seriez depuis un mois.*" The Duc d'Angoulême, when he joined the Allied army, was treated with all the respect due to him, but he remained incognito at headquarters and did not accompany the Duke on any public occasions, the latter being desirous not to implicate any person in the danger of acknowledging him till the conditions of peace were known. But their ignorance of the Bourbons in that part of the country was very great, and one respectable man asked the Duke *who the Duc d'Angoulême was.*

The Duke had the government of eight Préfectures which devolved upon him after the Battle of Toulouse. The *Préfets* decamped, but the *Sous-Préfets* received his orders. "They were very easily managed. I sent them my orders by proclamation, like a General Order, so that what was said to one was known to the rest. They applied to me to know in whose name justice was to be administered – to lay a trap for me. But it would not do, and I directed it should be in the name of *Les Puissances Alliées.*"

After the peace, when the Duke was on the road one day between Paris and the Army in the South, the postillion stopped to change with another carriage, and that carriage was Soult's. The Duke was asleep, and Soult got out and walked round him and examined him – the first time he had seen him!

The Duke used to joke with Masséna when he met him at dinners at Paris, about their Peninsular campaigns; and one day contrived to compliment him upon the only success he had obtained against him, by reminding him that the Port they had open before them was not so good as certain Port of the Duke's which had been deposited in a fort in Portugal, when the Duke went from the siege of Ciudad Rodrigo to Badajoz, and which Masséna captured.

Sunday, January 7th Went to Lord Wilton's at Melton for one night . . . A hard frost.

267

Tuesday, January 9th Home, snowed all day.

Wednesday, 10th and following days Hard frost and deep snow. We remained quite alone at Hatfield.

Tuesday, January 16th Came to town for the opening of Parliament.

Wednesday, January 17th The Duke called upon me. He is just come from Drayton — says Peel more amiable than usual, but "had not made up his mind about anything, as usual" . . . *He* has a mean opinion of Lord Durham's talents.

[Lord Durham was sent out as High Commissioner to attempt to compose the endemic difficulties between Upper (mainly occupied by British settlers) and Lower (French) Canada. The Governor of Upper Canada had placed his troops at the service of the Governor of Lower Canada who had resigned after dismissing some militia officers and members of the Assembly on a charge of high treason. An Imperial Act was passed suspending for two years the Assembly of Lower Canada. Durham dismissed his predecessor's Executive Council and nominated another. Brougham, who was veering towards the Tory party, carried a motion censuring the Ministry's colonial policy. Durham, finding himself abandoned, resigned and returned home. He was succeeded by Sir John Colborne, afterwards Lord Seton (1778–1863), once military secretary to the Duke.]

He looked over the tenth volume of his Dispatches which had just come out and was lying on my table. I observed that the manner in which he attended to the details of every sort, and the multiplicity of affairs which developed upon him was even more wonderful than the victories he obtained. He said, "Oh! as to the victory, I had never any difficulty about *that*. That was always a matter of course. There never was the slightest doubt about the result of any action when we once engaged upon it. But it was the daily detail that was the weight upon me. I never walked out, or rode out, or took a moment's recreation without having some affair or other occupying my thoughts."

[Leaf torn out.]

Pozzo was not so amusing as usual. He told me, however, a curious anecdote of Napoleon which he had from Hortense, the Duchess of St. Leu, herself, that when her son was born, she told Napoleon it

268

would be reported that he was the father, and he said, "*Laissez-dire, Il y a pas de mal qu'on le croie ainsi.*"

[Hortense de Beauharnais, ex-Queen of Holland (1783–1837), daughter of Josephine and wife of Napoleon's younger brother, Louis Bonaparte, repeats this story herself in her Memoirs. Her own account differs in detail. It was after the death of her eldest son and before the birth of her third (who became Napoleon III) that her step-father said he was generally believed to have been the father of the deceased boy. "It was perhaps just as well to have people think it, and so I look upon his death as a calamity."]

The Duke's speech in the House last Thursday containing a qualified approbation of the conduct of Ministers in Canada has raised a storm in our party. He is aware of it, but in his usual way says that he is sure he is right, and that "he does not care sixpence", and that it was his duty to support them on this occasion; he should have been inconsistent in blaming them.

Thursday, January 25th All the party went away, and we were left with the Duke alone. I walked with him for some time today. He told me the late King had consulted him upon his offer of the allowance to Princess Victoria, and he had advised him to do everything in concert with his Ministers. The Duke saw the first letter written by the King and altered some expressions in it which he thought reflected upon the Duchess of Kent. He saw also Victoria's answer, saying it was the first attempt that had been made to separate her from her mother etc., and he thinks it was in her handwriting. Whether there was any farther correspondence he does not know.

[On May 19th, 1837, Princess Victoria received personally from the hands of Lord Conyngham a letter from William IV offering her £10,000 free of her mother's control, an independent Privy Purse and the right to appoint her ladies. Conroy and the Duchess attempted in vain to intercept this letter. They prepared a draft reply for Victoria to copy accepting the £10,000 but pleading her youth and inexperience as her reason for wishing to stay "in every respect as I am now". On returning to her room after signing this she dictated to Baroness Lehzen, her governess, a statement that she had not written the letter. William IV spotted this. "Victoria has not written that letter . . . The Duchess and King John (Conroy) want money." The Duchess was offered by Melbourne £6,000 for herself, the remaining £4,000 to go to her daughter. She sent a refusal without consulting her daughter. Lord Liverpool had interviews at Kensington Palace on June 15th with Conroy, who told him that the Princess must have a private secretary, she was "younger in intellect than years" and had silly tastes for dress and fashion. He wished Lehzen to be dismissed. Lord Liverpool saw the Princess who refused to consider Conroy even as Keeper of the Privy Purse and agreed with Lord Liverpool that she should do without a private secretary. After her first council Lord Melbourne received Conroy's terms for retirement – a peerage, £3,000 per annum, the Grand Cross of the Bath and a seat on the Privy Council. He got the £3,000, a baronetcy and a promise of the first vacancy in an Irish peerage. He did not retire.]

Friday, January 26th Walked again with the Duke. He seemed deeply hurt at Peel's speech of last Tuesday which throws him over certainly about Canada; and altogether I think he feels sore. I told him a conversation I had had with Lord Aberdeen at Burghley in which he assured me of Peel's reverence and regard for the Duke. He listened coldly, declared his entire unbelief in Lord Aberdeen's statement, and added that he was of opinion that Peel wished to do everything he could to thwart and oppose him.

He talked a good deal on politics this evening – said it was impossible the Government of this country should ever go on without a virtual repeal of the Reform Bill – that Parliament did not represent the opinion of the intelligent classes, and that therefore in fact there was no such thing as public opinion.

In our conversation this morning he told me in the event of the Tories coming in, he did not wish to take office; that he should be very reluctant to be Secretary for Foreign Affairs, "But it is impossible for a man in my situation to say positively what he would or would not do." I suggested the idea of President of the Council or Privy Seal, which he rejected almost indignantly, and said he should prefer to lead the House of Lords without office, or rather, not to lead them at all. I said they could not be kept together without him, that they would not follow Lord Lyndhurst. He said, "No – but Aberdeen." I said that nobody could have the same advantage as he had, from his great name and influence, and the respect of the Peers for his opinions. "I beg your pardon. I have no influence. There is no respect for my opinion, *none I assure you.*" This only shows how hurt and irritated his feelings were at the moment.

He considers Lord Grey as infinitely more guilty than Lord Melbourne, and said the country would never prosper till it prepared to impeach him.

Saturday, January 27th Left S. Saye at nine o'clock for town that Lord S. might have time to go down to Hatfield afterwards. I dined with Mlle. D'Este . . .

Sunday, January 28th Lord Aberdeen called upon me. I told him the Duke was annoyed at Peel's speech. He answered that the Duke had hitherto been in the habit of confiding his griefs against Peel to him, but that he had not heard from him on this occasion and feared the Duke might have withdrawn his confidence from him as he had been heard to say that Aberdeen was the person for whom Peel had the most esteem. He added that in consequence of what I had said to him at Burghley, he had induced Peel to write to the Duke from Drayton and tell him his opinion on the state of affairs — that Peel was anxious to conciliate the Duke and should do anything amiable that I should recommend. I advised that he should upon all occasions go and consult the Duke in person and tell him openly and frankly (if it be possible to make Peel open and frank), his opinions, never allowing them to [be] transmitted through a third person. Straightforwardness and direct communications are the only way with the Duke. Nothing can be more degrading than the position of Ministers . . .

Wednesday, January 31st I told the Duke after dinner an anecdote I heard this morning from Lord Fitzgerald, and which I believe to be true, that Lord Aberdeen had applied to the Ministers to have an office created under him in Canada, a sort of lieutenant to govern in his absence. They refused on the ground of injustice to Sir John Colborne, upon which he sent Stockmar with the same request to the Queen, and the additional one that Conroy should be appointed to the office. The Queen was very angry, and, supposing the Ministers privy to it, wrote a furious letter to Lord Melbourne who, on the receipt of it, flung the paper on the floor and exclaimed it was impossible to go on if such proceedings were allowed.

[Baron Christian von Stockmar, was an Anglo-Belgian statesman of a Swedish family, born at Coburg. He had been medical attendant to Prince Leopold on his marriage to Princess Charlotte and become his secretary and controller. He was sent to England in 1837 by her uncle to advise the young Victoria.]

Saturday, February 3rd The storm about the Duke's speech is subsiding, but it has been really very great. In the City, some of the more violent proposed to abandon the petition against the sitting members "as it was no use – the Tories only supported Government". I think the prospects of our party very bad; it will be impossible to keep them together if they are not brought to action, in the H. of Commons particularly. On the other hand is the doubt whether a Tory Government, when formed, could stand – the risk and impoverishment of a dissolution, and the formidable strength that would be given to the now insignificant democratic party by the junction of Whigs and Radicals in opposition.

Wednesday, February 7th Went to the Olympic – capital fun . . .

Wednesday, February 14th A small party at dinner here – the Bishop of Exeter, Henningsen, Lockhart, Croker, Bankes, the Hardinges and G. Wortleys. Bankes and Croker sat next each other at dinner, each watching when the other should launch forth, that he might pounce upon him. At last the silence broke and Croker eventually gained a complete victory: altogether very agreeable. . .

Saturday February 17th A dinner and evening party at home.

[This appears to be the occasion on which Disraeli (for whom Lady Londonderry had asked for an invitation for the evening party following the dinner), had "a great deal" of conversation with Fanny, who received him with "great cordiality". He described it as a most brilliant party, and the first in the house since it had been re-opened. He had been there in the days of the old Marchioness and said her receptions had contained as many stars as a tale from the Arabian Nights – "The Duke, in his Garter ribband and Golden Fleece." The affability of the young Marchioness made an indelible impression upon him.]

The Duke and Lord and Lady Lyndhurst dined here. There is nothing to object to about her, but one cannot help saying, when she comes into the room, "*Why* did he marry her?" She is not handsome, but looks intelligent and *got through* very well.

[Lord Lyndhurst's second marriage, to Georgina, daughter of Louis Goldsmid, was happy though it did not bring him an heir, and lasted more than a quarter of a century.]

Lord Aberdeen is in despair at the pacific sentiments of the Duke and lamented it to me. He is quite for supporting Molesworth's motion on the 6th. Peel, he says, is undecided, and the only hope of influencing him is thro' the Duke—who is worse than he is. But he (Lord A). still hopes they may decide on active measures.

Wednesday, February 19th The Duke called here. I never saw him so annoyed. He sat the whole time, leaning back in his chair, with his finger between his teeth, and scarcely looking at me who sat on one side of him. I found him very decided in his opinion of the impolicy of supporting Molesworth. "I should like to know, when they have carried the motion, and turned Ministers out, what is to be the next step? Eh? What is to happen then?" He said the immediate consequence would be a rebellion excited by O'Connell in Ireland — our troops being absent in Canada. *That this* Parliament would not grant troops to put it down, and serious mischief would happen before you could assemble another. Besides, how to carry on Irish elections in a state of civil war? I could not deny the difficulties that would attend a Tory Government and could only oppose the danger of the party splitting on Molesworth's motion.

[On March 2nd he moved a vote of censure upon the Colonial Secretary, Lord Glenelg. Lord Sandon proposed an amendment, condemning the Government's Canadian policy, and Molesworth's original motion was withdrawn. The Government got a majority of twenty-nine; Molesworth did not vote.]

Duke "The party! What party? What is the meaning of a party if they do not follow their leaders? I don't care sixpence if they split! D---m! 'em: let 'em go!"

I said that if Peel were a more popular leader he might do a great deal to appease them. He might assemble them and reason with them on the state of things. That they complained of the want of personal communication with him; and that if no decision was announced, they would be apt to pledge themselves.

Duke "He cannot announce a decision till the last moment. I could not do so myself in his place. What I cannot bear is to hear a man blamed for what he cannot help. The great thing is to do what we think right, without caring for the party! What would they have? Do we not in fact legislate for the country now? Peel can carry any measure he pleases. Besides, I ask you, in common justice, in common morality, am I justified in forcing this poor girl into all these embarrassments, *against* her will. That's the thing — *against* her will. With William IV it was different."

He spoke also of the danger of driving the whole Whig party into the most violent opposition, by forcing out their Ministry; whereas if they break up of themselves some might be expected to join us.

Altogether he appeared to me settled in his determination against it. We had, as usual, a good deal of conversation about Douro. Peel and the Duke seem to be getting on better: Peel is more attentive to him, which seems to succeed. I cannot help hoping I have contributed to it. I am afraid there is a strong feeling in the party against the Duke just now.

Tuesday, February 20th Went to the Adelphi to see the Italian dwarf in *The Gnome Fly*. Curious and nasty . . .

Saturday, February 24th Dined at Lord Ashburton's and for the first time in my life met Lord Brougham. I thought him one of the most agreeable men I ever saw, and the more so as his conversation is without effort, *coule de source*, and appears to be only the overflowing of high spirits and a mind stored with ideas. The oddity of his face, and gestures, his Scotch accent, and affected freedom of manner in speaking to everybody, do not take off from the effect. Politics were not touched upon, except a *coup de patte* occasionally bestowed by Brougham upon the Ministers. The rest of the party were all strong Tories — indeed he professes now that he can bear no other society.

[A truly remarkable example of Brougham's talent for pleasing the most improbable ladies. He had become an embarrassment to Melbourne and his colleagues since his disappointment that he had not become Prime Minister.]

Tuesday, February 27th Majority against Ministers last night 9 — upon O'Connell's breach of privilege. A great triumph. Lord Ellenborough told me to-day that Lord Lyndhurst had all along been the person to set Brougham on to attack Ministers, and that he corresponded with him from Paris for that purpose.

Thursday, March 1st I have a letter from the Duke who says Lyndhurst must be mad.

Friday, March 2nd Lord Teignmouth has carried the Marylebone election by 400. This strong proof of reaction, coming just now, is very important.

Sunday, March 4th The Duke called here on his way to Peel's, where he was to meet Stanley, Graham and Aberdeen. His feelings are certainly a good deal changed about the course to be pursued on Tuesday. He says nearly the same things, but says them in a different way. He was in very good humour, said his decided opinion was to get rid of Molesworth's motion by the previous question — went over all the arguments against undertaking the Government and the unreasonableness of our party, and declared that the Tories could not form a Government, that nobody would dare vacate their seats to be re-elected, and went so far as to say that there was no reaction anywhere but in Marylebone. However, when I repeated my observation that the worst evil was to have a split in the party, he listened patiently and made no reply.

He called upon me again on his way from Peel's, two hours after — very well pleased with the meeting, and told me he thought a course had been determined upon which would satisfy the party, at which he was evidently pleased. An amendment censuring the Colonial policy of Government is to be moved — the exact circumstances to be regulated by the conduct of Ministers. But the Duke seemed perfectly content, and all irritation has subsided as if it had never been.

I am very glad it has ended so well, for I am convinced Peel would have done nothing without his consent, and then the party must have broken up. He still said he thought we could not form a government, and that if we did, there would be great difficulties to encounter in the reluctance of the Queen, and her probable intrigues with her former Ministers . . .

Thursday, March 8th A majority of 29 against us last night upon Molesworth's motion, much increased by casualties, which were all against us. Upon the whole, we are well out of it, and our party at last voted together, and kept clear of the Radicals. However, I have no doubt this will keep the Ministers in much longer than they could otherwise have remained . . .

Friday, March 16th Lady Maryborough's. Brougham talked to me of the general feel in favour of the abolition of slavery — said it was the only question on which people of this country took any real interest — that owing to *that* chiefly, and to other causes, four-fifths of those in the lower and middling classes, who last year supported Ministers, are now hostile to them, and that the only policy for the Conservatives was to take up the Anti-Slavery cry.

Lord Fitzgerald, who was by, seemed to acquiesce in this, and when Brougham was gone, went on speaking in the same *sense* . . . Lord Lyndhurst's behaviour since his new conjunction with Brougham is really so childish, that it is difficult to form any conjectures respecting him; but I suspect there is a party in the House of Lords ready to desert the Duke, and that Lyndhurst is *quite* ready to be put at their head.

Saturday, March 17th A dinner and party at home. The Prince and Princess of Capua (née Smith) were here. She is very handsome, and infinitely more royal in her manners and appearance than our real Royalties. Strange, that a wild Irish girl, turned into a Bourbon princess, should come out so well.

[In 1816 when Ferdinand of Naples was restored to his patrimony by the Allies as Ferdinand IV of Naples, III of Sicily and I of The Two Sicilies, he created his heir the hereditary Prince, Francis, Duke of Calabria, and the sons of Francis, the Duke of Noto, the Prince of Capua, the Count of Syracuse and the Count of Lecce. The Princess of Capua had been born Miss Penelope Smythe, of Ballynatray, Co. Waterford. The Capuas wandered about Europe, their Gretna Green marriage stigmatized as morganatic, for twenty-seven years. In 1862 Victor Emmanuel granted the widow the title of Duchess of Capua, and the Villa Marlia, Lucca. Palmerston gave the lead to English society to accept them, to annoy Ferdinand II.]

Lord Aberdeen told me that he had no doubt that the Duke's famous speech upon Canada, which made so much noise, kept the Ministers in, upon that occasion, and that they would have gone out that night if it had not been made. Lord Robert Grosvenor called the other day on Lord John Russell and remonstrated with him upon putting down the yeomanry. Lord John said, "I will tell you the real fact. The Tories are so powerful in the counties, they must be got the better of; and this is the best way of doing it."

Wednesday March 28th Lord S. went to Hatfield on his way to Scotland.

Thursday, March 29th Dined at Pozzo's. I sat next him and he was very agreeable and communicative. He told me that he communicated everything that passed between him and the Ministers to the Duke — that he was convinced of Louis Philippe's wish to have a Conservative Ministry here, but that he had no influence over Leopold, who guided this Court, and who had his personal predelications to gratify — that the Anti-Jacobin party on the Continent would prove stronger than it was supposed, when it was tried and that our Ministers were mistaken if they relied upon the strength of the opposite side.

[Leopold had married Louise of Orleans, daughter of Louis Philippe in 1832. She was seven years senior to Queen Victoria and a close friend. She wrote at once in 1848 commending her unfortunate parents to the Queen when Louis Philippe and family arrived in England, turned out by his Radicals whom Pozzo represented as so uninfluential.]

He was the person who induced the French Ministry to make the invasion of Spain under the Duke of Angoulême. He talked of this favourite subject — the campaign of 1813–14 — and assured me that he stood alone against all the *Puissances* in advocating that things be brought to extremity — that the two Emperors, Metternich and Castlereagh, Aberdeen were all for making peace . . .

Friday, March 30th The Duke called here. He gave me an account of the visit Lord Melbourne made him the other day, which has caused many conjectures. Some time ago, Lord G. Lennox made a motion, supported by some of our party, for interfering with promotion etc., in the Marines, which was carried. Lord M. wrote to the Duke stating the difficulties in which this vote had involved them, and requesting that he would allow himself to be placed at the head of a commission of inquiry, which was the only mode by which they could extricate themselves. The Duke replied that the subject required great consideration, and it was agreed that Lord M. should call upon him, which he did. The Duke disapproved of the instructions to the Commissioners, as going too far. Lord M. however, sent them back to him some days after, unchanged. The Duke then said he would not be at the head of the Commission, and in consequence of that threat they had to be altered . . .

I dined at Sir F. Burdett's — a strange mixture of Papists, Bishops, Whigs and Tories.

Saturday, March 31st A party at the Duchess of Cambridge's.

Sunday, April 1st The Duke called here to settle with me who was to go to S. Saye to meet me. I gave him my opinion of his colleagues, in the course of our conversation — that Peel and Aberdeen were thoroughly honest and honourable men, Ellenborough without political principles, Fitzgerald a jobber, Hardinge for whichever side he would make most by, and Lyndhurst a double dealer. He said nothing, but seemed to assent. Speaking of the contrast between his character and the Duke of Marlborough's, with respect to sensitiveness to popular applause and censure, he said, "I never cared about it, not even in the beginning, and my feeling *now* is (it may be a feeling of vanity, and I daresay it is) that nobody can do me either good or harm except myself. Therefore I am very careful what I do. But I care very little what is said." He went this morning, as he frequently does, to the Chapel Royal at 8 o'clock — nobody there but himself and a girl of fifteen . . .

Sunday, April 8th The Duke called here. He talked of Mme. de Lieven, told me that the great service he had rendered her, which I had heard him mention before, was getting back her letters to Metternich. Metternich was her lover, and when she took up Canning, they quarrelled, and after his death she applied to the Duke to get back her letters. He wrote to Metternich, who agreed to return them on condition of receiving his own. Accordingly, they arrived in a great box at Apsley House, docketed and arranged in the most official manner. Mme. de Lieven came there to be present at the unpacking of the box, inspected them very carefully, and carried them off. I asked the Duke how she came to apply to him to render her such a service after the infamous way in which she had behaved to him. "Because I am the Duke of Wellington, and because they knew I was an honest man."

He said he did not believe Canning had ever been her lover. He went on to talk of Canning — traced all the troubles of the present day to his Ministry. The Duke spoke of Canning, Peel and Lord Castlereagh, and of their several abilities, and I was much struck with his manner of *valuing* them, which was wholly in reference to their habits of business, common sense and information on necessary topics. What one should describe as genius or talent seemed to go for nothing with him. He said Canning was "a man of imagination, always in a delusion, never saw things as they were; that he had wonderful powers of speaking and writing and in that was superior to Mr. Pitt (who could speak but not write), but that he was wholly uninformed as to foreign affairs" — in short, spoke of him as a charlatan. Peel also, he said, knew nothing of foreign affairs; but they were not in his province; and he was thoroughly acquainted with official business at home.

Lord Londonderry[1] could neither speak nor write, but he was completely master of all our foreign relations, and knew what he was about. I observed that the two latter were honester men than Canning. He said Lord Castlereagh was completely so, but Peel was not always scrupulous as to the means he used to gain his object, and his object was often a mean and petty one.

Tuesday, April 12th Went to S. Saye with Mildred, Blanche and Eustace. Found the Duke alone and walked with him a little while before the others came. He told me that he thought Leopold inclined to give good advice to the Queen, but that probably Ministers would mislead him.

The De Ros's and Lord Ellenborough came to dinner. Douro and Charles also in the house. It is grievous to see their neglect and inattention towards the Duke, or rather their repugnance to speak to him or approach him. During the whole time I was in the house on this visit, I never heard either of them *lui adresser la parole*. Gerald dined with us every day and his conduct is most advantageously contrasted with that of his cousins. Speaking of military education, the Duke observed that "the best education for all professions was the common education of the country they were in".

Good Friday, April 13th In the evening the conversation turned upon the campaigns. The Duke told us a curious anecdote of some Cuirassiers at Quatre Bras. It was towards the end of the day, when he was observing the troops from an eminence, and he saw forty or fifty Cuirassiers turn down a road, and, finding themselves too much exposed, dash off into a sort of walled farmyard of which the gate was standing open. They disappeared, and he concluded they had got off through the enclosure into a wood behind. But in about quarter of an hour they reappeared, galloping out as hard as they could along the road; and most of them got away. They had found the exit from the yard and remained *perdus* till they supposed that the enemy concluded they had escaped.

[1] The Duke is referring again to Castlereagh here.

The Duke went over and saw the Prussian position on the morning of Quatre Bras. "I told them they would be beat, but they treated me as an ignorant fellow; and it was no business of mine. I pointed out to them the faults of their position, and to Hardinge also, who was there; and he did not perceive them till I had remarked them to him. There was a marshy rivulet between them and the enemy, which neither party could cross. And they had posted their men on a declivity, so as to expose them in detail to all the fire of the enemy, without the possibility of acting themselves."

This day the Duke read to me his Memorandum on the government of the Army which he had previously mentioned to me — most clear and excellent.

Saturday, April 14th The Duke went hunting. I took a sketch of the house and afterwards a ride with Lord Douro. Lord St. Vincent and Miss Jervis arrived to dinner, also the Cowleys.

Sunday, April 15th, Easter Day At breakfast the Duke was speaking of the shameful use made by the Whigs of patronage in the Army and Navy for party purposes, and the contrast it presented to former practice. King George IV, after the war, objected to giving a regiment to a violent Whig, Sir Ronald Fergusson.[1] "But I told him he *must*, and he *did*."

After church I had a conversation with the Duke which I shall always [A leaf is torn out of the Diary here. It apparently refers to Miss Jervis]. singing, but scarcely considers her as a rational person. She has certainly great musical talent, but is very mad and extremely vain, and anxious to give out that she has a great power over him, and to show him off. I was afraid his good nature would lead him to allow her to take liberties, and to comply with her caprices in a manner which might seem to give foundation to the reports she is anxious to spread. He was not all offended, but laughed and said it was all nonsense.

We have now eight children in the house — three of mine, three De Ros's, two Grosvenors — and the rush of delight they make when the Duke enters the room, and the way in which they surround his chair is quite *touchant*.

[1] General Sir Ronald Crauford Fergusson of Raith (1773–1841) performed distinguished services in Flanders, India, at the Cape and in the Peninsular. As Member for Kirkcaldy burghs, spoke against the Duke of York.

Tuesday, April 17th The Tyrolese singers came down and sung this and the following evening. Some of the neighbours dined here as they have done every day except Sunday, for the last two or three days.

I rode with the Duke this morning to Farley Hill.

Friday April 20th The Duke went early to a meeting of the Board of Guardians, which occupied him till the middle of the day. I took a walk with Rogers.[1]

Saturday, April 21st The St. Vincents and Rogers went away. The Duke out hunting. I took a ride with Lord Mahon. At dinner, the Duke was speaking of the ball that wounded Lord Anglesey, at Waterloo, and which passed over the neck of his horse. He was never touched, but at Orthez. "But I have had horses killed under me — at Assaye, and I *think* at Talavera."

Sunday, April 22nd Croker came down early. I walked a little after church with the Duke and Lady Robert.

In the evening, Lord Mahon and the Duke were talking in a low voice about the plan of jurisdiction for election questions, when the Duke, warmed by the subject, and totally forgetting for the first time Lord Robert's presence (for we had all been models of discretion, never alluding to politics since he had been in the house), jumped up as he often does when he is excited and was just going to utter, in his most emphatic tone "What d – – – d rascals they all are!" when his eye caught Lord Robert and he sunk suddenly down in his chair as if he had had a fit. The whole scene was *impayable*.

Monday, April 23rd Lord and Lady Robert left us after breakfast. We all went round the house afterwards viewing the improvements the Duke intends to make — everybody giving their opinion, and he full of good humour and enjoying the laugh that was sometimes raised against his own propositions. There was a print of himself in one of the rooms, with the title of *"Invictus"*, which Croker told us the Duke had sent home from Portugal, but with this note under the title in his own hand, "Don't holloa till you are out of the wood."

I walked with the Duke after luncheon in the pheasantry; our conversation was chiefly on Douro and Charles.

Speaking of Soult's conspiracy in Portugal, and of Napoleon's

[1] Samuel Rogers (1763–1855), poet, and banker; renowned for his breakfast parties, his mordant wit and genuine kindliness.

281

seeming confidence in him afterwards, he said "Napoleon was right in many things, and especially in one thing — he forgave everything but want of success". He told us a curious anecdote of General Wrede, who was with Napoleon at the time of the Battles of Eylau and Friedland, and asked him what was his plan of campaign. He answered *"Je n'en ai pas. Je n'ai point de plan de campagne."* "And it was true", the Duke added, "he had no plan; all he required was that his troops should be assembled and posted as he directed, and then he marched and struck a great blow, defeated the enemy, and acted afterwards as circumstances would allow." If the war had gone on after the Battle of Toulouse, the Duke would have taken Bayonne and Bordeaux, and have marched along the coast toward the Loire, attended by the transports.

He said he knew what the Whigs would have done if they had come in after Perceval's death — they would have sent out Lord Hastings to examine how things were going on in the Peninsula, "And I should have received him very well, and he would soon have found out that I knew all about it and he knew nothing."

Speaking of Ney, he said it was absolutely necessary to make an example.

Lord S. arrived today to dinner, from Hatfield, where he had spent a day or two on his way from Scotland.

Tuesday, April 24th The melancholy day of leaving S. Saye. The Duke came up to town at the same time. The children returned with me. Lord S. went on to Dorsetshire. Got to town about four o'clock and dined with Mlle. D'Este . . .

Thursday, May 3rd Dined at the Duke's. The Jerseys, Beckets, De Horseys, Esterhazy, Prince and Princess Chorinsky, Lord Hertford, the Zichys, Lyndhursts, Lord Wilton, Croker, Lord Jocelyn, Chas. Bagot, Lord Lowther. The Duke terribly deaf.

Friday, May 4th Went with the Duke to the private exhibition of the Royal Academy the first time of its being placed in the National Gallery.

[The Royal Academy, instituted in 1768, held exhibitions in Pall Mall and Somerset House, till 1838. The first exhibition in Burlington House took place in 1869. The National Gallery was founded in 1824 and also held its first exhibitions in Pall Mall. Completed and opened April 9th, 1838. Peel was an original Trustee.]

Some beautiful pictures of Landseer's (who has decidedly the best). The Queen's favourite animals, the Highland hunter and a portrait of a Newfoundland dog, are the finest things of the kind I ever saw. Wilkie's is a sad falling off — Hayter's portrait of the Queen abominable — like, but disagreeably so.

Saturday, May 5th Went with the Duke to the panoramas of St. Sebastian, Canton and New Zealand. He seemed particularly interested in that of St. Sebastian, and thought it like.

Thursday, May 10th The Queen's Ball. She looked remarkably well, almost pretty, and I think is grown.[1] She did the honours with much grace, and danced quite well enough for a Queen. No distinction of party in the invitations. The apartments had a brilliant effect — rather too theatrical. They are certainly in bad taste, but looked well for the occasion.

Sunday, May 13th I hear Peel's dinner, given to him yesterday by the Conservatives of the House of Commons, went off admirably.

Monday, May 14th The Duke has an attack of deafness which has occasioned the debate in the House of Lords of to-night to be put off. He writes me word, however, that he is not otherwise ill.

Lord S. all this week with the Yeomanry at Hatfield. I dined at Lady Tankerville's.

Wednesday, May 16th The Duke wrote to desire I would call upon him. I took Mildred with me, and went. I walked with him up and down the Gallery the whole time I remained, which is his exercise now he is confined to the house. I think he is very well in health, but very deaf and has a rheumatic stiffness in his neck which makes him look bent, and worse than he really is. He told me he had been to see Lord Wellesley the first time for some years. Lord Wellesley sent him a message, thro' Lady Wellesley; in consequence he rode immediately down to Fulham. There was no *explanation*, but the two brothers met most cordially.

[Richard, Marquis Wellesley (1760–1842), eldest of the Duke's five brothers, was Governor-General of India 1797, Ambassador to Spain 1805, Secretary for Foreign Affairs 1812, Lord-Lieutenant of Ireland 1821–8. His second wife was an American Roman Catholic widow from Baltimore. His first wife had been French and he had lived with her and had children by her for nine years before their

[1] The Queen had not attained five feet.

283

marriage in 1793. A man of mercurial temperament, he was a great trial to the Duke. They had differed openly in the Lords on Catholic Emancipation.]

Peel was announced while I stayed, and the Duke went down to him, but returned shortly after to finish *his walk*. At half past five he sent me away, having letters to write. I dined at Lady Carnarvon's.

Thursday, May 17th The Birthday. An immense crowd.

Friday, May 18th Went again to see the Duke. Found his deafness better. Dined with Mlle. D'Este.

Wednesday, May 23rd A dinner at home and assembly in the evening. A regular drag-net — between seven and eight hundred people. Heard of Mr. Barham's death — a great blessing.

Sunday, May 27th The Duke called here. He certainly looks better and is much less deaf, but there is a stiffness and stooping about his neck that I do not like.

Wednesday, May 30th Went to see the Duke. Dined at the Duke of Devonshire's — afterwards the Duke of Sussex's party. I saw his reception of O'Connell. He shook him cordially by the hand, exclaiming, "Ah! Dan, my boy. How are you? You see we never forget you." The Queen merely made him a courtesy.

There were, it is said, two thousand people asked — the crowd and heat excessive. An extraordinary piece of luck happened to me. Having lost a diamond brooch of considerable value, on the grass opposite the Palace, where I walked to find my carriage, it was found the next morning by one of my servants whom I sent to make the search, lying on the same spot.

[The Duke of Sussex had a splendid *suite* in Kensington Palace, so "the Palace" alluded to was Kensington.]

Saturday, June 2nd Lord S. at Hatfield for a few days. I dined with Mlle. D'Este.

Monday, June 4th The Duke called here. He looks *much* better in consequence of going down to S. Saye yesterday. Dined with the Cravens. Lady Jersey's in the evening.

Tuesday, June 5th Lady Willoughby's.

Saturday, June 9th Dined at Lord de Grey's. A dinner of twelve only — Peel, Stanley, Lord Ripon, Lord Aberdeen — very pleasant.

Monday, June 11th Lady Manver's concert.

QUEEN VICTORIA

By Sir George Hayter. Reproduced by permission of the National Portrait Gallery

"Went with the Duke to the private exhibition of the Royal Academy, the first time of it being placed in the National Gallery. Hayter's portrait of the Queen abomin-able — like, but disagreeably so."

(From the Diary of the 2nd Marchioness, May 4th, 1838)

Tuesday, June 12th The Duke, the Clanwilliams, Mlle. D'Este, Lord Aberdeen, Lord Fitzgerald, Lord Stuart and Mr Bankes dined here. The Duke terribly deaf — as bad as ever.

Wednesday, June 13th I went to see him. He was less deaf today, but he stoops very much. I questioned him about it. He acknowledged feeling some pain and stiffness in his neck, but positively denied that there was any swelling or inflammation. We dined at Lady Falmouth's.

Friday, June 15th Esterhazy's ball. An enormous squeeze. The first sample of the Coronation fêtes — foreigners from all parts of the known and unknown earth — like the Tower of Babel. The Duke very much cheered by the mob . . .

Monday June 18th Went to see the Duke. Found him in great force and spirits and looking remarkably well and less deaf. It always does one good to see him on this day. The weather being fine, there were immense crowds of people in the Parks etc., the whole day, partly attracted by the expectation of a review which did not take place, but they all seemed gay and good humoured.

Friday, June 22nd Dined with the De La Warrs. The Queen's concert. The Duke and Soult met in the music room for the first time for many years, and shook hands. Soult's appearance is different from what I expected. He is a gentleman-like old man, with rather a benevolent cast of countenance, such as I should have expected in William Penn or Washington — tall, and rather stooping, the top of his head bald. He does not look above 64 or 65. The Duke, though the lines on his face are deeper, has a fresher colour and a brighter eye.

The Duke is extremely annoyed at Croker's having brought out that article in the *Quarterly* on the Battle of Toulouse just at this moment. Besides, he says it is full of inaccuracies, which may, however, be excused as founded professedly on the French accounts. The Duc de Nemours was at the concert.[1] He is more like a white sheep than anything I ever saw.

The influx of foreigners into London is something prodigious. The streets and parks are actually blocked up with people, and the noise and movement and confusion are incessant.

The Ambassadors are extremely annoyed at having to go in the

[1] Louis-Charles-Philippe (1814–96), second son of Louis-Philippe.

Queen's train, in the procession. Pozzo complains bitterly, and with reason.

Tuesday, June 26th Dined at Lady Kinnoull's.

Wednesday, June 27th The Duchess of Buccleuch's breakfast. It was almost impossible to get there, the streets are so crowded. Piccadilly was actually blocked up today for an hour and a half.

Thursday, June 28th The Coronation Lord S. and I and the two girls started at a little before nine, and found little difficulty in getting to the Abbey, which we reached in about half an hour. Mildred and Blanche were taken to The Duke's box (Lord High Constable) for which we had given them tickets, and we repaired to our places.

[The Duke had considered asking for "my friend Bobby" as a page but decided he was too small for a uniform coat.[1] But he was undoubtedly present, for his daughter, Lady Gwendolen Cecil, in her biography of him[2] recounts that he had said he would have remembered nothing but the weariness of the long ceremony had not a good-natured neighbour lifted him on to his shoulder at the moment the crown was actually put on the head of the Queen. Her future Prime Minister received an abiding memory of the slight lonely girl, the centre of a scene of gorgeous colour and light.]

Nearly all the peers and peeresses were assembled. The spectators had already been many hours in their places. At ten, the guns announced the Queen's departure from the Palace, and about half past eleven the head of the procession, the Foreign Ministers, began to arrive.

The Queen entered about twelve, attended by the great officers of State. She looked well, and, as far as I could see, perfectly composed, her manner graceful, with as much dignity as her want of height allowed her to display. She was loudly cheered, but I should say, not enthusiastically.

The day was fine, and occasional gleams of sunshine falling upon the different groups of assistants thro' the long Gothic windows of the Abbey produced a beautiful effect. The peers and peeresses were very numerous, more so, I think, than at the last Coronation, and the whole effect finer. When the crown was put upon her head, she seemed to suffer under its weight, but went very well through the homage and the remainder of the ceremony. When the Duke touched

[1] Cecil Papers, Wellington Letters, 278. [2] Vol. I, pp. 19-20.

the Queen's crown, a burst of applause resounded throughout the Abbey. It was impossible to mistake it, it was the burst of real feeling, not the applause of form. Lord Melbourne coloured and grew pale again. A faint applause was raised for Lord Grey, but the tail in the House of Commons gallery endeavoured in vain to raise one for the Minister. Lord Rolle in ascending the steps to do homage fell back. The Queen with great grace and presence of mind advanced to assist him, and this occasioned much applause, which was again renewed when the Duke walked down the aisle after the ceremony.

[John, 1st Baron Rolle of Stevenstone [1750–1842), was an old Pittite Tory, who had voted against the Reform Bill. Queen Victoria mentioned his fall in her Journal, and her advance to help him on his second effort to ascend the steps of the Throne. The incident was immortalized by several artists, including John Martin. The Queen believed him to be eighty-two but he was eighty-eight.]

The whole was over by four o'clock, but we did not get to our carriage till half past six, and we were an hour getting home, such was the throng of carriages to avoid the crowd. I only stayed to dine and change my dress and went at nine to the Duke's ball. The candles were not lighted, but I found him, and had half an hour's conversation with him before anybody arrived — much the pleasanter part of the evening. The ball was infinitely better for the Coronation, as fatigue and fear of a crowd prevented many people from coming and made it less unpleasantly full than his usually are. The Duc de Nemours, Soult etc. were there. I was amused at hearing the Duke of Osuna complimenting the Duke upon the applause he had met with in the Abbey, evidently thinking it must be a most gratifying subject to him. *"Vous avez eu un acceuil très flatteur, Monsigneur, ce matin."* *"Oui"*, said the Duke, with the utmost indifference. *"On me reçoit toujours très bien dans ce pays-ci."* *"Ah! mais c'est trop juste!"* said the Spaniard bowing to the ground. *"Oui toujours, très bien, n'est-ce pas?"* addressing me.

I think, however, although he always despises mob popularity, that he was gratified with the applause which came from the most respectable people, judges and privy councillors included, which attended his leaving the Abbey. He remarked upon it to me. But a feeling — a real and sincere feeling, tho' almost a romantic one, that the chief attention and homage is on all occasions due to the

Sovereign when present (the effect of that extraordinary devotion to the Crown which I never saw approached in any other person) diminished his gratification, and even gave him a degree of annoyance. He looked back to see if the Queen was coming, with an air of vexation, as if to say, "'This is too much; this belongs of right to her.'" I left him at supper at half past two in the morning, apparently not the least tired.

He had written twice to Croker to endeavour to prevent his publishing that article. "I am a very clever man, a very clever man indeed, except when any gentleman happens to differ in opinion with me on any point – and then I am not a clever man at all." He told Croker, in one of his letters that this was a gentlemanlike country, and the Tories were the gentlemanlike party in that gentlemanlike country, and therefore, not at this time to publish such an article.

[The Duke had postponed the publication of the eleventh (Toulouse) volume of Gurwood's edition of the Dispatches, on purpose to avoid offending Soult who was coming as Ambassador Extraordinary for the Coronation.]

Monday, July 2nd Dined at Lord Londonderry's – the Austrian, Russian, Prussian and Swedish Ministers, the Duke, Peel, Lyndhursts etc. in all eight and forty. We dined in the Long Gallery; very handsome and well done. The first time the Duke has been asked to dine there these three years, but I suppose they have seen at last the folly of their conduct and *he* is always ready to be reconciled.

In the evening, the Queen's ball.

[The Hertfordshire *Reformer* reported that Her Majesty's State Ball at the New Palace surpassed any which had been given since the reign of George IV. Her Majesty, who opened the ball with the Duc de Nemours, was attired in a blue satin dress covered with white silk lace, and wore the insignia of the Garter on her left arm, also the star. Her head-dress was a wreath of white roses with a cluster of diamonds in the centre, and diamond drop earrings. The local notabilities present were the Duchess of Bedford and the Marquess and Marchioness of Salisbury.]

Tuesday, July 3rd A ball at home. I had about 600 people, and it went off very well, and lasted till between 3 and 4 in the morning. I saw the Duke present Hardinge to Soult – "*J'ai l'honneur de vous présenter le Chevalier Hardinge qui était avec l'Armée quand"* (he might have added *"quand j'ai eu l'honneur de vous battre"*). Soult replied, *"Tout ce qui me vient de votre main, m'est toujours agréable."*[?]

The Duke is disinclined to give the foreigners a dinner because Soult must necessarily be among them, and he does not like to ask him to a table covered with trophies won against the French — a reason that certainly would not have occurred to anybody else. I told him I hoped he would ask them, notwithstanding; that they would expect it of him, and that as to trophies, it was impossible to avoid them; in fact he was a trophy himself. He said he should try at all events to make out something for his table that had no relation to the war.

Wednesday, July 4th Another great dinner at Lord Hertford's, in the Regent's Park — the same number as at Lord L'.s.

[Francis Charles Seymour Conway, 3rd Marquess of Hertford (1777–1842), had electoral influence which made him a Tory peer of weight. He was caricatured by Thackeray in *Vanity Fair* as the Marquis of Steyne, and by Disraeli in *Coningsby* as Lord Monmouth. He possessed three houses in London, and died in Dorchester House, Park Lane, but Hertford House, Manchester Square, housed the best of his and his successor's collection of French works of art.]

The Duke dined there, Mme. de Stroganoff, and the Princess Schwartzenburg. The husbands were at a Ministerial dinner at Stroganoff's. Princess Schwartzenburg very pretty, but with that disagreeable affected Viennese manner which I cannot like.

The Duke called upon me this morning. Speaking of the *Life of Wilberforce* lately come out,[1] I asked him if he did not think Wilberforce, tho' he carried his opinions too far, had done good to the morals of Society. "Not the least in the world." He was equally of opinion that he had increased the general traffic in slaves by procuring its abolition in England.

Speaking of the present strictness of keeping the Sunday, he observed that he could not give a dinner on that day without being watched and attacked by anonymous letters, and that if he dined out, he never had his carriage, but went in his cab, to avoid observation. "It is astonishing," he said, "how much power may be obtained by

[1] The five-volume *Life of Wilberforce* by his sons, Robert, Isaac and Samuel, appeared first in 1838.

any body of people in this country who have a good end in view, and persevere in working together."

With respect to Wilberforce's observations on the desirableness of making Sunday a day of rest to those engaged in official occupations etc. he said, "But what *is* a day of rest? You may rest from manual labour, but you cannot rest the mind. Lord Castlereagh might have abstained from opening his despatches, but he could not prevent his mind from being anxious about their contents. He would be thinking what they contained — and would that be rest to him?"

Thursday, July 5th Duchess of Gloucester's ball. I never saw such a crowd — quite terrific — 600 people crowded in a house that holds 200.

Friday, July 6th Soult's ball. Another great mob. He asked everybody who had left their names with him.

Saturday, July 7th I went to see the Duke and stayed with him near an hour, walking as usual up and down the gallery. His neck is certainly much better, by the application of mustard poultices, and the deafness quite gone. He is engaged to Lord Beresford on the day appointed for the great City dinner, which annoys me. He *ought not* to be absent from a great national festival given to foreign powers. Such a thing *should* not and *must* not be without the Duke of Wellington . . .

Sunday, July 8th I spoke with Lord Aberdeen about the Duke's engagement and he quite agreed with me that it must be put an end to, and undertook to manage it with Lord Beresford.

The Ministers have been obliged to apologize for their outrageous conduct in causing the Ambassadors of the four Revolutionary Powers — France, Spain, Portugal and Belgium — to be asked alone and before the others, to dine at the Palace. So like the Whigs! First to commit an unnecessary folly and then to have to sneak out of it.

Monday, July 9th A great dinner and assembly at Count Stroganoff's. All Conservatives at dinner — the Duke, the Peels, Lyndhursts, Londonderrys, Jerseys, Buccleuchs, Northumberlands etc. etc. They have managed the two houses put together extremely well — Lord Stuart's and Lord Caledon's — the reception room in one and the dining-room in the other, and the staircase was beautifully ornamented with a sort of *treillage* of artificial flowers.

[Lord Stuart de Rothesay bought 4 Carlton House Terrace in 1837 on his return from the Paris Embassy. In 1841 it became the Prussian Embassy. Lord Caledon was his brother-in-law.]

They say Stroganoff has a particular turn for giving *fêtes* and nearly ruined himself in that way in Russia. Afterwards, Lady Cadogan's ball.

Tuesday, July 10th Duchess of Buccleuch's breakfast. Afterwards went to the House of Lords with Lady G. Somerset and Lady Clanwilliam. There are only four places where women can sit, but they are very convenient and one hears well. Brougham opened the debate (on the orders given to attack Sardinian vessels conveying arms to Don Carlos), with a capital speech. Lord Melbourne's reply weak – or rather no reply at all. Lord Ripon good – Lord Minto, a wretched speech in which he laid down the doctrine that such orders would be justified by the Quadruple Treaty. This induced the Duke to abandon his first intention of not supporting Brougham's motion, and to resolve upon dividing – very few of our Peers in the House – messages sent off in all directions to collect them, and Lord Redesdale [Tory whip] running to and fro, when Lord Melbourne gets up and throws over Lord Minto entirely. This induces the Duke, who forgets he is not at the head of troops who can wheel about and retire with as much ease as those of the line, to get up again and recommend Their Lordships not to divide. At the conclusion of which word of command he retired, followed by Lord Aberdeen, to dine with Soult. The peers on our side were furious, and though some abstained from voting a great number (among whom, I regret to say, was Lord S.) divided in support of Brougham's motion, which was lost by the numbers being even.

I never was more annoyed in my whole life. There is no doubt the Duke was right in the principle of policy, and in not pressing the motion, but in a party view nothing could be more fatal than such a sudden change after the Lords has been summoned from all parts for a division.

Wednesday, July 11th The breakfast at Sion. This storm will blow over, I hope. The Duke takes it very good humouredly, at least in appearance. I had a walk with him in the evening to see the fireworks.

Friday, July 13th The Duchess of Cambridge's ball. Lord S. went with the Duke to the City dinner, that City dinner which I have been moving heaven and earth to get the Duke to go to, by having the

Beresford dinner put off. And a pretty result it has been! After a long delay in giving the Duke's health, the Lord Mayor at last gave his and Soult's *united*!!! "His Grace the Duke of Dalmatia, and His Grace the Duke of Wellington!!!" Lord Londonderry instantly got up and left the room, observing to those about him that he would not stay to be insulted. Lord S. would have followed him but that he depended on the Duke. The Duke got up and made an excellent answer in very good taste. But he could not do otherwise than feel the insult, and expressed it to Lord S. on his way home. It was proposed to the Duke to give "The French Army". "D – – m 'em," he said, "I'll have nothing to do with 'em but to beat 'em."

All high feeling, all sense of national honour, even all good taste and common sense seem swallowed up in this rage for magnanimity and liberality, and the greatest recommendation to the applause and gratitude of the people of England is to have been all your life their bitterest enemy, to have loaded them with calumnies, and claimed their most incontestable triumphs as your own.

Saturday, July 14th We had a great dinner at home for the foreigners . . . altogether 33.

Monday, July 18th Went early to see the Duke. He is going to have the foreigners to dine on the 28th and showed me some vases he intended as ornaments on the table. They are presents from the King of France, Louis XVIII, and therefore *trophies*, but they have no inscriptions or representations to betray their origin . . .

Tuesday, July 17th Mrs. Damer's children's breakfast. Took Mildred, Blanche and Eustace. In the evening Lady Londonderry's ball.

Wednesday, July 18th The Duke called here while I was out. I went to see the National Gallery with Lord Haddington and the children and was delighted, particularly with the Murillo in the first room.

[St. John with a lamb. Prince Albert's Italian primitives had not yet reached the National Gallery.]

Friday, July 20th The Duchess of Somerset's breakfast. Took Mildred and Blanche there. Returned with the Duke in his carriage.

Monday, July 23rd Princess Schwartzenburg's breakfast at Richmond. A magnificent *fête*.

Tuesday, July 24th Lord Chesterfield's ball. We have received an invitation for that of the Queen on Thursday.

Wednesday, July 25th Went at twelve o'clock to a christening party, at Lady Ravensworth's[1] at Percy's Cross: took the three children.

Thursday, July 26th Went to see the Duke. The Queen's ball. ["Her Majesty wore a white satin costume covered with a figured blonde (silk lace) being ornamented down the front with geranium blossoms. Head-dress of flowers with centres of jewels. Her Majesty also wore the purple ribbon of the Order of the Garter with the Star, suspended from the left side. Her Majesty led off a country dance with the Marquess of Douglas, who wore the Highland national dress."[2]] She received me civilly.

Friday, July 27th Lady Wilton's ball and concert.

Saturday, July 28th I went to see the Duke.

His great dinner to the foreigners, altogether about 48. We dined in the Gallery, between the candelabras. On the table were two large porcelain vases, given by the King of France, and two candelabras by the City of London, and some smaller ornaments, but nothing *personal* to Soult. Of the silver plate some bore "Assaye", and some "Duque de Vitoria" upon them. But one could not help feeling whatever care might be taken not to suggest such ideas, that it was a proud moment to witness Napoleon's great General sitting at his Conqueror's table — equally *his* conqueror and of the master whom he served. Everything that surrounded us was a trophy, even the very room in which we were sitting, the pictures that adorned its walls, the splendid furniture, the magnificent plate, everything was the gift of a grateful nation in recompense of the triumph obtained by the victor over him who was now sitting at his table, and over the deadly and malignant foe to England whose instrument he was. There was a pleasure even in contemplating the figure of Victory that crowned the candelabras and seemed each to hold out her laurel wreath before Soult and his companions — before them, but above their reach, reserved for a greater than they.

Prince George of Cambridge sat next me and a delightful neighbour he was. He entered into all my feelings and enjoyed the day to the utmost. Curiously enough, when Soult entered the house, the

---

[1] Isabella Horatia, eldest daughter of Lord George Seymour, m. 1820 Henry Liddell, 1st Earl of Ravensworth and had issue five sons and eight daughters.
[2] *Reformer*, August 4th, 1838.

band (probably supposing it in their ignorance particularly appropriate) played *"Vive Henri Quatre!"*

Soult went away rather early. There was no taking leave between the Duke and him. The Duke had declined to go tomorrow to a breakfast at Sir R. Otway's given to him on his departure.

Monday, July 30th All the foreigners are gone or going. London is suddenly *tombé à plat* – nothing more to be done or given, most people hurrying out of town. The few that remain seem fallen asleep with their past exertions.

Went with Lady Stanhope and a party to Vauxhall. Weather cold and rainy, gardens not half lighted, whole thing miserable.

Wednesday, August 1st Went to see the Duke. In the afternoon went down to Panshanger. The children all removed this day to Hatfield. Cranborne arrived two days ago. He has almost entirely recovered the hearing of one ear which is a great blessing, but his sight continues much the same.

Thursday, August 2nd At Panshanger. An agreeable party – the Schwartzenburgs, Esterhazy, Erdödy, the Cannings, Mrs. Damer, Lady de Grey, Lord Clanwilliam, Lord Clements, Mr. Ponsonby, Lord Leveson, Lord Harry Vane, Lord Robert Grosvenor. Unluckily it rained all day.

Friday, August 3rd Returned to town.

Sunday, August 5th Went to see the Duke. His rheumatism is not yet removed and he had rather a return of it today. I wish they would send him to Buxton.

Tuesday, August 7th Went to see the Duke. Went to the House of Lords. Rather an amusing speech from Brougham, attacking Lord Durham's proclamation. Afterwards a dry debate on Irish Municipal bill and I came away

Wednesday, August 8th Dined with the Duke. Lord S. out of town. Met the Jerseys, Lord Lyndhurst, Lord Ellenborough, Lord Haddington, Lord Wharncliffe and Lord Ripon.

Note. At this period Lady Salisbury's illness began. She was never really well afterwards and died on the 14th of October, 1839.

(*Signed*) *Gascoyne Salisbury*

[The abrupt cessation of the diaries and the statement of her husband that her fatal illness had already begun cannot be disregarded, but to

294

the Duke and her children she mentioned nothing. That she accompanied Lord S. on a visit to the Duke of Rutland in Derbyshire is confirmed by the following letters, and by letters to her from the Duke, September 2nd–19th.]

Longshawe,

Jeudi.

Mes chères filles,

Je vous suis très obligées de vos lettres: elles sont cependant assez courtes et je soupçonne que Mildred n'a point relu la sienne, comme j'y trouvé une faute grave. Nous sommes arrivés ici Lundi à neuf heures du soir. J'aime beaucoup cet endroit. La maison est fort petite mais elle est située dans un pays fort sauvage et fort romanesque à une élévation de 1500 pieds, au dessus du niveau de la mer. Vous pouvez penser que le climat est assez froid. En effet, les fraises n'y ont pas muri cette année. Il fait un très mauvais temps, et beaucoup d'orages, et les grouse ne sont pas aussi abondans qu'à l'ordinaire. Le Duc de Rutland m'a prêté un petit cheval de la grandeur à 'Blacky', avec lequel je me promène toute seule sur les moors. Il s'y connait parfaitement et sait marcher en sûreté parmi le heather. Ce qui n'est pas toujours très facile: et il tient tranquille comme un rocher pour me laisser monter et descendre. Seulement, il est terriblement broken-winded.

Faites mes amitiés à Cranborne etc. Je crois que nous serons de retour Jeudi prochain. Dites au servantes de chercher dans ma chambre à toilette, un petit fermoir à perles blanches que je crains y avoir perdu.

Votre tres affectionnée . . .

In a postscript to a second letter she added: "Tell Eustace I am much obliged to him for his letter. He behaves better in that respect than his two brothers."

[Eustace was now four years old, Mildred sixteen, and a fine horsewoman, Blanche thirteen, the artist and scholar of the family, though Cranborne, seventeen, had marked scholarly tastes so far as his disabilities allowed. The Library at Hatfield possesses most beautifully bound books bought by him at Roederer's sale. They had come from Malmaison. One set, *Crimes de la Révolution*, 1796, bears on the cover the Imperial coat of arms and on the fly-leaf the signature of Gourgaud. He bought largely elsewhere in Paris. He died aged forty-four, unmarried. A report on him by a German surgeon,

Dr. Franz, October 5th, 1840, deposed that his defects of sight and hearing were due to checked brain development, probably before birth.

Robert, aged nine at the date of his mother's last mention of him, had no taste for field sports or even riding.]

EPILOGUE
1838-9

Her illness was at first described as an ague, and on October 29th the Duke of Rutland wrote to say that he was glad to hear that she was convalescent. She had been ordered to Brighton. The Duke thought that she had been already ill when she had quitted Walmer. "That circumstance, and the subsequent accident to the carriage, and the necessity for walking two or three miles probably occasioned the disorder." The accident took place in Kent. The axle-tree broke and the carriage bowling along at a considerable pace overturned. Lord and Lady Salisbury suffered only shock and contusions, but two servants travelling outside had more serious injuries. The party got into two postchaises to reach town and then Hatfield.[1] Lord Ellesmere held always that she had caught "the fatal chill" at the first splendid assembly given at the re-built and re-decorated house in Arlington Street. He had noticed that the walls had still been wet.

The family went to Burghley as usual in January, and on to Strathfieldsaye. "Bring your daughters and Bobby and Eustace with you, or as many of them as you please. You know how happy I shall be to take care of you, and I think that you will be quite well before you have been here many days." The Duke had been making alterations, and she could have the bedroom through which all the warm water pipes were carried. But in April only Lord S. was present at the marriage of Douro. The Press took alarm.

"*May 14th, 1839* The health of the Marchioness of Salisbury is unsatisfactory. The air of the Mansion in the Green Park having been pronounced to be prejudicial, her Ladyship was removed to Apsley House ten days ago, the faculty having decided on its being the purest spot in the Metropolis.

"It is doubtful whether the magnificent family mansion in Arlington Street will be thrown open to the *beau monde* this season, owing to the indisposition of the Marchioness."

Four days later, only Lord S. attended Her Majesty's State Ball. He had been to Apsley House to be shown and pronounce upon the rooms which her concerned host was having prepared – on the first floor – easy access to the garden – new curtains. "My house will

[1] Cecil Papers: XIII, 154.

acquire a great reputation. It will be deemed the Montpelier of London." She was on her way to Broadstairs, for sea air.

While she lay under the Duke's roof the Season was at its height, and carriages whirled in eternal procession around the great house which was the centre of London. She could not walk at all.

By June 21st she had arrived safely at her marine hotel and the Duke mentioned that Lady Flora Hastings was said to be dying and that Lord S. would tell her when he came down tomorrow the details of a scrape in which the Duchess of Montrose (?) and Lady Sarah Ingestre had involved themselves. They had said Mrs. Norton hissed Her Majesty at Ascot. Lady Flora Hastings, a lady-in-waiting to the Duchess of Kent had appeared to be pregnant and the Queen had believed this and that Sir John Conroy, her bête noire, was the culprit. The "unfortunate young lady" as the Duke called her, had been obliged to undergo the humiliation of a medical examination which had disclosed that she was suffering from a tumour, from which she died. The Duke had been called in by all parties. He advised the Duchess of Kent to keep the affair hushed up, and advised the Queen that the Duchess had the right to keep Conroy if she found him reliable, but that he must not be allowed to intrude at Court. Her Majesy had said, "Duke, I thank you for your good advice," and the Duke had replied "If ever you want me, or I can do you a service, you may depend upon me." But the story got into the press. The Hastings family took umbrage. During the period that this miserable affair dragged its course the Queen lost Melbourne (but only temporarily). She refused to change her Whig ladies of the bed-chamber for Tories, which resulted in the resignation of Peel. The little Queen had temporarily lost her popularity. There had also been cries from the crowd of "Mrs. Melbourne". The appearance of Albert the Good in her life-story was becoming necessary. Prince Albert landed in England five days before the death of Fanny and Her Majesty proposed to him on the day of the funeral at Hatfield. Personally, the Duke did not believe that she liked her Prime Minister to be a Whig, but to be Melbourne.

He had just succeeded in a business in which Melbourne had failed – got Sir John Conroy to resign. Nobody knew how he had managed this. The old man could be very terrifying. He had been much criticized when he had asked the favourite to an Apsley House banquet. But at the end of it Sir John had come up to resign and had been congratulated by his host on a manly resolution.

The last letter in her younger daughter's collection of letters from the beloved mother belongs to this period.

Bedford Hotel.

Ma chère Blanche

Je vous remercie de votre lettre bien qu'elle ne fut pas trop longue. J'espère que vous profitez beaucoup de Mlle. Dorrall.

J'ai quitté mon premier hôtel à cause du froid. Je suis très bien établie ici avec deux petites chambres qui donnent sur la mer. Il n'y a que la distance qu'il y avoit devant Beach House. *Mais la mer ici est triste en comparaison de celle de* Walmer. *On n'y voit que quelque barques de pêcheur; les grands vaisseaux n'osant approcher, et les bateaux à vapeur n'ayant qu'y faire. Cependant, c'est toujours* la mer: *et quelquefois peut-être cette absence de toute animation fait un effet plus sublime et plus frappant dans* "the wild waste of waters" *comme l'appelle un de nos poètes.*

La ville est un grand Douvres, ou plutôt un mauvais Londres: le pays absolument dépourvu d'arbres. Les petits jardins qu'on aperçoit sont composés entièrement de parterres de tamarisk *en différentes formes, et ceux là même paroissent avoir une répugnance très forte à croître excepté à l'abri d'une muraille. Je crois qu'il fait ici un vent éternel comme dans un des cercles de* l'Inferno *où vous n'êtes pas encore arrivée. De ce côté ci de la ville il n'y a pas de rochers et le rivage ressemble à celui de* Walmer.

Votre Affectionnée

The *Globe* took up the tale again on August 10th. "The Marquess of Salisbury has accompanied the Marchioness to Germany where it is their intention to pass several months. It was entirely on account of her Ladyship's health that induced the Marquess to leave this country, for although her Ladyship derived considerable benefit during her sojourn at Broadstairs, her health is not fully reinstated."

Dr. Lewis Powell, the specialist who had been called in in February, had written to Lord S. that he agreed with Dr. Hume and Dr. Paris and Dr. Chambers in recommending a course of Carlsbad waters. A new French governess had been added to the staff at Hatfield to continue the education of the daughters. Eustace was still in the nursery with his *bonne*. Bobby's holidays presented a problem. This was solved most happily for him by sending him to

Devon to Dr. Lyte, whose report before returning him to Dr. Faithfull's for the autumn term was one of the few rays of sunshine on the scene at this date. "We are all delighted with him. Indeed, I do not think I ever met with so promising a boy, and I have no doubt of his distinguishing himself hereafter in life. His constitution is, I fear, a little delicate, and he requires a stimulus to induce him to take exercise. This we endeavoured to give him by interesting him in Geology and Botany and he was quite rosy while scrambling about among our rocks."

The Duke, as Master of the Elder Brethren, arranged that the Trinity House steam yacht should waft his friends to Antwerp, the opening stage of a journey which proved tedious and exhausting. In their first days at the German Spa Lord S. did nourish hopes that his wife was gaining strength; there was at any rate, no sign that the waters were disagreeing with her. "To be sure," he told Lord Ellenborough, "the practice of German is diametrically opposed to that of English physicians." They found Carlsbad very pretty. "But a more extraordinary collection of faces of every hue and nation never was brought together . . ."

They left so suddenly that the Henry Wellesleys at Stuttgart, who would gladly have gone to meet them at Frankfort, missed them entirely. For the cure was not agreeing with the invalid and it became hourly clearer that she was declining. Dr. Karl Pffeifer of Bamberg spoke good French. His gentle last words would have told anyone but a husband hoping against hope that this wise man had been called in to a hopeless case. He said that the journey to England could be undertaken without ill effects, but should be made rapidly, to avoid getting in and out of the carriage as much as possible. He supplied a simple diet sheet. Finally, he believed that Madame would find her strength increased more and more as she approached her native land.

She was coming home. Lord Aberdeen did not know what to think from his newspapers on October 4th. There were paragraphs saying that the Salisburys were hourly expected in London, that Lady Salisbury was much better, and on the same day that she was very unwell. All the friends began to shower letters of enquiry and advice again, on Hatfield and Arlington Street. The Duke wrote unhappily to Lord S. almost daily. "The journey is long and the season unfavourable . . . She is still young . . . I don't write to Lady Salisbury but beg you to give her my kindest love . . . Thank God! that she is come home. She has youth on her side, and I cannot lose hope . . . We must not despair." Lord S. replied with news of an improvement and then a check.

Dr. Lyte, who had just sent up Robert, in charge of one of his sons, was not entirely surprised by a request that Cranborne should come at once. His last glimpse of her ladyship as she had passed through the hall in Arlington Street, had filled him with painful forebodings. Miss Nightingale's nurses did not yet exist. The De Ros family did not wait to take action. A discreet figure presented herself at Arlington Street with a hasty note addressed to Lord S. signed G. De Ros, dated October 14th.

"The bearer is the maid who has been used to nursing, and will be found very quiet and obedient. Will be happy to take charge of Eustace if he is at all in the way.

"Nothing can ever repay the kindness we have received from you both, and I should be glad to show you that we are sensible of it."

Lord S. kept a Diary from October 9th till the 15th. It recorded brief better daylight hours and worse nights and much pain. About midnight on the 14th after a violent spasm he thought she was gone. But she revived to ask for the children, and blessed them in a faint voice. She could join in Dr. Faithfull's prayer only by clasping her hands. At her grief-stricken husband's desire she agreed that they should pray that his end might be like hers. She asked for scissors and tried in vain to cut off some of her long dark hair. She ceased to breathe, without a struggle, about seven a.m. on Tuesday, October 15th. The press announced, "The disease to which her Ladyship fell a victim was the dropsy." Dr. Powell's diagnosis was inactivity and enlargement of the liver. The autopsy, which she had herself desired, performed by Dr. Edouard Meissner from Prague, disclosed disease of the pancreas. (Diabetes was not mentioned, and the word Insulin is noted in the Oxford Dictionary as first appearing in the English language in 1922.)

"In her I have lost a loving friend. During the nineteen years that we have been married, we have hardly had a difference. She set me an example of the performance of every duty, and it is to her education that I owe the excellent disposition of my children."

303

Lord S. took the children down to Hatfield the same night. Before they left, Blanche asked him to take her in once more to see her mother. The little girl was still only fourteen, but the face of the Gascoyne Heiress was unalarming, unforgettable, "beautifully calm". "The traces of her illness seemed to have almost disappeared."

The funeral *cortège* which set off on the Great North Road at nine a.m. on October 22nd had a look of almost mediaeval pageantry. It was led by six horsemen in cloaks, carrying wands, followed by a horseman bearing the coronet of the lamented Marchioness on a velvet cushion. Her emblazoned hearse was drawn by six horses, as was her own private carriage which was preceded by three mourning coaches and four. The carriages of three children of George III (Princess Mary, Duchess of Gloucester, Princess Sophia, and the Duke of Cambridge), came next; those of the Prime Minister, Lord Exeter, the Duke of Wellington and "about thirty others of the nobility", closed the mournful cavalcade.

It arrived at "The Greyhound", Woodside, about a mile and a half from Hatfield House at four p.m. where the local magistrates and gentry were waiting. The road to St. Etheldreda's church was lined on each side by thousands of tenants, and tradespeople come from miles around. At the farm, the widower stepped into the first of the three mourning coaches.

Lord S. noted in his diary that both Cranborne and Robert behaved very well and calmly. The church was crowded to excess. Dr. Faithfull preached. (*The Reformer* was indignant that London newspapers had described her as "a leader in our fashionable world." "She was more, infinitely more!" A few of the immense concourse of mourners might have been brought by curiosity, but the vast majority were there to testify to their gratitude and regard for "a woman of no ordinary stamp".[1])

Lord S. continued the education of his children strictly on the lines that his wife had laid down. He had them in his dressing-room for history lessons, while he dressed. He corrected their essays. He saw to it that they did not lose touch with any who had been close friends of their mother. He had written on the night of her

[1] The letters, press reports and accounts of the illness and death of the second Marchioness are to be found in Cecil Papers, Index volume XIII, pp. 71–125, 154. See also Letters of the Duke of Wellington, 285–7, 288, 293, 295, 298, 315.

death to tell Lady Westmeath of his loss of his "poor Fanny, leaving me almost broken-hearted". His list of people to whom he had sent pieces of her jewellery was formidable. He waited until Mildred and Blanche were married. He waited eight years before he took a bride of twenty-three — a daughter of the De La Warrs who had made frequent appearances in his first wife's diaries.

He was fifty-six but her family considered that Lady Mary had made the best match of the three Sackville girls. He had always been peppery, and there was little hope that this was a failing which time would improve. His habit of returning from the House of Lords at eleven p.m. and telling his children to get up and dress, they were off for Hatfield, had been, at least, unusual. But his more beautiful and gentle younger daughter evidently accepted what she called "explosions of temper" as a normal prerogative of the Early-Victorian male. She chose a bridegroom who gave way to an alarming display on their road to her new home after a honeymoon at Strathfield Saye. (She afterwards confided in Miss Louisa Faithfull that she anxiously watched her own infants to see if they had inherited the tendency, and was relieved to find that they seemed no worse than most.[1])

The figure of the old Duke of Wellington, with a little Cecil daughter in either hand, was long a familiar sight on the terrace at Hatfield, at Apsley House, and in places of entertainment in London. No other *confidante* replaced their mother. Mr. Arbuthnot reported that when the fatal news had reached Walmer the Duke had appeared much affected, but he had kept an appointment for which he was just setting forth, to review Lord Cardigan's regiment at Canterbury, and as far as Mr. Arbuthnot knew he had not expanded on his grief to anyone, then or thereafter. He put on mourning and sealed his letters with black wax. He was still in mourning when his *valet* found him speechless and blind on the floor of his study three weeks after the ordeal of the funeral at Hatfield. But he recovered, and lived a further thirteen years.

The person to whom the loss of the Gascoyne Heiress seemed irreparable was her younger son, Robert. He had a dark period before him.

[1] Cecil Papers: *Some recollections of my mother Lady Blanche Balfour* and *Letters of Lady Salisbury to Lady Blanche Balfour*, 1832–9.

Index

Abercromby, James, afterwards Baron Dunfermline, Speaker of the House of Commons, 144, 152

Aberdeen, George Hamilton Gordon, 4th Earl of; statesman, 73, 85, 137, 166–7, 229, 230, 244, 248, 265; Wellington thinks Tories would follow, 270; Fanny discusses Peel with, 271; Molesworth's motion, 273, 275; tells Fanny Duke's famous Canada speech kept Melbourne ministry in, 276; she tells Duke he is a thoroughly honest and honourable man, 278, pleasant dinner with, 284–5; a tactful go-between, 290; dines with Soult, 291; enquires for Fanny, 302

Aberdeen, Harriet, *born* Douglas, Countess of, widow of James, Viscount Hamilton, 2nd wife of George Hamilton Gordon, 4th Earl, 63, 71, 85–6

Adelaide of Saxe-Meiningen, Queen consort of William IV; childless, 59–60, 65; advised by Wellington not to go abroad, 135; her husband ill, 169; visits Stratfieldsaye, tolerably civil, 179–80, widowed, "unamiable", 243; mentioned, 79, 84, 162

Albert, Prince of Saxe-Coburg-Saalfeld; arrives in England for first time, 202; his patronage of art, 292; arrives in England and becomes engaged to Queen Victoria, 300

Alexander I, Czar, sends 14 packing-cases of models to Stratfieldsaye, 111; Pozzos' anecdotes of, 199; receives the Londonderrys, 221; Wellington's opinion of, 236

All Souls College, Oxford; Fanny admires quadrangle and library, 118; dances Scotch reels in the library, 122

Althorp, *see* Spencer

American beauty, Mrs. Wansworth, 166

American institutions, "the end of us", 156

American Minister, *see* Stevenson

Anglesey, Henry William Paget, 1st

Marquess of, 84; Duke of Wellington's strictures on, 213, 261; wounded at Waterloo, 281

Apethorpe, Northamptonshire, an abode of misery, 107

Apsley House; described 81; Fanny at, 63, 123, 168, 204, 253, 293; "Miss J." at, 136; attacked by mob, 73; coronation banquet at, 293; Conroy at, 300–1; Fanny's last stay at, 299–300

Arbuthnot, Charles, M.P., prejudiced but honest, 111–12; a broken-hearted widower, 134, 177, 182, 188, 211; his portrait of Wellington, 205; at Walmer, 209, 256, 261

Arbuthnot, Mrs. Harriet, *born* Fane, wife of Charles Arbuthnot, 40; tells Wellington Cranborne is said to have married the Gascoyne heiress, "a very pretty girl", for her money, 53; stays at Childwall, 71; Sir Henry Hardinge says is mischievous, 95, 115; at Belvoir, 105; at Stratfieldsaye, 107; at Oxford, 115–23; dies of cholera, 132–3; anniversary always kept, 211, Duke's description of, 216

Arlington House, the Cecil family mansion in London, 43, 60, 112, 134; must be sold, 188; Lord S. decides not to sell but to repair, 195, still in the builders' hands, but moved into, 239; opening party at, 272; theory that Fanny caught fatal chill at, 299; dies at, 303

Bamber, Dr. John, of Bifrons, Barking, Essex, and Mincing Lane, great-grandfather of the Gascoyne heiress, 25; his monument in Barking church, 28

Barham, John Foster, M.P., courts Lady "Katty" Grimston, 94; engaged to, 97; married to, 107; Salisburys dine with, 130; becomes insane, 202, 205; dies "a great blessing", 284

Barham, Lady Katharine, *see* Grimston

Bathurst, Lady Susan, bosom friend of Sally Price (Mrs. Gascoyne), 24

309

D'Este, Mlle (see Sussex, Augusta Emma), daughter of Prince Augustus, Duke of Sussex, and Lady Augusta Murray, afterwards wife of 1st Baron Truro, Lord Chancellor, 105, says Queen Adelaide has influence, 159; William IV will not accept Peel's resignation, 101–2; reports unfavourably on Queen Adelaide as widow, 243; on the young Queen Victoria, 250; mentioned, 165, 224, 232, 241, 271, 282

Delmé-Radcliffe, Amelius, one of the best shots in England, 68; stays at Hatfield, 217

De Ros, Charlotte, Baroness, wife of Lord H. Fitzgerald, her sketches, 59

De Ros, Lady Georgiana, born Gordon-Lennox, wife of William, afterwards 23rd Baron De Ros, 92, 108, 201, 214, 221, 232; quite overwhelmed by her brother-in-law's guilt, 233; Duke kindly asks her and her children to Stratfieldsaye, 235, 279, 280; sends a nurse to Fanny's death-bed, 303

De Ros, Hon. Henrietta, afterwards Mrs. John Broadhurst of Foston Hall, Co. Derby, 63

De Ros, Henry Fitzgerald, 22nd Baron "The Sarpent", "sad affair of", 214; accused and convicted of cheating at cards, 217, 221, 232–4; mentioned, 205

De Ros, Olivia, afterwards Countess Cowley; her caricatures, 38, 115; her marriage, 84–5, 88–9, 92, 94; bears a son, 134; sister of Henry, Baron De Ros, 214; disappointed not to see Salisburys in Germany, 302

de Staël, Germaine, born Necker, Baronne, "the most agreeable woman you ever saw, if you kept her light", 238

Devonshire, William Cavendish, 6th Duke of, "that sovereign idiot", 159; entertains Salisburys, 284

Disraeli, Benjamin, afterwards Prime Minister and 1st Earl of Beaconsfield; author of Vivien Grey, 61; "evidently clever but superlatively vulgar" 240; attends opening party at Arlington House, 272; mentioned, 289

Dino, Dorothea, Duchess of, born princess of Courland, French ambassadress, 79, 116

Douro, Arthur Richard Wellesley, 1st Marquess of, afterwards 2nd Duke of Wellington, 108; makes a declaration to Fanny, 162; his engagement and marriage, 162–3; arrives unexpectedly at Apsley House, 203–4, makes a gaffe in sending a message to his father by Fanny, 246–7; his father complains of, 208, 223, 274, 279; wedding of, 299; mentioned, 286

Drayton Hall near Tamworth, Staffs., Salisburys stay with Peels at, 219–21

Drummond, Edward, M.P., private secretary successively to Ripon, Canning, Wellington and Peel, 88, 146, 170, 188, 204, 224

Drummond, Henry, banker and Irvingite, 61

Duncombe, Thomas, M.P., 75

Durham, John George Lambton, 1st Earl of, friend of Duchess of Kent, 96; sent for by her, 240; Peel has a mean opinion of, resigns as High Commissioner in Canada, 268; attacked by Brougham, 294

Eden, the Hon. Emily, authoress, 50, 70, 180, 214

Egerton, Lady Francis, Harriet, born Greville, wife of Francis, afterwards 1st Earl of Ellesmere, 107, 151, 154, 157, 181, 265

Ellenborough, Edward Law, 1st Earl of, 73, 145; "wants India", 147, 157, 159, 165; curls his hair, 188–9; runs wild about clauses in Acts of Parliament, 206; at Drayton, 220; Fanny tells Duke has no political principles, 278; "Lord S." writes to about her last days, 302; mentioned, 209, 234, 241, 244, 279, 294

Erroll, William Hay, 18th Earl of, proposes by letter to the Gascoyne heiress, 47–8

Esterhazy, Prince Paul, Austrian Ambassador, 108, 169; his Coronation ball, 285, 294

Evans, General Sir George de Lacy, commands British Legion in Spain, 235–6, 261

Evelyn, see Glanville

Exeter, Brownlow Cecil, 2nd Marquess of, 63; his cats, 220; Salisburys spend New Year with, 195, 265; attends Fanny's funeral, 304

310

Lady F. Egerton and Duchess of Sutherland, 181; reports he will resign, 203, 231; at Queen Victoria's first council, 242; she relies upon him, 243–4, 251; his dealings with Conroy, 270, 271; with the Duke, 277; at Queen Victoria's coronation, 287; speaks weakly, 291; "Mrs. Melbourne", 300

Melville, Robert Dundas, 2nd Viscount, 138

Metternich, Prince Clement, Austrian Foreign Minister, 98, 158, 198, Wellington on, 278

Molesworth, Sir William M.P., friend of Jeremy Bentham, John Stuart Mill, his articles in the *Westminster Review*, 231; his motion of censure, 273, 275

Murray, General Sir George, Wellington's opinion of, 257–8

Napier, General Sir Charles, 90

Napoleon I; Emperor, 31, 79, 81–2, 155, 161; his legacy to man who had attempted to murder Duke of Wellington, 212; his tactics at Waterloo, 216, 260; on his first campaign in Italy, 259–60; tells Captain Frederick Maitland that Wellington excelled him in caution, 261; his cynical comment to Queen Hortense, 268–9; did not forgive Soult, 282

Ney, Michel, Duke of Elchingen, Prince of Moskowa, Marshal of France, shot for re-joining Napoleon; "absolutely necessary to make an example", 282

Nicolson and Longmore, Messrs; solicitors in Hertford, 75

Northumberland, Charlotte, *born* Herbert, Duchess of, wife of Hugh Percy, 3rd Duke of; state governess to Princess Victoria, 85; delighted with her pupil, 172, 249; admired by Duke of Wellington, 229; "The Grand Duchess", 250; mentioned, 290

O'Connell, Daniel, M.P.; Irish politician, 144; at Lansdowne House, 166, 181; his party increases, 256; Wellington thinks will excite first rebellion, 273; at Kensington Palace, 284

"Old Sarum", nickname of the 1st Marchioness of Salisbury, 97; a rotten borough abolished by the Reform Bill, 198

Oxford University; Fanny's visit to for installation of Duke of Wellington as Chancellor, "a fairy vision of beauty, and delight", 116–23

Ouseley, Sir Gore, diplomatist, 69, 204, 258

Panshanger, Whig stronghold, pictures at, 88; agreeable party at, 294; mentioned, 134

Peel, Miss Julia, afterwards wife of 6th Earl of Jersey, a clever intelligent girl, 219

Peel, Lady, *born* Julia Floyd, wife of Sir Robert, Prime Minister; "no politician", 98; not a clever woman, 163, Fanny calls upon, 197; her *Chapeau de Paille* portrait, 219

Peel, Sir Robert, Bart, Prime Minister; first appearance of in Diary, 61; caricature of, 73; going to Rome, 90, 95; defended by Wellington, 128; correspondence with William IV, 132; on better terms with Wellington, 136; dramatic recall from Rome, 143, 146, 153; grows in stature, 151–8; has scenes with the Duke, 158–60; resigns, 163; loyal to Duke, 164; Fanny praises, 168–9; his cold manners and shyness, 97, 98, 114, 123, 167; opinion of Apethorpe, 107; speaks powerfully, 171; Duke visits, 196, 268; Salisburys visit, 219–21; his favourite period in history, 204; ready to have served under Canning, 211; his picture collection, 219–20, 282–3; Fanny wishes the Duke to stay with, 222, 231; at Queen Victoria's first council, 242; the Duke thinks has behaved with duplicity, 256; gets on better with Duke, 274; Fanny says is thoroughly honest and honourable, 278; Duke says ignorant of foreign affairs, 279; not always scrupulous, 279; gives successful party dinner, 283; mentioned, 113, 147–8, 191, 202, 254, 288, 290

Pepys, Sir Lucas, Bart, President of the Royal College of Physicians; connected by marriage with the Prices and medical adviser to the family, 29, 31

Perugini, confectioner at Hatfield House, attends "Lord S." as *valet* on the Continent, 141; at Hatfield fire, 185

scribes £2000 to elections, 245; attends funeral of William IV, 247; supports Brougham's motion, to his wife's regret, 291; accompanies Duke to Coronation City dinner, 291; states his wife never really well from August 1839, 294; takes her to Carlsbad, 301, his diary of her last illness, death and funeral, 303–4; almost broken-hearted, 305

Salisbury, Frances Mary, 2nd Marchioness of, the Gascoyne heiress; born, 32; a charming child, 33–5; her albums, 36, 75; a young lady, 37; receives proposals of marriage, 38–51; marries Lord Cranborne; "her decided choice", 48–52; births of her first four children, 55, 59; her son Robert, 70; happily married for 13 years, 112; birth of her fourth son, Eustace, 114; another wedding anniversary, 152; her kindness to Charlotte Sneyd, 89; Katty Grimston, 202; is shown letters of "Miss J" by the Duke, 136; grief at 1835 Election results, 134; Duke tells her "with you I think aloud", 145; Douro makes a declaration to, 162; she wishes him at the bottom of the sea, 246; her husband shows her an anonymous letter, 216; her account of the fatal fire at Hatfield House, 184 et seq.; has influenza, 230; taken violently ill at Stratfieldsaye, 238; sends for Dr. Hume, 239; admires first public appearance of Queen Victoria, 249, and her natural manners and dignity, 292–3; advised by the Duke not to stay at Walmer without "Lord S.", 255; discusses his political prospects, with Duke, 270–1; never saw him so annoyed, 273; all irritation subsided, 275; gives him her frank opinion of his colleagues, 278; at Queen Victoria's coronation, 286–287; at Buckingham Palace, 252–3, 282, 288, 294; her indignation at slight to Duke, 292; taken ill again, 294; carriage accident, 299; stays at Apsley House, 299; Broadstairs, Carlsbad, 301–3; her last letters to her daughter, Blanche, 295, 301; says farewell to her children and dies, 303; autopsy on, 303, her husband's eulogy on, 303–4; funeral of, 304: her appearance, 53, 167; diaries, 56, 59–64; sketches, 37, 71,

134, 141 (of Stratfieldsaye), 280; her charities, 65, 134, 179; far more than a social leader, 304; her rousing address to the Hertfordshire Yeomanry, 74; her foreign tours, 66–8, 71, 140–2; her theatricals, 70, 89; portrait by Lawrence, 68; conversations with Talleyrand, 79–82, 124, 130; conversations with the Duke, 73, 114, 125, 215, 223, 247, 256, 280; description of his appearance, 168–70; see also London homes of, Arlington House; regular visits to Apsley House, Burghley House, Belvoir Castle, Belton House, Ingestre, Walmer Castle, Stratfieldsaye

Salisbury, Mary Amelia, born Hill, wife of 1st Marquess of Salisbury; mother-in-law of the Gascoyne heiress; her fox-hunting, 23, 40; her interview with Bamber and Fanny Gascoyne, 43–4; attends her son's wedding, 52–3; a bitter pill, 53–4; gives an excellent christening party, 55: as a widow resides at Arlington House, 60; described by Creevey, 69; her Album, 70–2, 75; her carriage attacked, 75; has a fall at a ball, 97; shaken but recovers, 100–1, 105, 112; gets on very well with her daughter-in-law, "business never mentioned", 134; her mad dog, 165–6, arrives at Hatfield, 178: failing, 179; her debts, 184, 187; burnt to death in Hatfield House fire, 184 et seq.; autopsy and funeral of, 189–90; Hatfield memories of, 190, relics of, 195

Scott, Sir Walter, 88–9, 91, 156–7, 167; his meeting with Wellington, 183–4, 196

Sebastiani, Comte François, French Ambassador to Great Britain, 151, 240

Sefton, William Molyneux, 2nd Earl of, 35, 72; cynical about Queen Caroline, 207

Sion House, Middlesex, breakfasts at, 169, 291

Smith, Abel, M.P., of Woodhall Park, 75, 151

Sneyd, Charlotte Augusta, of Keele Hall, Staffs; artist and author, 89, 107; her account of fatal fire at Hatfield House, 185 et seq.; at Hatfield, 195, 217, 224

FIVE HEIRESSES

Isaac Greene 1678-1749
of Prescot and
Childwall, Lancs.   172?

Thomas Blackburne = Ireland Greene
of Orford, Lancs.   1728-95 Lady of
d. 1768   1752   the Manor of
                         Hale

Bamber Gascoyne II   =   Sarah Bridget Frances
1758-1824 of Childwall,   1766-1820 heiress of
Bifrons and 10 Great   1794 Chase Price M.P. of
Stanhope Street M.P. for   Knighton, Radnorshire;
Liverpool 1780-96   d. 1777 he married
                             1765 Sarah Glanville daughter
                             of William Evelyn-
                             Glanville M.P. of St.
                             Clere, Wrotham

THE GASCOYNE HEIRESS

THE DIARIST
                                            =
Frances Mary 1802-39   1821   James Brownlow William Cecil
    heiress of Childwall, West   1791-1868 Viscount
    Derby, Wavertree, Everton,   Cranborne 1791 2nd
    and Much and Little Woolton,   Marquess of Salisbury 1823
    Lancs., and of Price property   who upon his marriage
    in Salop and Radnorshire,   assumed the additional
    and of Bamber property at   surname of Gascoyne
    Barking, Ilford and Enfield
    and 10 Great Stanhope
    Street
    2nd Marchioness of Salisbury

1   2   3
James Emilius   Mildred Arabella   Arthur George
    William Evelyn   Charlotte   Villiers 1823-5
    Viscount Cran-   Henrietta 1822-81   no issue
    borne 1821-65   m. Rt. Hon.
    no issue   Alexander
                                  Beresford-Hope
                                  M.P., P.C. and
                                  had issue